POLAND'S RETURN TO CAPITALISM

Poland's Return to Capitalism

From the Socialist Bloc to the European Union

Gavin Rae

Revised paperback edition published in 2012 by I.B.Tauris & Co Ltd
6 Salem Road, London W2 4BU
175 Fifth Avenue, New York NY 10010
www.ibtauris.com

Copyright © 2012, 2007 Gavin Rae
First published in hardback by Tauris Academic Studies, an imprint of
I.B.Tauris & Co Ltd, 2007

The right of Gavin Rae to be identified as the author of this work has been
asserted by the author in accordance with the Copyright, Designs and Patent
Act 1988.

All rights reserved. Except for brief quotations in a review, this book, or any
part thereof, may not be reproduced, stored in or introduced into a retrieval
system, or transmitted, in any form or by any means, electronic, mechanical,
photocopying, recording, or otherwise, without the prior written permission of
the publisher.

ISBN: 978 1 78076 039 1

A full CIP record for this book is available from the British Library
A full CIP record for this book is available from the Library of Congress

Library of Congress catalog card: available

CONTENTS

List of Tables   vii

Acknowledgments   ix

Preface   xi

Introduction   1

1. The Politics of Transition   10
2. Poland and the Under-development of Eastern Europe   27
3. The Socio-Economic Effects of the Transition to Capitalism   50
4. Poland's Fragmenting Consensus   79
5. From Stalinism to Social Democracy   112
6. Beyond European Union Accession   142

Conclusions   163

Appendix 1   Parliamentary and Presidential Election Results (1990 – 2005)   167

Appendix 2   Glossary of Main Political Parties   172

Notes   177

Bibliography   197

Index   215

LIST OF TABLES

TABLE 2.1: Average Rate of Growth (NMP) CEE, 1950-89 (%)   43

TABLE 3.1: Imports and Exports to Poland 1990-2003 (%)   56

TABLE 3.2: FDI and Privatisation in Poland 1989-2004   59

TABLE 3.3: Ownership Structure of Polish Banks 1993-2003 (%)   60

TABLE 3.4: Financial Result of Public and Private Sector 1992-2003 (Million ZŁ)   63

TABLE 3.5: Basic Economic Indicators in Poland 1989-2005   64

TABLE 3.6: Budget Spending 1989-2003 (% GDP)   68

TABLE 3.7: Poverty in Poland 1989-2002   71

TABLE 3.8: Social Groups' Income as a Percentage of National Average Income 1990-2003   73

TABLE 3.9: Incomes in Economic Sectors as a Percentage of National Average Income 1995-2003   74

TABLE 4.1: Opinions about Foreign Capital and Privatisation   92

TABLE 4.2: Attitudes to Government Spending   92

TABLE 4.3: Attitudes to Government Intervention   93

TABLE 4.4: Opinions Concerning Egalitarianism   94

TABLE 4.5: Opinions about the Transition   95

TABLE 4.6: Attitudes towards Public Institutions (2005)   95

TABLE 4.7: Opinions about Democracy   96

TABLE 4.8: Attitudes towards the Church   96

TABLE 4.9: Attitudes towards Abortion   96

TABLE 4.10: Attitudes towards EU and NATO Membership   97

ACKNOWLEDGMENTS

This book was researched and written with the help of a grant from the *Barry Amiel and Norman Melburn Trust*. I would like to thank IB Tauris and in particular Elizabeth Munns for their help and support in publishing this book.

Large amounts of the material and information included in this book are drawn from my PhD thesis, which was written on the topic of Polish Social Democracy for London South Bank University and completed in 2004. I would like to thank all the staff and my colleagues who helped me during my time at LSBU and in particular express my gratitude to my PhD supervisors Kate Hudson and John Solomos.

A number of individuals have read part or all of the book manuscript, including Tadeusz Kowalik, Kate Hudson, and Kevin Hadley. Also both Maciej Dębski and Michał Wenzal helped me collect and compile the statistics that I used in the third and fourth chapters. Obviously the content of the book and any errors included in it are the responsibility of the author.

I would like to extend my thanks to my parents who have continuously given me support and encouragement. I must also thank Dorota and Amelia Rae for putting up with me while I was writing this book.

I have spent the majority of the past decade in Poland and I incur a debt of gratitude to the countless people I have met there that have inspired me to write a book on the transition in Poland and have helped to make the country my home. I must also give mention to the students from the sociology faculty at Warsaw University, who attended my courses on the Polish transition in 2006/7. The comments, questions and discussion during these meetings were a valuable lesson and greatly helpful when considering the content of this book.

PREFACE
TO THE PAPERBACK EDITION

The first edition of this book concluded with the statement: 'The liberal phase of capitalist development in Poland is drawing to a close, politics will decide how its next chapter shall look.'

During this time, shortly after joining the EU, Poland was governed by a conservative-nationalist coalition, led by the Law and Justice Party (PiS). A new political divide had crystallised around historical and cultural issues, with PiS actively attempting to form a new Fourth Republic in Poland.

One could claim that a new, more positive chapter in Poland has since been written. In 2007, the electorate, particularly young urban voters, mobilised to elect a new centre-right government led by the Citizens' Platform party (PO). PO promised a new economic miracle in Poland and offered to represent the concerns and needs of the young and entrepreneurial sections of society.

Poland was taking its place in a new expanded Europe, in which the new member states from Central-Eastern Europe had the fastest-growing economies. In Poland, the economy expanded rapidly and unemployment fell sharply. Poland and Central-Eastern Europe's moment seemed to have arrived, but then the global financial crisis struck.

Central-Eastern Europe was disproportionately hit by the global economic crisis, as capital flowed away from the peripheries and back to the centres of the world economy. Poland's economic situation worsened, as economic growth significantly slowed and unemployment once again rose into double figures. Yet despite these difficulties Poland has been the only EU country to have avoided falling into an economic recession since the outbreak of the global economic downturn. Prime Minister Donald Tusk has sought to claim credit for this success and has painted Poland as being Europe's economic 'green island'.

To understand how Poland has managed to retain its positive course of economic growth, it is necessary to return to the transition from socialism to capitalism that is outlined in this book. These experiences show us that when economic liberal reforms were speeded up (as at the beginning of the transition and in the late 1990s) then economic growth slowed and unemployment soared. The most prosperous period during the transition came in the mid-1990s, when the centre-left government led by the Democratic Left Alliance (SLD) slowed the course of reform and strengthened the economic levers of the state.

Tusk had promised to repeat the Irish 'economic miracle' in Poland, through copying its policies of liberalisation and deregulation. Yet, despite his neo-liberal background, once it had taken office Tusk's government proved to be more cautious in its approach to economic policy and did not embark on any far-reaching programme of liberal economic reform. Furthermore, the positive experience of Poland to some extent answers another question raised towards the end of this book, which is whether EU membership would provide some form of counter-movement to the mechanisms of a liberal free-market economy.

In the EU budget (2004-13) Poland has been eligible to receive the greatest amount of EU structural funds (€67bn) of any member state, as well as a large sum in subsidies for farmers. This has allowed Poland to implement a programme of public investment in areas such as transport, at a level not seen in the country since the 1970s. During a global economic crisis that has primarily been driven by a slump in investment, Poland has increased its level of public investment, thus partly offsetting the negative effects of the steep decline in private investment.

This positive economic performance allowed PO to become the first governing party in Poland's democratic history to be re-elected. Yet since winning the presidential and parliamentary elections in 2011, the new administration has promised to speed up the course of liberal economic reform and adjust itself to the policies of austerity and strict fiscal discipline being pursued throughout the EU. However, as described in chapter 3 of this book, when liberal reforms have previously been pursued in Poland, its socio-economic situation has tended to deteriorate.

Chapter 4 also shows that when economic liberal policies have been pursued, and living standards have consequently dropped and unemployment and social inequalities risen, support for liberal democratic ideals have also declined. Despite its defeat in a series of elections in recent years, PiS continues to command the support of over a quarter of the electorate. This is compounded by the fact that since its crushing defeat in 2005 (described in chapter 5) the left has failed to challenge the hegemony of the two main right-wing parties in Poland, allowing PiS to remain the main opposition to PO.

Since the publishing of the first edition of this book, the symbols and slogans of the conservative right have changed. In April 2010, President Lech Kaczyński, alongside over 90 other prominent politicians and states-people, were killed in an air crash in Smoleńsk en route to a commemoration of the war-time massacre in Katyń. The symbolic and historical significance of this event has provided a new unifying theme for the conservative right. It is therefore unlikely that the contours of political division (described here particularly in chapter 6) will dissipate but will rather intensify in a new form.

The post-socialist transition in Eastern Europe transformed not just the region itself but also the rest of Europe and the world. It was perhaps the greatest and most coordinated series of transformations of socio-economic and political systems in world history. It helped to forge the globalised capitalist economy that expanded to previously unforeseen levels, with its accompanying ideology of neo-liberalism. Yet this global economic order is undergoing a crisis greater than any seen for a generation. This book analyses the events in Poland, in their global context, that transformed the largest and most strategically important of the Central-Eastern European countries that joined the EU from 2004. It is only in this context that we can understand the difficulties and successes of Poland during this time of global economic and political turbulence.

Gavin Rae
June 2012

INTRODUCTION

The revolutions in Eastern Europe (EE), between 1989 and 1991, changed the world. Just as the French revolution and the Bolshevik revolution were the defining moments of the eighteenth and twentieth centuries, so the overthrow of socialism in EE has moulded political and economic life at the advent of the twenty-first century. These events took the world by surprise, with representatives of all the different political camps claiming the revolutions as their own. Many on the left declared that they signified a renewal of socialism in a Europe without borders, while those on the right perceived them as the final victory of the liberal free-market over its socialist and social democratic rivals. More often than not, the collapse of socialism was accompanied by assertions that a new, post-modern era was evolving, where the fixed concepts of left/right and worker/capitalist would dissolve and the conflicts born out of the industrial revolution superseded. However, the collapse of socialism in EE did not signify the resolution of the contradictions of capitalism, but opened up a new stage in its development.

1

Over the past 17 years, the countries of the ex-Socialist Bloc have been defined in many ways. They have been termed post-socialist or post communist countries; transition, candidate or accession states, emerging markets or free-market economies. However, they have rarely been called what they actually are: capitalist. This in itself is a curious thing, considering that the resounding victor of the Cold War was the capitalist system itself. The transition in EE has involved the destruction of the socialist elements of the region's economies, in order for alternative capitalist structures to grow. The former socialist countries were absorbed into the international division of labour and their economies quickly became a part of and dependent upon the global capitalist system. The economic and political transitions in EE have not been formed in an insulated environment, but within a world capitalist economy. For nearly 50 years, over half of the world's population had been separated from the global capitalist system; whose insatiable thirst for these countries' resources, labour and markets grew ever stronger. The phrase globalisation had barely been spoken before the fall of the Berlin Wall, but came into common usage as capitalism expanded eastwards. In order to understand the countries of the former Socialist Bloc, one must comprehend how they have become a part of the world capitalist system; and in turn realise how this has changed global capitalism itself.

The overthrow of socialism in EE, like all revolutions in history, had its idealistic phase. Writers and dissidents assumed positions of power; the cities of Central-Eastern Europe (CEE) became magnets for idealistic youth and the 'peoples revolutions' provided inspiration for change in the West. A new united Europe was envisioned, with free and dynamic economies, open and diverse civil societies and democratic and accountable political systems. The ideals of fairness and equality were to be incorporated into this new Europe and realised within open and meritocratic market economies. However, this optimistic juncture was short-lived. Promises of prosperity and growth were replaced with the largest peacetime recession in history and the appearance of mass unemployment and poverty. The rapid opening of the EE economies to the capitalist world created the conditions for the strong and connected to prosper, with a new affluent (and often criminal) social layer gorging on the sale of the region's assets and flaunting its new gained wealth. After ushering in the shock therapy economic reforms the former oppositionists were quickly removed from office and the new political systems became rapidly infected by corruption and instability. Old nationalist and religious rivalries reared their heads, as nations divided, some torn apart by civil wars. At the same time, the bourgeoisies in Western Europe (WE) seized the opening in the East to launch a new offensive against their welfare systems at home. Free from the constraints of the Cold War, the West embarked on new military offensives to the South and the East, with the USA appointing itself the policeman of the New World Order and divisions widening between the major capitalist powers.

The re-introduction of capitalism in EE instigated a recession, in all the post-socialist states of unprecedented proportions. However, the depth and length of these recessions varied, with the majority of the countries in the ex-Soviet Union suffering the worst socio-economic regressions. By the mid-1990s, many of these countries had partly closed their economies to the influx of foreign capital and had begun to centralise their political systems. On the other hand, the countries in CEE and the Baltic states furthered their assimilation into the world capitalist system, which was institutionalised through their entry into organisations such as North Atlantic Treaty Organisation (NATO) and the European Union (EU). This has allowed for the globalisation of their economies, states and political systems, with large areas of their industrial and financial sectors brought up by foreign capital. They have generally become dependent capitalist economies, with their social structures reflective of a transition that has rapidly destroyed the socialist system of production and replaced it with a strategy of importing capital, consumer goods and services from the highly developed capitalist economies. The relative historical economic advancement of WE was partly achieved through the exploitation of the less developed economies in EE. The entry of the post-socialist countries into the EU is the latest phase of this process, and creates a new chapter in the combined development of Eastern and Western Europe.

2

By far the largest and most strategically important CEE country is Poland. With a population of nearly 40 million and a landmass of over 312,000km, the country borders Germany, the Czech Republic, Slovakia, Ukraine, Belarus, the Russian province of Kalingrad and has a sea crossing with Sweden. By the end of the sixteenth century Poland had become one of the largest and most powerful countries in Europe. In 1791 the Polish-Lithuanian Commonwealth adopted Europe's first written constitution, which was the second in the world after the USA. Shortly after, however, Poland was divided up; its different parts incorporated into Russia, Prussia and Austria and for 123 years the Polish state ceased to exist. A sovereign Polish state was once again formed in 1918, out of the ashes of World War One (WW1). This republic lasted just 21 years, before the country was once again torn apart by a world war. Some of the most horrific acts of the twentieth century occurred on Polish soil, with the majority of the holocaust carried out in the concentration camps, which the Nazis had built in

Poland. The country emerged from World War Two (WW2) 20% smaller in size and its borders shifted westwards, forcing the migration of millions of people. For the first time in its history, it had become an ethnically homogenous society and presently over 96% of the country's populace declares itself to be Polish and nearly 90% Catholic. The desolation of Poland during WW2 further pushed back the country, which had only begun to rebuild itself after the partitions. Poland lost around 1/5th of its population during WW2 and many of its cities lay in ruins, with just 15% of Warsaw's buildings surviving the War. Therefore, Poland entered the socialist period at a lower level of economic development than most neighbouring CEE countries. Its economy was still predominantly agricultural and its infrastructure, communications and industry underdeveloped and disjointed. After WW2, Poland underwent a period of rapid industrialisation and urbanisation. There were vast changes in its social class structure, the mass entry of women into the workforce and free and comprehensive health and education services made available. At the same time, the construction of socialism met a number of specific obstacles in Poland. The large agricultural sector meant that collectivisation did not advance to the extent that it did in most other Eastern Bloc countries. Low personal consumption was particularly acute in Poland, with the economy of shortage reaching extreme levels during the 1980s. The large size and influence of the Catholic Church differentiated Poland from the other countries in the Socialist Bloc, acting as an alternative social institution to the socialist state and enjoying a relatively high level of independence. Also, a significant private sector continued to operate alongside the state sector. Importantly, the socialist system was perceived as being imposed from outside, which contributed to the creation of the largest and most coherent opposition movement in the whole of the Socialist Bloc.

Poland became the first CEE country to move from socialism to capitalism, with its shock therapy economic reforms replicated throughout the region. These sought to dismantle the socialist elements of the economy as rapidly as possible and open up the post-socialist countries to the world capitalist market. The objective failings of the socialist system in Poland, and the hostility of large sections of its population towards it, meant that the reforms initially enjoyed wide social and political support. It was believed that the destruction of the command, protectionist economy would facilitate the development of a neutral and fair market economy, which would complement the corresponding growth of a political democracy. However, millions of people soon found themselves opposed to the practical reality of the reintroduction of capitalism in Poland. Workers in state enterprises discovered that their livelihoods were at risk; local entrepreneurs struggled to compete with the newly arrived multi-nationals and a population that had come to rely on the county's public services (and anticipated their improvement and modernisation) saw their very existence threatened. This did not mean that all of these people turned against the reforms and sought a way back to the previous order. Yet, what it did ensure was that society became divided and while the living standards and opportunities of many improved they declined for others, with large areas of poverty appearing in the country. This corroded support for the ideals of political liberalism and led to disillusionment and declining participation in the democratic process.

3

This book describes the transition from socialism to capitalism, focussing particularly on the period up to EU entry. Although the transition continues after accession, the form of capitalism in Poland and CEE had by then mainly been determined. In fact, it may no longer be sufficient to talk about a transition in the post-socialist states, but rather to consider the form of capitalism that has been created. This book looks chiefly at the transition to capitalism up to EU entry, with its later consequences considered mainly in the last chapter.

The theoretical framework for understanding Poland's return to capitalism is laid out in chapter one. Rosa Luxemburg's theory of the Accumulation of Capital is used to understand the transition from socialism to capitalism. Luxemburg believed that capitalism expanded through an extension into non-capitalist markets and she was one of the first to grasp the significance of this imperialist expansion. Coming from Poland, she lived on the periphery of the advanced capitalist world and could understand how the underdevelopment of EE contributed to the growth of the advanced capitalist economies in WE. In recent years, capitalism has expanded into EE through destroying the socialist elements of the economy and gaining a monopoly over large areas of its industrial and financial sectors. This is a contemporary example of primitive accumulation in EE. Luxemburg's theory is complimented by Antonio Gramsci's concept of hegemony and the historical bloc. Gramsci had sought to understand why the world's first socialist revolutions had occurred in EE and how the advanced capitalist countries in WE had managed to create a form of consensual political rule. He analysed the differing relationship between the state and civil society in Eastern and Western Europe and at how the intervention of the state had helped to create a well-formed civil society in WE that could absorb antagonistic social classes. Within the post-socialist reality the leading ideology, neo-liberalism, has subjectively clothed the opening up of the EE economies to world capitalism. This process of primitive accumulation has been most developed in the post-socialist countries, but has also had an international dimension as capitalism has sought to remove barriers, both domestic and global, that block the advance of monopoly capital.

In chapter two, the historical development of Poland is placed within the context of relations between Eastern and Western Europe. As some WE countries began their process of industrialisation, so Poland and other CEE nations became incorporated into an expanded world market, as suppliers of agricultural produce. This strengthened the feudal character of their economies and determined the nature of their Absolute States. The partition of Poland, its inter-war version of capitalism and its particular brand of socialism, were all partly generated by this historical reality; and it provides a context for understanding the capitalist system built in the country after 1989.

Chapter three examines the socio-economic effects of Poland's return to capitalism. It shows how the re-introduction of capitalist relations of production and the opening up of the country to the world capitalist market facilitated a sharp economic slowdown. We then observe how this began to reverse only when some of the protective elements of the socialist economy were strengthened; and that a further economic slowdown occurred when a new wave of neo-liberal reforms was once again implemented. A form of dependent capitalism has been created, with large swathes of its economy owned by foreign capital. This has depleted its productive base and deepened the under-developed nature of its agricultural sector. It has resulted in the creation of large social inequalities and the appearance of mass, structural unemployment; with enlarged areas of absolute poverty existing alongside a new urban middle class. The protective elements of the state are almost entirely connected to the previous system and diminish along with the socialist system of production.

The creation and dismantling of the liberal consensus in post-socialist Poland is considered in chapter four. This examines the organic cohesion of neo-liberalism, crafted at the beginning of transition, and then looks at how this disintegrates as the effects of the neo-liberal reforms are felt. The divisions created by the practices of primitive accumulation erode the social cohesion needed to sustain a healthy democratic system. Also, the association of political liberal ideals with neo-liberal economics severely weakens the former. The fragmenting of the liberal accord has allowed for the growth of a conservative-nationalist ideology and political parties.

In chapter five, the question of the Polish left is studied. After the collapse of socialism, it was widely perceived that there would be little political space for the left, especially those parts of it that were connected to the previous system. However, Poland was the first post-socialist country where a successor to a former ruling party during socialism was elected into office. This party was able to partially realise its newly adopted social democratic ideology through slowing the pace of the reforms and using the inherited socialist economic structures and protective elements of state to lessen the effects of the transition to capitalism. However, when it returned to office in 2001, the remaining elements of the socialist economy had been greatly diminished and it was unable to utilise them as it had done previously. By then, the dependent nature of Polish capitalism had been established and the government was adhering to a Blarite *third way* policy of attempting to combine neo-liberal economics with some elements of social conciliation. This policy led to the dramatic decline in support for the left and opened the way for the election of a government from the conservative-right.

Chapter six, returns to looking at the international context of Poland's return to capitalism and at how recent developments within Polish politics can be understood through wider changes within the international historical bloc. The socio-economic consequences of the two decades of neo-liberal supremacy in the world and the widening divisions between the major capitalist powers opened the way for a more conservative ideology to gain ascendancy in the world. Before joining the EU, Poland and the other Candidate States were politically compelled to remain within the European liberal framework. However, many of the reforms that these countries were obliged to introduce contributed to the growth of a significant, although minority, conservative and Euro-sceptic current. After entering the EU, these political forces have gained power in Poland and have presented a political agenda that breaks decisively from the liberal consensus that dominated throughout transition. This comes into conflict with many of the accepted principles of the EU and is to an extent institutionally restrained by it. However, this conservative turn is not an isolated development and the Polish conservative-nationalists find political allies within the EU and beyond, with Poland becoming one of the USA's major strategic partners in Europe.

****

Throughout this book a number of terms are employed that need some prior explanation. The term Eastern Europe is used to describe the whole of the region in Europe that was part of the Socialist Bloc, while Central-Eastern Europe depicts those post-socialist countries that have recently joined the EU, which includes the Baltic States and Slovenia. The post-socialist countries that have joined the EU are described as Accession States. The CEE countries that joined the EU in 2004 are termed the Accession Eight (A8) states. The systems existent in EE before 1989-91 are described as being socialist. This is of course problematic, as these were not developed socialist societies and many of their deficiencies and deformations were far removed from the socialist ideal. Also, millions of socialists, inside and outside of these countries, actively opposed the Stalinist bureaucracy and supported a democratisation and revitalisation of these systems. However, these systems still possessed certain socialist characteristics and were distinct from the capitalist world. The experience of the past decade and a half has dismissed the myth that the systems on either side of the Berlin Wall were somehow the same. There has since been a transformation of the entire socio-economic and political orders in EE, with the introduction of capitalist relations of production powering and shaping this process. The word socialist is therefore taken up in order to distinguish them from the capitalist world. A more common description of these countries has been communist. However, this definition is even more confusing, as communism describes a stage of development beyond socialism. Communist and communism came into common usage after the split in the Socialist International prior to WW1 and the creation of the Communist International following the Russian Revolution. The victory of Stalinism in Russia and within the international communist movement meant that the common usage of the words communism and communist became distorted. In this book the words communist and communism are used to describe those political forces that belonged to the former ruling parties in EE. The phrases post-socialist or post-socialism define the systems after the transition; whilst post-communist or post-communism describe the political currents that inherited the organisational and political mantle from the former ruling parties. These words have sometimes been used by some authors in a way that implies that socialism or communism are historical facets and that these ideologies are outdated in the modern world. In this book they are deployed simply to describe the countries, parties and ideologies that emerged out of the former Eastern Bloc.

This book is primarily concerned with the period between the collapse of the socialist system and Poland's entry into the EU. However, there is some description and analysis of events before the socialist period and after EU Accession. The book was finished at the beginning of 2007 and it has been my intention to make it as up to date as possible. Due to the unstable and fluid nature of Polish politics, events change extremely quickly and often unpredictably. Therefore, the episodes covered after EU accession should be considered as descriptions of temporal events that allow for some conclusions to be drawn about the future direction of Poland's development.

1

THE POLITICS OF TRANSITION

The transition in EE closes the chapter on the world's first attempt at building an alternative socialist system to capitalism. It also ends a period when the EE countries were endeavouring to take an alternative path of development to that in WE. This chapter shall outline the historical and international implications of the transition in EE and provide a theoretical framework for our study of Poland's return to capitalism.

1

The transition from socialism to capitalism in EE has opened up a new and unique phase in capitalism's history. From the moment of its birth capitalism spawned its potential successor: socialism. The rise of productive forces to previously unimagined levels and the rapid growth of the proletariat, created the conditions for the rise of this economic and political alternative. Socialism offered a negation of capitalism's contradictions and the promise of a more just and prosperous future. Until the beginning of the twentieth century it had generally been assumed, within the international socialist movement, that capitalism would first be superseded within Europe's most industrially advanced societies. However, developments within the advanced capitalist states, most notably rising wages, eroded the basis for this assumption. The profits gained from colonialism allowed for the growth on an international form of monopoly capitalism and thus imperialism. These changes also brought into questions a second presumption contained within socialist and Marxist thought. This was that the pre-capitalist or early capitalist countries would logically replicate the course of industrial development that the advanced capitalist nations had previously undergone. It was now becoming apparent that the inexorable rise of industrial capitalism in the advanced WE states had been built upon a conquest of resources, labour and markets in the less developed nations, which blocked industrial development in capitalism's periphery.

The rise of monopoly capitalism and imperialism deepened and cemented the developmental divide between Eastern and Western Europe. This division replicated itself in a political and organisational split within the European socialist movement (see next chapter), with the axis of Marxist thought shifting to the eastern half of the continent (Anderson, 1976a). The Polish Marxist Rosa Luxemburg wrote the *Accumulation of Capital* (1913) as an attempt to explain capitalist development through its relations with pre-capitalist states. She argued that due to declining domestic opportunities for the profitable sale of goods, the developed capitalist states were forced to expand their trade to the underdeveloped, pre-capitalist states. Luxemburg adapted the theory of primitive capital accumulation, inherited from Marx to describe the genesis of capitalism. Primitive accumulation describes the process of divorcing the producer from the means of production, which is a necessity for the free development of capitalist relations of production. In the transition from feudalism to capitalism this meant 'freeing' producers (peasants and small manufacturers) from feudal bonds and subsistence. This had traditionally been understood as something that occurred only when capitalism was being formed; but Luxemburg re-interpreted primitive accumulation as being a continuous element of capitalist development ('untrammelled accumulation'), seeing it as a component of capitalism's expansion into pre-capitalist countries, regions and branches of production. The core capitalist states therefore use pre-capitalist areas as markets for their goods, a cheap supply of labour and a supply of raw materials.

Europe's developmental divide also shaped the political and social structures in Western and Eastern Europe, which became a focus for those seeking to understand the differing types of political system evolving in Europe. When Antonio Gramsci began to develop his theory of hegemony, he also did so in recognition of the divide between Eastern and Western Europe. Gramsci was concerned with how capitalism in the advanced western states maintained rule through consent and why it was that a revolution had first occurred in Russia and not in the more advanced capitalist states to the West. Gramsci undertook to employ the concept of hegemony as a way of looking at how the bourgeoisie exercises its rule in the advanced capitalist states. Through hegemony he was attempting to understand how rule is exerted through 'consent' or 'direction' in contrast to 'force' or 'coercion' and to comprehend this he considered the evolving relationship between the state and civil society.

According to Gramsci the superstructures of civil society, in the developed WE capitalist countries, protected the state and helped to maintain consent without the regular employment of the direct repressive instruments of the state. This was in contrast to the state in EE where civil society was weak or non-existent and the state dominant and coercive.[1] From its creation the Absolute State in EE differed to that in WE. For whilst the Absolute States of WE were infected by the existence of a rising bourgeoisie and mercantile class, the eastern states were characterised by the overwhelming control of the nobility pursuing anti-urban policies; as economic underdevelopment, a strong coercive state and a feudal social structure set the political framework in EE (Anderson, 1996). In turn, the state in WE became characterised by its dual nature of being both repressive and interventionist. Gramsci counter-poses the concept of the 'state as a policeman' with that of an 'ethical' or 'Interventionist' state.

Gramsci saw the state as having both a coercive function and one of protecting its own national bourgeoisie against international competition and the working class against the extremities of capitalism.[2] Gramsci describes this as the state acting as an 'educator'.

> [The state attempts to create] a complex and well-articulated civil society, in which the individual can govern himself without his self-government entering into conflict with political society – but rather becoming its normal continuation, its organic complement (Gramsci, 1991:268).

Therefore, the educative, interventionist and protective activities of the state help to create a sturdy, well-formed civil society. The coercive element of the state is only revealed when the bourgeois class is no longer able to absorb other social layers. Therefore, the Interventionist State strengthens the hegemony of the bourgeoisie, assisting in its creation of a wider historical bloc.

The concept of the historical bloc describes how leading social forces, at a national level, establish a relationship over contending social forces. Gramsci understood the limitations of any historical bloc as being determined by society's economic base and that a starting point of analysis should be the social relations of production. A ruling class must develop a hegemonic project that transcends particular corporate interests and binds antagonistic social classes. Therefore, state power rests upon a changing configuration of social forces that is continually shaped by the class struggle. This is expressed at the level of the superstructure, above all politics, which provides the basis for the bourgeoisie's cultural hegemony. Gramsci indicated, for example in his analysis of Fordism, how such a hegemonic bloc could extend outwards from the national sphere onto an international plane.

The concept of the historical bloc has been utilised to describe the global changes that have occurred since the mid-1970s, including the transition from socialism in EE. Starting from an analysis of the international relations of production, it is argued that after WW2 the USA directed the formation of an international historical bloc, based upon the principle of 'embedded liberalism', which combined international free trade with national government intervention (Cox, 1987). Nation states were characterised by the existence of comprehensive Welfare States, full employment and a mixed economy. However, the internationalisation of the economy created the conditions for the erosion of this post-war historical bloc, which was precipitated by the crisis in the world economy in the 1970s.

The collapse of socialism, in EE, was the defining moment in the transformation of the world historical bloc and has determined the course of capital accumulation pursued globally over the past decade and a half. In recent years, some attempts have also been made to reintegrate the theory of primitive accumulation into an understanding of contemporary capitalist development[3] (De Angelis, 1999; Perleman, 1997). It has been argued that primitive accumulation occurs any time that producers place themselves as an obstacle to their separation from the means of production. Capitalist expansion can be blocked by restrictions into certain geographical areas and also by the historical gains of the working class that restrict the dominance of monopoly capital. The transition from socialism in EE is a contemporary example of capitalist expansion, through primitive accumulation. Capitalism contains within itself elements of a future socio-economic system that negate capitalism and lead to it being superseded. However, in the ex-socialist states components of a 'future socialist system' exist as structural features from a previous order. Furthermore, these survive alongside pre-capitalist elements, which in many respects have strengthened since the collapse of the socialist system. It is upon these socio-economic and political structures that capitalism is being (re)created in EE. These were not advanced socialist societies and the workers were not direct owners of the means of production. However, the working class and peasantry were protected from the world market both by the state and by the socialised and protective nature of the economy. One of the driving forces behind recent capitalist development and so-called globalisation has been its extension into *post-capitalist* areas, whilst driving back social-welfare protections in the core capitalist states.

2

During the post-war period, the world was dominated by the existence of two competing historical blocs. Furthermore, these were organised around two antagonistic modes of production, with their corresponding social structures, forms of state and ideologies. The defining feature of world capitalism, in the post-war era, was that it had managed to stabilise and then expand despite losing huge amounts of territory. International capitalism was able to rebuild itself principally due to the strength of the American economy, which had come through WW2 virtually unscathed and industrially strengthened. It was the aid provided by the USA to Europe after WW2, that ensured both the continent's political stability and its consolidation as a US export market (Hudson, 2000). Keynesianism promoted the stabilisation of capitalism through demand management and the mixed economy and within the radical post-war atmosphere this meant the nationalisation of many utilities deemed to be in the national interest. Phenomena such as de-colonisation, the growth of the Welfare State in WE, the civil rights movement and the extension of women's rights could all occur due to the existence of an alternative historical bloc with which international capitalism had to contend. The post-war historical bloc was a stage of development when the major contradictions of capitalism were partially suspended and its essential movement blurred.

The post-war consensus in WE is the highest form to date of consensual capitalist rule, where the Interventionist State allows for the flourishing of an independent civil society. The working classes of WE were absorbed into support for and participation in the political system through the social democratic parties, trade unions and their bureaucracies, which rested upon the working class and won certain reforms within the parliamentary system. This post-war consensus incorporated an ideological convergence between parts of the reformist socialist movement and liberalism in WE (Padgett and Patterson, 1991). From the latter tradition, T.H. Marshall (1950) argued that there was a historical movement within capitalist society towards greater equality and that this is inherent in the evolution of the concept of citizenship. For Marshall citizenship has three parts: *civil, political* and *social,* with the civil and political rights (gained in the eighteenth and nineteenth centuries respectively) paving the way for the securing of social rights (in the twentieth century). Such social rights guarantee a 'civilised' standard of living for all and help to reduce social inequalities. They facilitate the creation of a certain cohesion in society whereby individuals feel part of and an obligation to participate in the democratic system. Similarly, Joseph Schumpeter (1942), again writing from a liberal perspective, argued that liberalism had become submerged into the socialist project and that liberalism had to take up some socialist ideals to retain capitalism. He believed that the state was becoming more active economically and that this was part of the natural progression of the capitalist economy. Concurrently, some writers from the socialist tradition began arguing, in the 1950s/1960s, that the WE societies were in fact no longer capitalist and that the traditional conflict between capital and labour had disappeared. Crossland (1967) wrote that capitalism had been changing since the turn of the century, enforced by a rebellion of the working classes against *laissez-faire* capitalism. The programme of nationalisation and creation of a Welfare State, introduced by the post-war British Labour government, could not be undone by future right wing governments because 'its causes lie much less in legislation, than in changes in social psychology, the moral consensus of opinion, technology and the internal structure of industry.' (1967: 27).

Various Marxist writers also exaggerated the extent to which capitalism had overcome some of its contradictions. A significant section of Marxism was drawn towards the ideas of controlled state monopoly capitalism, with the state seen to have regulated the destabilising tendencies of capitalism in the service of monopoly capital. Concurrently, the ideology of peaceful coexistence in the socialist states mirrored such beliefs, and ideas of an inherent convergence between the socialist and capitalist systems gained ascendancy. Frankfurt School writers, such as Adorno and Horkheimer (1997), concluded that science, technology and industry had combined to organise modern capitalist society so that any form of opposition or critical thought was excluded. Accordingly, the modern capitalist state had become so well developed and run, using the methods of scientific rationality, that there no longer existed, within civil society, any space for creative, critical thought. These processes led to some of the most influential Marxist theoreticians to turn their attention away from the economic and political sphere towards the search for negation in areas such as culture and aesthetics, biology and sexuality and language. Such thinking permeated the social sciences, with the sociological conceptions of embourgeoisement employed to argue that capitalism had structurally changed spurred by the growth in the middle class and disintegration of the industrial working class. From such conceptions emerged the argument that the working class was becoming more heterogeneous *(disintegration of labour)* due to high levels of social mobility (Dahrendorf, 1959). Famously, the thesis emerged out of American sociology that society's basic social and psychological needs had been met in modern industrial society, thus securing the conditions for a dramatic increase in social and political fluidity (Inglehart, 1984). Therefore, politics becomes dominated by the omnipresence of 'post-materialist values', which relate neither to class lines nor to the traditional left/right dichotomy (Giddens, 1998).

3

Hegel's analysis of *being* confirms that something only emerges when it is in contradiction with an obstacle that it must overcome. When there is no sharp contradiction there is no movement and the essential being of an object (its movement) is obscured. And so it was with regards to the disintegration of the post-war historical bloc. The major contradiction existent within post-war capitalism was that between the internationalisation of production and the welfarist/interventionist nature of the nation state. The existence of permanent inflation had been a feature of the post-war boom, but this situation became unsustainable, especially after the oil crisis in 1973/74. Capital responded to this crisis by seeking to remove the constraints on accumulation, imposed by the nation-state redistributional model. Furthermore, the opening up of the world economy and the transformation of its financial institutions, helped to facilitate an influx of capital into the USA, which in turn funded its drive to defeat socialism through an escalating arms race. Therefore, the ending of the post-war boom coincided with the reversal of fortunes for the US and European economies, with the USA absorbing capital from the rest of the world, in contradistinction to its post-war position as a supplier of capital. This situation could be tolerated by the USA's rival powers (e.g. Japan and Europe) when the focus of attention was on the destruction of socialism in the East. The break up of the post-war historical bloc in the West also disrupted the balance between the two competing historical blocs in the world and laid the ground for the destruction of socialism in EE. 'Really-existing socialism' in EE was a protective system, which sought to develop its productive forces beyond those of world capitalism, through a process of rapid industrialisation and the administrative suppression of commodity relations. EE governments prioritised the expansion of heavy industry at the expense of other sectors such as services and consumption. Despite the region's relative isolation from the world economy many of the factors that led to the disintegration of Keynesian interventionism in the West contributed to the decline of socialism in the East. For example, the oil crisis particularly affected CEE, as their economies were strongly reliant on heavy industry and thus oil. Also, in an attempt to reinvigorate their economies, some CEE countries became heavily indebted to the West in the 1970s. This was particularly the case in Poland, where foreign creditors became part owners of the economy and foreign banks began pushing for the implementation of market reforms. The rise in interest rates in the West during the early 1980s exacerbated this problem and by the mid-1980s the ruling parties in Poland, Yugoslavia and Hungary were introducing austerity measures that precipitated the reintroduction of capitalism throughout EE.

The transition from socialism is part of the negation of the post-war historical blocs and the emergence of a new, neo-liberal, historical bloc. The neo-liberal historical bloc was strengthened by the transition to capitalism in EE and the removal of obstacles to capital accumulation around the globe. However, the consolidation of this historical bloc is restricted in its scope and duration due to the nature of primitive accumulation and divisions between the major capitalist states. The policies of neo-liberalism have proven to be effective in opening up economies and drawing them into the global economy. However, the socio-economic consequences of this 'opening' mean that consolidating a consensual historical bloc becomes increasingly harder, as the 'free market' does not promote convergence but rather divergence and growing inequality. Income has become ever more concentrated in the richest states of the world and these divisions have widened since the collapse of socialism.[4] The decline of Keynesian interventionism and the move towards neo-liberalism was partly precipitated by the decline in capital accumulation and investment in the USA (Hudson, 2000). Whilst the huge inflow of capital into the USA could be accepted during the Cold War, thereafter divisions between the major capitalist states have grown (Freeman and Kagarlitsky, 2005). Therefore, the neo-liberal historical bloc is undermined, as the specific interests of American capital no longer coincide with those of capital in general, which underlies the present shift of the USA towards unilateralism.

4

The dominant ideology that initially accompanied the collapse of socialism in EE was an aggregate of the two historical blocs existent during the post-war period. The Glasnost and Perestroika reforms were presented as part of a wider progression towards a new, united, social democratic Europe, which would bring an era of peace and prosperity to the whole of the continent and beyond. However, what was occurring was not a synthesis of two historical blocs but rather the defeat of one, and the subsequent transformation and extension of the other. Therefore, once the political break from socialism had been achieved, capitalism not only moved further away from socialism but also attempted to break from social-welfare capitalism. This was accompanied by an ideological offensive of neo-liberalism, which permeated all areas of social and political thought. Famously, Francis Fukuyama (1992) argued that democracy and the market economy had found a self-identity, leading to his conclusion that the ideal of freedom was realised in the liberal-democratic system.

The hegemonic expansion of neo-liberalism is evident when we examine how it infused European social democratic thinking in the 1990s. Breaking from post-war social democratic accepted wisdom, *third way* social democracy endorsed the left's adaptation to the market, the scaling down of the Welfare State and rejection of long-held principles such as full employment and universal welfare guarantees. The *third way*, developed by British sociologist Anthony Giddens, is built upon many of the theoretical assumptions made during the post-war period; most notably that industrial capitalism has structurally changed, as it moves from first to second stage modernisation. Such ideas were given further impetus through the spread of the worldwide communications revolution, the arrival of the 'weightless' knowledge based economy and the realities of a post-1989 world, after the fall of socialism. Accordingly, the trading of information and knowledge is seen as the essence of this 'dematerialised' economy, as what is important is not how or where a product is manufactured but what its 'definition' is.

Modern industrial society is seen to have entered a 'post-materialist' era, accompanied by the downsizing of the industrial working class. Adopting Inglehart's thesis, Giddens argued that voting behaviour no longer conforms to class lines, which, alongside the decline in the size of the industrial working class, means that social democracy's traditional electoral base disappears. These 'shifting sands' cut the traditional connection between political parties and social classes and transcend the established left-right dichotomy. Accepting this reality means social democracy looks towards the political centre, termed by Giddens the 'active middle' or 'radical centre' (Giddens, 1998).

The *third way* scenario for post-Cold War capitalism is that the transition into a second stage of modernisation provides the conditions for continuous economic growth based on information rather than production. The successful market economy ensures that living standards rise and the role of the left is to make sure that socially excluded individuals are made competitive in this market. The superseding of 'old' class divisions and the strict left/right dichotomy allows the centre-left to extend its political reach beyond its traditional boundaries. For all sense and purposes the left abandons its socialist project and adopts the social-liberal concepts of meritocracy and individualism. Neo-liberalism, with its accompanying social conservatism, is criticised for excluding large sections of society and therefore the policies of the *third way* are portrayed as a more comprehensive hegemonic interpretation of neo-liberal ideology (Giddens, 1998).

However, post-Cold War politics have not been characterised by the growth of a 'radical centre' and liberalism, but rather by the escalation of conservatism. Neo-liberalism is an ideological fusion of the concepts of individual and political freedom with 'economic freedom'. However, from its conception, the *New Right* governments of Thatcher and Reagan, in the 1980s, targeted an offensive against liberal values as a way of breaking the post-war consensus (Gamble, 1988). The *New Right* expressed its support for the 'traditional family' against the liberal cultural values, which had grown from the 1960s. As noted above, the scope of liberalism widened in the post-war era, as social inequalities reduced; and previously excluded social groups were incorporated into the political system, encouraging diversity, freedom of choice and openness, thus deepening and widening civil society. The break from the post-war consensus has been accompanied by a rise in conservative, authoritarian values in society and politically there has been a distinct move away from the liberal consensus of the post-war era; symbolised by the growth of far right parties in Europe at a level not seen since the 1930s. Just as civil rights were strengthened through the extension of social rights, in the post-war era, the opposite process unfolds in the post-Cold War age. As the Interventionist State withdraws, the space for an independent civil society is encroached upon by the market, political stability is disturbed and the possibility of the repressive instruments of the state being applied increased.

5

The decline of liberalism and rise of conservatism was driven both by the socio-economic effects of the neo-liberal offensive and the growing divisions emerging within the historical bloc. Fukuyama's vision that the ideals of free market capitalism and liberal democracy had found a self-realisation was supported in the final years of the Cold War when the universal interests of international capitalism were embodied in the policies of the USA (Anderson, 2006). All this changed after the fall of socialism in EE. On the one hand, there was no longer a common enemy that compelled the leading capitalist states to remain united; and on the other, the collapse of the USSR and break up of the Socialist Bloc meant that the global reach of the American state greatly increased. In these conditions, American 'exceptionalism' and belief in unilateral political and military activities intensified. By the mid-1990s, Fukuyama had become a leading exponent of neo-conservatism and was urging the American government to promote its moral values abroad, through actions such as militarily removing Saddam Hussein from power in Iraq. However, by the start of the second Gulf War, Fukuyama had broken ranks with the neo-conservatives, arguing that the sudden collapse of the USSR had embedded a sense of over-confidence within the American administration (Fukuyama, 2006). A growing rift with Europe emerged, and the USA became embroiled in a number of military conflicts. The principles of democracy, human rights and freedom, espoused by the American state, increasingly came to be seen as slogans to promote the interests of the USA abroad. In turn, a US administration, more aggressively promoting these values overseas, moved away from many liberal democratic practices and principles domestically; thus losing the moral authority it had gained at the end of the Cold War as the ostensible promoter of liberal-democratic rights internationally.

The divergence between the major capitalist powers is evident in CEE. During the Cold War the populations in the Socialist Bloc viewed the West as one united entity, with any divisions between Europe and the USA rarely considered. However, after the collapse of the Berlin Wall, this relative unity began to break up, something that has been clarified after 9/11 and the incursions of the USA into the Middle East. Although the CEE transitions had the 'return to Europe' as their stated goal, the reforms were broadly based upon the assumptions underlying the *Washington Consensus*. At the end of the Cold War the USA faced huge budget deficits and was in no position to fund a developmental programme in CEE similar to the Marshall Plan after WW2. Other alternative major investment programmes, coming out of Germany and France, were rejected and the transition in EE proceeded along neo-liberal lines directed by the IMF and World Bank. The USA was able to consolidate its position as the 'victor' of the Cold War, via the expansion of NATO into CEE in 1997, which was then immediately consolidated through the war in Yugoslavia. The project of European expansion has been more protracted and one of its features is the fact that the new EU members from CEE generally maintain a pro-US foreign policy stance. At the point of the EU's expansion into CEE, divisions between Europe and the USA were widening, which has in turn created further discords within Europe itself.

The major effect of the EE transition in WE has been the erosion of the Welfare State. From the 1970s, European capital became convinced that there needed to be a transformation of the WE economy to make it more competitive with the USA and Japan. High wages, trade union rights and welfare benefits were once again viewed as being particularist and something that restrained further economic growth. However, a class compromise had existed in WE since WW2 and in the 1980s the dismantling of this compromise was seen as being politically dangerous. The collapse of socialism in EE provided the grounds for the WE bourgeoisie to launch a new offensive against their own Welfare States. Policies such as extending the working age, privatising public services and imposing new pay structures have been pursued. These have conflicted directly with the interests of public sector workers, who are most affected by the practices of primitive accumulation in WE. The demands of these workers relate directly with the living standards (in health, education, pensions, etc) of the majority of the population, along with the progressive social policies that allowed for the broadening of civil and political rights after WW2.

The transition in EE provided the opportunity for the project of European integration to proceed on a neo-liberal basis, which also shaped the course of the EU's eastward expansion (Bieler, 2003, Hudson, 2000). The process of monetary union, through the Maastricht

Treaty and creation of the European Central Bank, was based upon the principles of price stability and low inflation, to the exclusion of full employment. From the beginning of transition European institutions set a framework for EU expansion that served as an impetus to the liberal market reforms in CEE. The major European economies in particular sought to open up the CEE economies, in order to gain access to their resources, labour and markets. Therefore, by the time the CEE states entered the EU, their economies had been largely opened, the ownership structure transformed and large sections of their economies bought up by international capital. However, once inside the EU a new situation emerges. As well as pressure for further liberalisation, the possibility also exists that there will be a transfer of resources, through direct aid and subsidies to CEE from the EU. The question facing CEE and the EU is whether expansion will facilitate the extension of European social standards eastwards or, in contrast, whether it will deepen the liberalisation of the EU economy as a whole.

6

The strategy of primitive accumulation in EE resulted in a region-wide recession of unprecedented proportions. The majority of the EE states have still not crossed their pre-transition level of GDP and there has been a huge rise in poverty and social inequalities across the region. A recent World Bank report shows that in 1988 only 4% of the region's population were poor (defined as having an income of less than £1.25 a day), while in 2003 poverty affected 12% of society.[5] By opening up to the world economy it was assumed that the ex-socialist countries would be able to import some of the prosperity from the West. In this context a globalisation of the CEE states occurred, with their governments geared towards serving the interests of international capital (Gowan, 1997). However, the immense economic slump, following the collapse of socialism, meant that a number of states resisted this process and, notably in Russia, governments were formed that secured a form of corporate (semi-criminal) capitalism, which blocked the globalisation of their economies and institutions.[6] These systems are now characterised by the existence of an oligarchy that draws huge profits from their countries' natural resources. However, the blocking of international capital has also meant that some of the extreme levels of poverty in EE have reduced. For example, according to the same World Bank report, between 1998 and 2003 poverty in Russia declined from 20% to 12%. Also, the country where poverty has fallen the most has been Belarus, which has most resolutely resisted the influx of foreign capital. Between 1996 and 2003, poverty in Belarus reduced by a half.

The post-socialist countries are shaped by the historical legacy of socialism and feudalism in the region. The countries in which capitalism was overthrown in the first half of the twentieth century were characterised by the underdevelopment of capitalist structures and the endurance of pre-capitalist forms, upon which socialist structures were now being built. These continue to have a material presence, after the collapse of socialism, and are also deeply rooted within social consciousness, exerting themselves politically, socially and culturally. Although, the industrial expansion made during socialism was limited, it did achieve a level of development surpassing that made during capitalism. The policy of the transition, after the collapse of socialism, has been to demolish the socialist aspects of the economy as rapidly as possible, in order to allow for the growth of capitalism. However, the obliteration of the socialist economy has often not been matched by the growth of advanced capitalist structures, leaving the CEE economies reliant upon the world economy, with some socialist elements among the most advanced areas of the post-socialist economies. These include sectors of industry, agriculture and social welfare, upon which millions of people rely.

Socialism also created social structures that replicated these countries particular level of development. Due to the structure of a command economy and rapid industrialisation, the working class was officially proclaimed as the spearhead of society in creating socialism. The policy of rapid industrialisation led to the quantitative development of the working class, which benefited under socialism from such things as the full employment policy and from the fact that manual labour was highly valued. Simultaneously, farmers and peasants were faced with a paradoxical situation where the development of an independent farming sector was controlled and even reversed. However, those working in agriculture, whether on state or private farms, were also protected from the world market and were dependent upon the state monopoly of supplies and marketing of agricultural produce. Similarly, the intelligentsia was negatively affected by the fact that salaries were not linked to education and that they had to deal with state censorship. Yet on the other hand, the state financing and sponsorship of science, culture and art protected them. Thus the social structure, system of differentiation and network of class interests and relationships were fundamentally changed during the socialist period (Mokrzycki, 1997). The neo-liberal reforms have met the obstacle of this existing structure of class interests. Literally millions of people; ranging from industrial workers to peasants, teachers, pensioners and health-workers have an interest in defending elements of the inherited socialist system. Moreover, those social classes that were most instrumental in overthrowing socialism, have often fared the worst after its collapse; the prime example being the industrial working class in Poland.

7

When examining the transition from socialism one necessarily returns to the relationship between the state and civil society. Overwhelming emphasis was placed on the importance of civil society in the overthrow of socialism and the need for a strong civil society thereafter.

> For if one thing had seemed clear, it was that the post-socialist period in Eastern Europe would be marked by an explosion of civic association and new interest representation. 'Civil Society', after all, had been the democratic (and revolutionary) password of the opposition since the mid-1970s. Many of its theorists came to power throughout the region after 1989 (Ost, 1993: 455).

The socio-economic role of the state is invariably bound with post-socialist politics to a much greater degree than in the West. This is both because of the universal role played by the state during socialism and the relative economic underdevelopment of the region, which has historically led to the state having a more dominant role. It became a general *a priori* that for the CEE societies to become secure and functioning liberal democracies they must develop sturdy, well-formed civil societies and to achieve this the 'constraints' of the state needed to be removed to allow for the full development of market forces. Neo-liberalism harnessed the former opposition's preoccupation with civil society, as a counterweight to the socialist state, using it as a wedge to drive through the market reforms. In the post-socialist discourse the terms market, democracy and civil society became synonymous.

The reintroduction of capitalism in CEE coincided with the high point of neo-liberalism's popularity internationally. Neo-liberalism was nowhere as strong or omnipresent as in EE during the early stages of reform and the free-market and democracy became the antithesis of the command economy and one-party state; with the reform weary population offered a complete break from the previous system and a seemingly proven model of development. It created an *organic cohesion* with which all social and political forces were compelled to comply. The notions of 'freedom', 'openness', 'liberalisation' and the 'primacy of the market' were all presented as neutral concepts, yet corresponded to the course of primitive accumulation that was being embarked upon in EE. However, as the reality of the economic liberal reforms became clear, so dissatisfaction with the social and political liberal reforms grew. The political scene in the post-socialist countries is shaped by changes within the world historical bloc. The social divisions caused by a decade and a half of neo-liberal economic reform; divisions between the major world powers and the international offensive of conservatism, exert their influence. Increasing social divisions and the alienation of large social classes have the potential for destabilising the political systems in CEE and making possible the return of the coercive instruments of the state. This takes on a particular form and importance in the CEE countries after they have joined the EU, with the new EU members becoming incorporated into an enlarged superstructure with the WE states.

As long as EU entry remained the destination point for the transition in CEE, then the ideological dominance of liberalism and the unity of liberal democratic and economic reform were assured. The allure of joining the EU, already excluded to many neighbouring states to the east, pulled the CEE nations through a series of intense structural and institutional reforms. However, once inside the Union much of the impetus for continuing along this course has been removed and the subjective unanimity of liberalism broken. With the left immersed into this liberal framework, conservatism has arisen as the most coherent and consistent alternative mode of political thought in many of the CEE states. Conservatism in the post-socialist states combines a critique of both socialism and liberalism. Liberalism is criticised for its cultural relativism, secularism, unconstrained modernism and for its inherent tendency towards social levelling. In the post-socialist reality it is blamed for not carrying through a consistent policy of 'de-communisation' and for allowing ex-communists to retain prominent positions of power. Conservatism thus proposes instigating a joint campaign against the remnants of socialism and the fledging liberal democratic system. The pragmatism, relativism and pluralism of liberalism are seen to have created an individualistic and immoral society. Contemporary post-socialist conservatism refers back to the work of inter-war conservatives, such as Carl Schmitt and Leo Strauss, and the opinion that the world is divided into friends and foes. It proposes that the state takes a more active role in public life, fixing the nature and frontiers of a community and actively promoting a moral alternative to both socialism and liberal individualism.

****

When studying Poland's return to capitalism we are looking at an element of the wider changes that have been occurring within the global capitalist system. These include how the disintegration of the Socialist Bloc has affected the capitalist system and, consecutively, how this system has extended into the ex-socialist states. This is based upon the historically uneven development of capitalism and the relative underdevelopment of the EE economies. The historical weakness of capitalism, the bourgeoisie and civil society in the region contribute to the imbalance within the region's socio-economic and political systems. The attempt by the EE states to close the developmental gap with WE has been ongoing since the fifteenth century. During socialism a regional structural and superstructural developmental path was taken, in counter-distinction to that in WE. The short history of post-socialist capitalism has been one of attempting to replicate western models at a superstructural and structural level, which involves the integration of the CEE states into the EU. In the next chapter we shall examine in detail the question of underdevelopment in Poland and CEE, which will provide an historical context for Poland's transition from socialism to capitalism.

2

POLAND AND THE UNDER-DEVELOPMENT OF EASTERN EUROPE

Capitalism in the post-socialist states is built alongside pre-capitalist and socialist structures. This affects both the form of capitalism in CEE and the relationship between the state and civil society in these countries. This chapter shall focus on the historical underdevelopment of CEE vis-à-vis WE and at Poland's place in this dichotomy. It will describe how WE development has been intrinsically tied to the underdevelopment of CEE. We shall also examine how the state, and its relationship with civil society, differs historically in the two 'halves' of the continent and at how this has shaped political rule and thought in CEE and Poland. This will allow us to place the socialist period in Poland in its historical context, thus providing a basis for examining the country's return to capitalism.

1

At the turn of the fifteenth/sixteenth centuries WE began its dramatic ascendancy of modernisation, which opened up a developmental division with EE. This division was then accentuated by the English industrial revolution and the French revolution, during the 18th and 19th centuries, that helped pave the way for WE industrialisation and the emergence of strong bourgeois states and political systems (Berend,

1986). The fundamental demographic difference between eastern and western feudalism was the relative abundance of unpopulated land in EE. 'Peasant flight' was a constant threat in EE, compelling the nobility to restrict the mobility of the peasantry. The existence of independent (albeit weak) urban towns acted as a pole of attraction for peasants and therefore the autonomy of these towns was also curtailed, clearing the way for the imposition of serfdom (Anderson, 1996)[1] The agricultural character of EE was deepened as the eastern manorial estates began supplying cereals to western markets in the sixteenth century. For example, Poland exported 20,000 tons of rye at the start of the sixteenth century, which had risen to 170,000 tons by 1618 (Anderson, 1996). In return, the EE nobilities imported manufactured goods from the West, thus further reducing their dependency on the towns. This process accelerated as countries such as the Netherlands began specialising in areas of agricultural produce such as livestock, to sell on the world market. In order to feed their growing urban population such countries needed to import cereals, which further opened up a market for EE agriculture. The effect of this trend was that the eastern economies became further dependent on WE and the power of the lords against the towns, central government and peasantry was strengthened[2] (Kochanowicz, 1989).

Although, eastern feudal agriculture became more extensive during this period, it was never able to match the intensive gains in organisation or technology achieved in the West.[3] This technological unevenness meant that the West exerted a pressure on the East not only (or primarily) through trade but also militarily. Therefore, the eastern nobilities were forced to adopt equally centralised state machineries in order to survive (Anderson, 1996). The impulse for the creation of eastern Absolutism came from one of the newest and least developed western Absolutisms: Sweden. Sweden invaded Russia, Austria, Germany and Poland between 1630 and 1720 and the reactions of the different nobilities to these invasions helped to determine the future development of their states. In Russia the decisive phases of the introduction of Absolutism occurred during the Swedish expansion. In contrast, the loose aristocratic order in Poland was unable to repel the Swedish invasion, thus instigating a decline, which ultimately led to the country being divided into three parts controlled by the Russian, Hapsburg and Prussian empires. The growth of Absolutist States throughout the region decisively ended any hopes of urban independence and stamped the authority of the nobility over the towns.

The paradox of this situation was that while structurally the two halves of the continent were diverging, superstructurally they were converging. In turn, this meant that the form of these Absolute States differed (Anderson, 1996). In the West the state was infected by the existence of a rising bourgeoisie and mercantile class. In the East the emerging Absolute State was characterised by the overwhelming control by the nobility pursuing anti-urban policies. The relative underdevelopment and dependence of CEE was further underlined in the eighteenth and nineteenth centuries as industrialisation speeded up in WE, widening the gap between the eastern and western halves of the continent.[4] CEE did undergo some significant modernisation during this period as an inflow of surplus capital from WE began to transform agriculture, industry and (importantly) communications. In the fifty years before WW1, agricultural production in the region increased fifty times, stimulating other areas of the economy including the industrial sector (Berend, 1986). These industries were generally connected to agriculture, such as the milling industry in Budapest and the textile industry in Łódź. The western parts of the region (Germany, the Czech Lands and Austria) made significant developmental strides, catching up with (and in Germany's case surpassing in some areas) WE.[5] A second group of nations followed (e.g. Hungary, the Polish areas, Russia) experiencing some limited industrialisation, accompanied by a third group (e.g. the Balkan states of Romania, Serbia and Bulgaria), which underwent no significant structural change, with the traditional agricultural system remaining intact (Ibid.).

2

It is in this context that we can grasp the essential difference between the state and civil society in Eastern and Western Europe. In WE the formation of Absolute States, shaped by an emerging bourgeoisie, ensured that ideals of individualism gained dominance. Also, the fact that this was accompanied by a progression towards the creation of political democracies meant that individuals and social institutions sought to influence and participate in the activities of the state. In EE the situation was entirely different. Firstly, the dominance of the feudal empires in the region excluded the construction of citizenship based around a national identity. Additionally, the populations in many CEE countries saw the state and political system as being alien and imposed from outside. Polish society came to see itself as being a political, economic and cultural self-organising society, existing alongside or in opposition to the state (Kurczewska, 1995). Visions of a single united

Poland transcended the living reality of a divided nation and collectivist ideas of independence, patriotism (embodied in romanticist philosophy and literature) combined to create a vision of an ideal future life after independence was regained. Concurrently, due to external domination and economic underdevelopment, alternative institutions to the state, such as the Church and the family, gained a leading position in society. These both provided a social space where national identity could be preserved and social networks that provided support to communities and individuals. Therefore, the ideas of the nation and society became more dominant in Polish consciousness than those such as the individual and the state.

Two examples of how the relative underdevelopment of CEE influenced social and political relations are the position of Jews and the nature of the socialist movement. After being eliminated from commerce in Europe Jews moved into usury, where they could prosper within the confines of a feudal economy. However, the commodification of the countryside and the growth of capitalism rendered this situation impossible. As capitalism developed in WE, during the fifteenth and sixteenth centuries, so a large number of Jews were assimilated into these societies, whilst another section emigrated to EE. In Poland, the Jews enjoyed royal protection, as they provided the royalty with its main source of revenue and they supplied the Polish nobility (*Szlachta*) with luxury goods. However, as the *Szlachta* became heavily indebted to the Jews, so they sought to restrict the amount of money going to them in order that they did not challenge the nobility's position as landowners. Usury also brought the Jews into contact with the poor who became reliant on the Jews as moneylenders, which inevitably meant that the Jews became scapegoats for the impoverishment of the peasants and artisans. However, the class that was most hostile to the Jews was the emerging bourgeoisie, who perceived the Jews as representing a block to their own socio-economic advancement. The severe weakening of Polish feudalism from the seventeenth century meant that the royal protection of the Jews diminished and their persecution began. This was strengthened by the emancipation of the peasantry in 1863 in the Polish lands of Russia and the growth of the Polish bourgeoisie. However, the weakness of Polish capitalism meant that the Jews were not assimilated into society as had occurred in WE. Rather than being incorporated into society, the Jews were persecuted as a distinct social group and anti-Semitism grew within the EE societies, including Poland where more than one million Jews lived (Leon, 1946).

The weakness of capitalism in EE also affected the socialist movement in the region, which began to diverge from that in WE from the beginning of the twentieth century. Reformist socialism emerged first in England, with *Fabianism* commanding an ideological hegemony over the British Labour Party by the end of the eighteenth century. The major reason why reformist socialism emerged first in England was the monopoly it enjoyed as a colonial power in the middle of the nineteenth century. This dominant economic position meant that concessions could be given to the upper strata of skilled workers, who were involved in the first trade unions and by the late nineteenth century male universal suffrage had been granted (Nairn, 1965). Fabianism was founded on the utilitarian basis that socialism could be built piece by piece with state intervention and administration slowly extended to replace the anarchy of the market. In contrast to the British Labour Party, the German Social Democratic Party (SPD - formed in the late 1860s) spent its early years fighting Bismarck's anti-socialist laws. Consequently, the SPD came to be seen as the leading campaigners for democracy and as a result German socialism was not immersed into liberal-democracy as happened in England. After the repeal of the anti-socialist laws the SPD became a serious force in mass politics, standing on a Marxist political platform. However, the growth of German capitalism in the late nineteenth century, spurred by its own colonial exploits, began to provide the possibility for the German working class to gain greater civil and social rights. After being in contact with British Fabians, leading SPD member Eduard Bernstein concluded that the SPD should become a democratic socialist party of reform, seeking to win social reforms within the parliamentary system that would lead, step-by-step, to the implementation of socialism through the parliamentary system.[6]

It had previously been assumed, within the international socialist movement, that the less developed, semi-feudal eastern states would have to undergo a period of capitalist industrialisation, before being able to embark upon a socialist path. Russian Marxists, such as Georgi Plekhanov, believed that Russia had to imitate western development as socialism could only be built in a strong capitalist society with the working class organised independently through liberal social institutions. By the middle of the first decade of the twentieth century Russia had an impoverished peasantry, a small but concentrated and radical proletariat and a repressive political system embroiled in foreign conflict. These factors combined in 1905, creating revolutionary protests demanding economic and political reform. The combination of this growing radicalism, along with the absorption of growing sections of WE social democracy into the institutions of bourgeois democracy, led to a fundamental reappraisal of long-held Marxist assumptions. The issues at hand were to clarify why the revolutionary movement was not the strongest in the advanced industrial states, which demanded an explanation as to how developed capitalism had managed to appease its working classes. Tied to this was the question of what were the possibilities for socialism in the less developed countries, where the revolutionary movement was the strongest.

Along with the work of Rosa Luxemburg a number of criticisms of *revisionism* grew out of EE, especially Russia, with the works of people such as Vladimir Lenin, Nikolai Bukharin and Leon Trotsky revealing how Russian Marxism had evolved from the positions of its early leaders. One of Lenin's early theoretical works (*Development of capitalism in Russia* – 1899) challenged the *Narodniks*, who believed that Russia should pursue an alternative path of development, based around the peasant commune, due to the country's late entry into the process of capitalist industrialisation. Lenin at this time believed in the necessity and inevitability of the development of capitalism in Russia, although he suggested that this would be hindered by the competitiveness of the advanced industrial states. However, after the revolutionary events of 1905 and the rise of 'revisionism' in WE, Lenin (*Imperialism, the highest stage of capitalism* – 1916) began to argue that the 'super-profits' of imperialism were helping to create the conditions for the stabilisation of capitalism in the advanced industrial states and the assimilation of large sections of the proletariat, represented by a growing reformist labour bureaucracy. Also, the material basis for this reformism came from the exploitation of less developed countries, thus restricting the latter's ability to undertake a capitalist road of development. These developments in eastern (especially Russian) Marxism were part of the growing schism in the international socialist movement. It was in this context that Rosa Luxemburg developed her theory of the accumulation of capital and her critique of *revisionism*, which were created with the division of Poland and the incorporation of its eastern lands into Tsarist Russia in the background.

During the eighteenth and nineteenth centuries, early Polish socialist thinking concentrated on the recreation of an independent state, with the peasant commune (*Gmina*) envisaged as the core of this new state. This movement suffered a series of defeats in the nineteenth century culminating in an uprising in 1863, which was crushed by the Russian army. The Tsarist administration then introduced a set of measures intended to deny any semblance of autonomy within the Russian occupied part of Poland (known as the *Congress Kingdom*), simultaneously introducing a law to 'emancipate the peasantry' (*uwłaszczenie*). This destroyed the *Szlachta* and opened up a period of industrialisation. From 1863 to 1886 industrial workers grew by two to three times to become 8% of the population. Areas of industrial concentration grew up in towns such as Łódź, where 60% of the industrial population was based (Naimark, 1979). This initial industrialisation manifested itself ideologically in *Warsaw Positivism* and a shift in the locus of intellectual activity from the *Szlachta* to the new urban alliance of bankers, merchants and liberal professionals (Blit, 1971). These positivists were critical of the revolutionary idealism of the romanticists and instead argued that the highest form of patriotism was the economic and cultural advancement of Poles. As they observed the improved conditions of the working classes in WE, they believed that progress could be brought about in Poland through legislation. This theory (which expressed the hopes and aspirations of a rising and optimistic bourgeoisie) could not hegemonise itself into a political theory of the working class. This was due to the underdevelopment of the economy, a weak native bourgeoisie and the absence of an elected parliament. Similar situations were evident throughout CEE, with the one exception being the Czech Lands of the Austro-Hungarian Empire, which incorporated some of the most advanced industrial areas of the empire, although most of the industry was German owned. In this situation Czech nationalism acquired influence within the Czech working class, represented by T.G. Masaryk, who combined nationalism with ideas of economic progress and greater social equality and a significant *revisionist* wing arose within the Czech-Slovak Social Democratic Party.

3

The end of the WW1 heralded the collapse of the empires in CEE and the creation of independent nation states. However, the conditions in which these states were being formed differed greatly. Czechoslovakia had a level of economic development and a social structure comparable to many countries in WE, although there was an imbalance between the industrialised Czech lands and the rural based economy of Slovakia. After the war an independent bourgeoisie emerged in Czechoslovakia, accounting for 5% of the population, numbering around 22,000 families (Tiechova, 1985). In contrast, Hungary had a predominantly feudal social structure and the republic was formed in an atmosphere of reaction and repression as thousands were killed, deported or placed in concentration camps, after the defeat of the Hungarian Soviet Republic in August 1919.[7] All social legislation, passed by the Hungarian Soviet government, was reversed and limited suffrage was only introduced in 1921. Poland had a similar social structure to Hungary but its republic was born in an atmosphere of optimism, as the creation of an independent republic briefly realised the hopes of generations of Poles.

During the first three years of its existence the Polish Republic was involved in military conflicts with Germany, Czechoslovakia, Lithuania, Western Ukraine and Soviet Russia. The latter conflict was instigated after the Polish and Soviet armies moved into land vacated by the Germans. Conflicts between the Soviets and Poles had a wider international significance as the Poles aligned with the western armies seeking to defeat the Russian Revolution and in turn the Soviet Union looked to export its revolution to Poland, which was seen as a bridge between the USSR and Germany. With the Soviets pre-occupied by a civil war, the Polish army moved eastwards taking most of Lithuania and Belarus. As they moved into Ukraine the Soviet Army pushed them westwards and then progressed towards the gates of Warsaw, with victory seemingly imminent. However, the Polish army, led by Józef Piłsudski, defeated the Soviet advance, with Lenin subsequently admitting that it had been a mistake to expect the Poles to welcome the Red Army, which was not seen as a liberator but rather another example of Russian expansionism. This was part of the wider geopolitical tensions in the region and throughout its 21-year history the Polish Republic was constantly caught between the struggles of greater powers, which eventually led to its destruction.

Polish society was characterised by the presence of significant groups of ethnic minorities, especially the large Jewish community. The situation of the Jews in Poland, during the inter-war period, was determined by both the decline in feudalism and the problems associated with Poland's young capitalism, especially high unemployment. Jews were excluded from owning land and working in large factories; there were boycotts of Jewish goods and anti-Semitic campaigns waged in universities to exclude Jews from entering the intellectual professions. The Jews fared particularly badly in the large cities, where capitalism was most highly developed. While in 1914 72% of shops in the towns were Jewish owned, this had declined to 34% in 1935. Conversely, over 82% of shops in the less developed rural areas of Poland belonged to Jews (Leon, 1946).

Two major figures dominated political life during the inter-war period in Poland: Józef Piłsudski and Roman Dmowski. Although they had distinct political ideologies, they both offered an authoritarian solution to Poland's socio-economic and political problems. Dmowski, whose social origins were in the emerging bourgeoisie of the nineteenth century, is regarded as the creator of Polish nationalism. He helped to form the Polish National Democratic movement and its accompanying ideology, known as *Endecja*. He believed that the nation was a natural phenomenon, identifying ethnic and cultural variety as the source of conflict in society. His social-Darwinian thinking brought him close to inter-war fascist ideology and he openly praised Italian fascism in the mid-1920s. He identified Jews and the freemasons as sources of an international conspiracy and was an advocate of the anti-Jewish boycotts and exclusion of Jews from universities. Dmowski was close to the Catholic Church and he regarded Polish national identity as being synonymous with Catholicism. However, Dmowski and his supporters were isolated from the inter-war European fascist movement as they saw Poland's main threat being Germany, believing that the Slavonic nations should form a common front against it. Although he only held a government office briefly, Minister of Foreign Affairs in 1923, he was the main political figure of the nationalist right throughout the inter-war period.

In contrast Józef Piłsudski was born into a family descended from the old Polish nobility and intelligentsia. He helped establish the Polish Socialist Party (PPS) in 1893, leading the party's patriotic wing during partition. He was Poland's Chief of State and Commander in Chief for the first four years after the formation of an independent Polish state, and was the unofficial leader of the country after he led a coup in 1926 (see below). According to Piłsudski, the nation was a product of history and ethnic and cultural diversity a source of national strength and vitality. Piłsudski's main concern was not with nationalism but with national independence and, particularly from 1926, he promoted the idea of *Sanacja*, meaning a return to political health. As a registered protestant he was distant from Polish Catholicism and was open to other nationalities and religions. Also, in contrast to Dmowski, he believed that Russia was the main threat to Poland and supported the concept of creating a common anti-Russian front with the states to Poland's east. Due to his anti-Russian convictions, Piłsudski supported the central powers during WW1.[8] (Davies, 2001) Despite their differences, both Piłsudski and Dmowski offered authoritarian solutions to the crisis of capitalism in inter-war Poland.

4

The fundamental problem in Poland and CEE, during the inter-war period, was the lack of capital needed for economic modernisation, which was exaggerated by the break up of the empires and the loss of these 'internal' markets. At the beginning of the inter-war period large areas of the CEE economy were based on land tenure with millions of small peasants living next to large landowners employing landless labourers. The prospect of having to compete on a world market, along with the radical impact of the Russian revolution, provided an impetus for land reform. However, this land reform failed to significantly raise the productivity of farming, with rural unemployment remaining alarmingly high, especially during the recession of the 1930s.[9] In order, therefore, for the countries of CEE to modernise they needed to reduce their over-dependence on agriculture and accumulate capital for investment in industry[10]. The countries of CEE had an abundance of raw materials but lacked the necessary capital to exploit their potential. Some surpluses were extracted from agriculture but these were largely insufficient for serious capital investment. This search for capital defined the economic stages that the CEE states passed through during the inter-war years. These stages will be considered below in the context of Poland's inter-war experience, with the examples of Hungary and the Czech Republic given as a comparison.

The 1920s

During the 1920s the countries of CEE became incorporated into the world economy, looking to attract loans from the advanced capitalist states. Therefore, one of the priorities for these governments was to establish stable currencies and sound budgets. Most of the CEE economies had stabilised by the mid-1920s, after an initial period of high inflation and instability, and began to experience relatively rapid growth. The main problem for the new independent Polish state was that its separate parts were not incorporated, with the absence, even, of a self-contained transport network (Taylor, 1952; Zweig, 1994). Another major socio-economic imbalance was between agriculture and industry, as only 25% of the population lived in the towns, while 75% lived in the countryside (Davies, 1981).[11]

The new Polish republic was born in an atmosphere of optimism and radicalism, with strong support for greater social justice and fairness. The new Polish constitution (1921) paid special attention to social justice, under pressure from the peasant and socialist parties. The PPS was reformed as a united party in 1919 and gave its support to

Piłsudski's aim of building a federation with Belarus and Ukraine.[12] Soaring inflation and the attempt to form a national currency marked the initial period after the formation of the Polish state. This was accompanied by a series of strikes and a rapid turnover in government. In May 1926, the leader of the peasant movement Wincenty Witos formed a government. Dmowski and the National Democrats had participated in his government in 1923 and the left interpreted the move as being a sign of an impending dictatorial takeover. In response, Piłsudski joined a section of the army to fight the President's troops, leading to the 1926 May Coup, which was backed among others by both the PPS and Polish Communist Party (KPP).[13] Piłsudski was able to use his past connections with the left, and the standing he had as a military leader, to create a political programme that could win the support of large sections of society. During the inter-war period around 30% of Poles were non-Catholics, and if Dmowski and the *Endecja* had triumphed, it is likely that Poland would have been thrust into a civil war. Piłsudski's *Sanacja* regime sought the 'moral cleansing' of public life and the stabilisation of the budget and currency. He achieved his latter aim quickly, when in 1926 Poland registered a large export surplus (ZŁ707m) instigated by a currency depreciation (Zweig, 1944). A stabilisation loan was secured from American and European bankers, which helped to improve living conditions, with official unemployment falling from 304,000 (1926) to 185,000 (1928) (Ibid.).

By the end of the 1920s, Hungary was profiting economically from the healthy international market for agricultural goods and the $1000m loan (equal to one year's national income) it received from the USA (Borysanyi, 1968). During the same period, Czechoslovakia transformed itself into a country with more people employed in industry and trade than in agriculture. The government pursued a joint strategy of placing large private concerns into Czechoslovakian hands (in order to build-up the national bourgeoisie – *nostrification*), while introducing some social legislation such as unemployment benefit and land reform (Tiechova, 1988).

Recession

The impact of the 1929 USA stock market crash and the ensuing recession disproportionately affected CEE, with the prices of agricultural products collapsing and foreign loans drying up. Poland had managed to recover economically, during the second half of the 1920s, through an influx of foreign capital, which stopped after 1929. Therefore, between 1929 and 1933, national income fell by 25% (while for example in Great Britain it only decreased by 4%) and industrial production declined from an index of 116.1 (1929) to 71.2 (1932), one of the largest industrial collapses in Europe. Registered unemployment rose from 185,000 in 1928 to 466,000 in 1936 (Zweig, 1944). As an idea of how severe an impact the recession had on agriculture one can observe that the wages of agricultural workers fell to an index of 54 in 1931 from a national index of 100 in 1929 (Taylor, 1952). Before 1930 there had been a period of collaboration between Pilsudski and the parliament, but the depression marked a turn towards a more dictatorial political rule in Poland. From 1930 Pilsudski appointed his own cabinet, arrested eighteen members of parliament from the PPS and peasant parties and tightened his bureaucratic and military rule. Therefore, the historical ally of the PPS had turned against members of his former party as he established a more authoritarian government.

This collapse in international agricultural prices and the drying up of foreign loans led to a rising trade deficit in Hungary, taking the country to the verge of financial collapse.[14] This fed into industry, which began to slump in 1930 and reached a trough in 1932, by which time production was about 25% less than in 1929. These factors had catastrophic social effects, with the peasantry and agricultural workers hit worst, pushing them towards absolute poverty. Also, industrial unemployment reached 240,000 (or one third of its employed workers). This increased surplus of labour was then used to bring down wages, which were 42% less in 1932 than in 1929 (while price indexes dropped by only 14.2%) (Borysani, 1968). In Czechoslovakia the collapse in international agricultural prices affected the Slovakian areas most severely. However, the weight of the agricultural sector bore heavily on Czechoslovakian industry and slowed its climb out of recession. Industrial production (taken as an index of 100 in 1929) fell steadily to a low of 60.2 in 1934 and by 1937 it had still not recovered to its 1929 level (standing at 96.3) (Olivova, 1972).

Recovery

From 1933 the majority of CEE countries began to increase accumulation and industrial production. However, this was largely achieved through an internal process of capital accumulation stimulated by government intervention and a policy of protectionism through high tariffs. Combined with strengthening its political control, the Polish government also began to take a more active approach to the economy. This was necessitated by its inability to maintain the inflow of capital from abroad and the need for the state to initiate its creation internally.

This marked the beginning of an economic policy known as 'Polish etatism', where the government took control of savings banks, the foreign exchange operations, foreign trade and cartels.[15] Furthermore, the government started a huge investment programme in public works and the stimulation of private initiatives. Industrial production (taken as an index of 100 in 1928) grew from 45.5 in 1922-27 to 125.8 in 1939. Also, between 1921 and 1931, the percentage of people employed in industry increased by 25% and in 1939 mining and industry accounted for over 50% of the total value of production. Public financing of investment increased from ZŁ1,094m (1932) to ZŁ2,067m (1938). The most outstanding example of this policy was the programme of industrialising the Central Industrial District. This was designed to industrialise an area of high poverty but great potential, in the central areas of the country, which had previously been neglected during the partitions. This project was started in 1936 and was the beginning of a projected ten year plan which would start with increasing the country's military capacity; move to developing transport; next agricultural production; then industrialisation and urbanisation and finally be completed in 1951-4 with the balancing and completion of a new economic structure.

The ramifications of planning the Central Industrial District were clearly transforming the whole national economy to a planned economy when that development was ruthlessly cut short by foreign invaders in September 1939 (Taylor, 1952: 100).

Although, these policies helped to improve the country's socio-economic situation they could not completely reverse the effects of the recession. After the death of Pilsudski (1935) the government moved in a more radical nationalist direction, with the *Sanacja* regime forming a closer relationship with supporters of Dmowski and *Endecja*. The building up of the Polish war machine could not compete with the growing foreign aggression and in 1938 the country was divided up into spheres of influence between Nazi Germany and the USSR.

During the 1930s, the Hungarian economy became integrated into Germany's sphere of influence, which was coming out of recession under Nazi rule. This was combined with a policy of government interventionism, which increased as the war approached. This particularly applied to the armament industry, with the Hungarian economy directly serving the German military regime during WW2. These policies helped to pull Hungary out of recession, although the national economy only stood at 78% of its 1929 level in 1938 (Berend and Ranki, 1977). Although a new policy of government intervention helped to reverse the economic decline in Czechoslovakia, by 1937 the country had not regained its industrial production level of 1929 (Tiechova, 1985). The government introduced a series of devaluations; created work schemes and increased public spending. These policies were made necessary by a number of domestic and international pressures and were accompanied by a series of political measures designed to increase the government's powers.

During the inter-war period, capitalism was not able to instigate an industrial revolution in CEE and close the developmental gap with WE. The CEE states, with the exception of Czechoslovakia, were characterised as being relatively underdeveloped agricultural economies and were thus heavily dependent upon the world market. During the first few years after WW1 the CEE states attempted to integrate themselves into the world economy and attract foreign investment and loans. However, once the world economy entered a recession the CEE economies were forced to search for internal sources of capital accumulation and embarked on a process of state induced investment, which led to some socio-economic development. However, the political systems in CEE were generally unstable, moving steadily in a dictatorial direction. The weakness of reformist socialism in the region is an example of this. During the inter-war period social democratic parties entered government for the first time in CEE and in many cases it was the only political current openly supporting the principles of parliamentary democracy. Social democracy helped to stabilise capitalism in CEE, but often ended up supporting undemocratic and authoritarian measures. This was the case when the Hungarian social democrats compromised with the fascists and Polish social democracy supported Piłsudski. This was even more pronounced in the less developed states in southern-eastern Europe, with, for example, the Bulgarian social democrats helping in the overthrow of the elected peasant government of Aleksandur Stambuliski and the subsequent terror unleashed by the repressive conservative regime against supporters of the peasant and communist parties. Membership of social democratic parties was much lower in EE than in WE, with the lowest membership in the most underdeveloped and agricultural states, such as Romania and Bulgaria (Dauderstadt, et al., 1999). CEE social democracy was generally unable to assimilate the working classes into the democratic system meaning that an essential pillar of a stable bourgeois democracy was missing in CEE.

5

The Polish Peoples' Republic (PRL) was built upon the ruins of WW2 and the reality of a continent divided into two spheres of influence. In proportion to its size Poland suffered more damage and casualties than any other country during the War, with its cities razed to the ground and the holocaust carried out on its soil. The Polish nation lost over 6 million citizens, which equalled 18% of its total population.[16] The territory of the Polish state shifted 200km westwards, vacating lands in Lithuania and Ukraine and incorporating areas of pre-war Germany. Around 5 million Germans and large numbers of Ukrainians were expelled from the country meaning that, along with the physical elimination of the Jews by the Nazis, Poland essentially became a mono-ethnic society.

The USSR dominated post-war CEE, due to the immense contribution it made in the defeat of fascism in Europe, with the West having no choice but to accept Soviet hegemony in the region. However, this supremacy was questioned most vehemently in Poland for a number of reasons. Firstly, this reached back to the historical perception of Russia as an oppressor and that Poland was a country whose traditions and culture were closer to those in WE. Secondly, the Nazi-Soviet pact in 1939 carved up Poland between the Soviet Union and Nazi Germany and created deep distrust and resentment within the Polish population towards the USSR. Thirdly, communism was historically weak in Poland and a Stalinist purge had virtually wiped out the KPP by the late 1930s (see chapter 5). Finally, despite the Red Army's liberation of most of CEE, Poland and Auschwitz, a view has dominated in Poland that the Soviet Union allowed the Nazis to destroy Warsaw and defeat its underground army before taking control of the capital city. Along with the strong presence of the Polish Catholic Church in Poland, there was probably no country that opposed its assimilation into the Eastern Bloc as strongly.

Under pressure from the USSR, Poland rejected Marshall Aid in 1947, withdrew from the IMF and the majority of trade flows switched from the West to the USSR and EE. Economic policy shifted to one of modernising Poland as quickly as possible through rapid industrialisation, which brought impressive results, especially when compared with the inter-war period. National income grew by 76% (1947-50); gross agricultural and industrial production more than doubled (1946-50) and the share of agriculture in national income declined from 70% to 60.3% (1946-50). Investment grew as a whole by 35% (1947-50), doubling in industry but declining by 61% in agriculture

(Slay, 1994). Consumption lagged far behind investment and the postwar economic recovery was not matched by a corresponding rise in living standards. Therefore, while Poland was becoming more modern, industrial and urban; it was also developing inefficiencies, imbalances and shortages. There was a massive reallocation of labour and other resources from agriculture to industry and a virtual extinction of the private sector. However, the Cominform's collectivisation policy was implemented more slowly than in other CEE countries, due to the numerical strength of the peasantry.[17] By 1951 Poland, along with Bulgaria, was arguing against an overzealous policy in the countryside and for slower collectivisation. A unique feature of Polish socialism was to be the existence of a large number of small private farms and the relative independence of the Catholic Church.

It was this contradiction, between investment in heavy industry or consumption and services, which determined the debate on economic policy throughout the socialist period. Between 1953 and 1956 there was a rise in real incomes, throughout CEE, as more resources were diverted from investment into consumption. 1953 marked the peak of accumulation in Poland, and also the year of Stalin's death and the beginning of a political thaw. In Poland a 'national communist' current advanced in the ruling Polish United Workers Party (PZPR) and the General Secretary, Bolesław Bierut, attempted to redress some of the country's imbalances through reducing investment, diverting more resources to agriculture and consumer goods and slowing collectivisation. However, these measures were not enough to prevent the first upsurge in social discontent, as workers began to protest against the government's attempt to increase the level of exploitation in the workplace, through lowering real wages and reducing benefits such as overtime pay. In 1956 strikes by factory workers in Poznań, turned into a general strike in the town. This was co-joined by a demonstration of over 100,000 workers who then began to attack state buildings such as that of the Security Service. This was eventually repressed by the military, with 57 people losing their lives. Four months later a huge nationwide anti-bureaucratic movement erupted, resulting in the creation of workers councils in factories and firms (Kowalewski, 2006).

In response to these events, Władysław Gomułka was appointed General Secretary of the PZPR, advocating a 'Polish road to socialism.' After calm had been reintroduced the party began a new process of counter-reform, with the autonomy of workers' councils curtailed and the percentage of income devoted to industrial investment again increased. This again brought about a period of sustained economic growth. The countries of CEE enjoyed high growth rates throughout the socialist period, averaging 6.7 percent in Poland. However, in all of these countries growth was significantly faster during the first half of the socialist period (i.e. up till the mid-1970s), brought about through large-scale investment in heavy industry. By re-emphasising this form of investment, Polish GDP grew from 3% (1955-60), to 7% (1960-65) and 6.5% (1965-70). It is absolutely clear where this growth came from when it is considered that the share of national income devoted to investment grew from 15% (1956) to 70% (1970) (Slay, 1994).

TABLE 2.1
Average Rate of Growth (NMP) CEE, 1950-89 (%)

Country	1950-89	1st Phase of Growth	2nd Phase of Growth
Romania*	8.2	17.0	5.4
Bulgaria**	6.9	10.0	5.2
Poland	6.7	9.8	3.9
USSR	6.5	16.0	3.3
GDR	5.9	18.0	3.3
Hungary*	5.0	9.3	1.6
Czechoslovakia	4.8	10.0	2.4

* Average for 1953-89. ** Average for 1951-89.
Source: G.W Kołodko (2001) (reproduced with the permission of the author)

By the early 1970s the majority of CEE countries had reached the WE pre-war industrial level of production (Berund and Ranki, 1977) However, while mass consumerism was driving western development, the CEE countries were increasingly developing economies of shortage and falling further behind the West technologically. We can see *table 2.1* how economic growth in the Socialist Bloc was most rapid in the early period of socialism and thereafter growth significantly slowed. These contradictions were most sharply felt in the most economically advanced countries in the west of the region, as the course of 'socialist primitive accumulation' was exhausted here first. This helps explain why the major uprisings occurred in Hungary (1956) and Czechoslovakia (1968). Both of these uprisings were defeated through military interventions by the USSR. In Hungary a policy of political and economic relaxation was then pursued, with greater emphasis placed on raising living standards and more autonomy given to individual enterprises (Berend and Gygorgy, 1977; Kaser, 1986). However, in

Czechoslovakia a more 'orthodox' policy of extensive industrial growth and tight political control was undertaken, after *Prague '68*. As the region's most advanced industrial country, Czechoslovakia could maintain a degree of stability through this strategy, as it exported machinery to the rest of CEE.

In Poland the decline in labour and capital productivity meant that larger shares of income were devoted to investment and more labour resources used. Living standards stagnated during the 1960s, despite the sustained level of economic growth, leading to rising levels of discontent. Opposition first emerged from within the PZPR, when in 1965 two members of the party organisation in Warsaw University, Jacek Kuroń and Karol Modzelewski, published an open letter to members of the party. They argued that a new ruling class had emerged out of the ruling party bureaucracy, which had risen above the party and the working class. An intellectual opposition grew within the PZPR, but was suppressed in 1968, after the party organised a purge of the dissidents under the guise of anti-Semitism, with a number of prominent intellectuals (such as the sociologist Zygmunt Bauman) expelled from the country. In 1970, there was a wave of strikes throughout Poland, resulting in over 300 deaths and the resignation of Gomułka from the post of General Secretary. Nevertheless, the party leadership was able to prevent the cementing of an alliance between the intelligentsia and the working class, through pursuing a policy of raising the living standards of the working class.

New General Secretary, Edward Gierek, adopted a conciliatory policy of freezing prices of food for five years, having less censorship, developing a closer relationship with the Church and allowing more freedom to travel. The government proposed a 'New Developmental Strategy', which focussed on increasing living standards, consumption and international integration.[18] The question remained, how could production and consumption be shifted closer to the patterns in WE (i.e. in manufactured consumer goods)? With industrial output stagnating and the country lagging technologically, the government began accelerating investment through building-up its productive capacities. In 1975 investment, spurred by foreign capital, exceeded the 1970 level by 133% and was supplemented by a massive increase in the import of consumer goods from the West (Poznański, 1996). The government was following a policy of sustaining a large balance of trade deficit, financed through western credits. It was envisaged that Poland would be able to pay back these credits through exports, produced with imported machinery and technology. This policy was strengthened with the creation of large autonomous enterprises, which were given greater independence in matters such as prices and wages. In a further attempt at replicating western consumption patterns, real wages were raised. This 'demand led' type policy was also intended to increase labour productivity and buy political compliance. A period of remarkable economic growth ensued combined with surges in incomes, consumption and living standards. Between 1971 and 1975 national income grew (on average) by 9.5% a year, consumption by 17.5% and real wages by 6.8%. Also, between 1970 and 1974, gross agricultural production rose by 22%, due to increased investment and an abandonment of compulsory deliveries. However, the balance of trade deficit switched from a surplus of ZŁ451.2m (1971) to a deficit of ZŁ8.9m (1975). Foreign debt had also risen from $1.2bn (1971) to $7.6bn (1975) (Slay, 1994).

This growth of foreign debt and a rising trade deficit was not unique to Poland, but was common throughout CEE.[19] The situation in the region worsened, due to the huge rise in oil prices following the international oil-shock in the mid-1970s. This particularly hit the countries of CEE, who were reliant on heavy industry and therefore unable to reduce the amount they spent on oil.[20] Growing debt and recession in the West meant that the amount of imported consumer goods and investment products began to slow, and the western market for Polish exports started drying-up. The government reasoned that, in order to avoid an economic crisis, there needed to be a freeze in consumption and an increase in fresh supplies of credits to complete their investment projects. The latter aim was curtailed by the worsening international situation, while at home any consumption cuts were met with political opposition. Nevertheless, the government announced food price rises in 1976, leading to strikes and demonstrations. The government was forced to retreat and with no alternative plan its economic problems worsened. By the end of the decade, Poland had the largest foreign debt of any CEE country, which had increased 23.5 fold during the 1970s and was three times larger than the annual value of exports (Tittenbrun, 1993). Whilst Gierek had previously tried to stimulate the economy through credits and consumption he was unable to redirect the economy to debt re-servicing. During the period of economic growth he was able to co-opt the political compliance of a number of social groups, but this proved impossible as economic conditions worsened. National income declined by 25% (1979-82), inflation hit triple digits and the government became increasingly unable to service its debts (Slay, 1994). This led to new surge of social protests and the creation of the largest and broadest opposition movement to appear in any CEE country throughout the socialist period.

6

One result of Poland's growing debt was that foreign creditors were becoming part owners of the Polish economy. Foreign banks were pushing, in the late 1970s, for the government to reduce food subsidies and increase exports to pay for rapid debt repayment.[21] As Poland was also progressively falling behind the West technologically it was dependent on importing technology in order to raise the competitiveness of its exports. This problem was accentuated by a dogma, which lay at the heart of the PZPR's (and other CEE leading parties') economic ideology, which assumed that the most productive area of economic growth was in the production of the means of production (i.e. heavy industry). This presupposition arose from a generalisation of the early conditions of 'socialist primitive accumulation', which were conditioned by CEE's underdevelopment and defence considerations (Tittenbrun, 1993). The Polish government continued to invest in inefficient industries, preventing Poland from moving from *extensive* to *intensive* economic development. This 'technological gap' meant that the West had increasing influence on Poland, with the government adopting a western supported policy of debt repayment through decreasing consumption and living standards, while increasing exports.

The worsening economic situation once again led to a growth in social dissatisfaction and protest; but this time at a level that threatened the system's very existence. The historic strikes at the Gdańsk shipyards, in August 1980, sparked a wave of similar protests throughout the country. Crucially, an alliance between the intelligentsia and the working class was cemented, with the Workers' Defence Committee (KOR) providing support for the strikers and the new independent trade union Solidarity (Solidarność) was created.[22] The Gdańsk strikers won a series of concessions including the right to form an independent trade union, the right to strike and have access to the media, a five day week, a tightening of price increases, the raising of the minimum wage, lowering of the retirement age, three years paid maternity leave and an agreement that exports would be limited to surplus production.[23] However, the ruling authorities were neither in a position to control the situation nor to offer the country a way out of the enveloping crisis.

Within a few months *Solidarność* had grown from a trade union into a political movement that commanded huge social support. In 1981 *Solidarność* boasted around 9.5 million members and over 700,000 people participated in strikes. The first congress of *Solidarność* was probably the most democratic and representative congress of Polish labour in history. It created a programme that sought a genuine socialisation and democratisation of the socialist system. It demanded the democratic control of the planned economy; workers control of production and distribution; and workers self-management of enterprises, that would form the basis for a self-managed republic. This programme came into direct conflict not only with the party nomenclature in Poland but also with that in the USSR. The *Solidarność* demands amounted to a revolutionary agenda seeking a transformation of the entire system of power and privilege in the PRL.

Therefore, by the beginning of 1981 Poland was faced with a revolutionary situation, with the balance of power shifting decisively in favour of *Solidarność*. Nevertheless, the *Soldarność* leadership, centred around Lech Wałęsa, calculated that they were unable to take advantage of this opportunity. The reason for this was the international balance of forces, primarily the fear that the USSR was preparing an invasion similar to that carried out in Hungary (1956) and Czechoslovakia (1968). At the peak of the revolutionary crisis, in March 1981, the *Solidarność* leadership decided that rather than pushing forward towards a conquest of power, that they would sign a compromise agreement with the government. From this moment support for *Solidarność* began to decline (Modzelewski, 2006).

The events of 1980/81 also instigated a huge crisis and shift of power within the state and PZPR. Worsening economic conditions meant that it was impossible for Gierek to revive his corporatist strategy and in December 1980 Stanisław Kania replaced him as General Secretary. However, the crisis within the PZPR deepened as its membership declined by 17% between December 1980 and July 1981 (Poznański, 1996). With the party weakened, power moved to the state administration and the military; and in September 1981 General Wojciech Jaruzelski was appointed as the party's General Secretary. Jaruzelski came under intense pressure from the USSR and only managed to maintain his position thanks to the support of the military members of the Central Committee. In turn, the Polish military sought to take control of the situation and on 13th December 1981 Martial Law was announced, which lasted until July 22nd 1983. In February (1982) prices of most consumer goods went up by 300-400%, the cost of living index rose by 100% and throughout the year real wages dropped by 25%. Production had begun to recover by the mid-1980s, but investment was again concentrated in heavy industry.[24] The technological gap between Poland and the West was therefore not bridged and by 1985 Poland had become the third largest debtor in the world.[25] By the mid-1980s, the situation had reached absurd levels, with Poland exporting raw materials and in return receiving poorly processed goods. This outflow of capital halted any process of modernisation and helped consolidate the backward nature of the Polish economy. In 1985 (compared with 1979), the percentage of exported raw materials and low processed goods rose by 6%, while high processed goods declined by 12%. Such conditions ensured that Poland could not pull itself out of the 'debt loop', with debt rising to 43% of GDP (five times the annual hard currency exports) (Tittenbrun, 1993).

Martial Law both prevented a revolution and broke the opposition movement. Millions of people withdrew from political activity and *Solidarność's* role as a mass movement of the working class at the head of society declined. Simultaneously the political character of *Solidarność* changed, with the leadership adopting a more anti-socialist stance. It should also be borne in mind that Martial Law also sounded the death knell for the PZPR. The political control of the military could only be a temporary situation and the party leadership calculated that the system had to be transformed and sought a compromise with the opposition. This process was facilitated by changes within the USSR, with Gorbachev making it clear that they would not interfere in Poland's internal matters. Combined with continued social discontent and the increased influence of western creditors and bankers in the economy, far-reaching reforms were agreed at the PZPR's tenth party congress in 1986, which paved the way for the restoration of capitalism.

The reforms were designed to establish the environment for the market to function, including the removal of price restrictions, the implementation of enterprise self finance and the liquidation of unprofitable enterprises. Along with this it was decided to commercialise the banking sector and reduce subsidies. Central to these policies was the decision of the government to join the IMF and World Bank.[26] The government planned to phase in a 110% increase in food prices over three years but in the first quarter of 1988 prices of rents, heating and fuel went up by 140-200% (Poznański, 1996). These reforms led to further inflationary pressures and thus greater social discontent. Towards the end of the socialist period the government rapidly developed the private sector and reduced price controls and subsidies. This ended in the Round Table talks with *Solidarność* in 1989 and the gradual reform of the system from within, until the PZPR gave up its monopoly of political power and the first 'non-communist' government was established in 1989. Both the PZPR and *Solidarność* agreed to the package of shock-therapy economic reforms implemented from January 1st 1990, which prescribed a rapid leap to a capitalist economy. It is totally inconceivable that the original *Solidarność* movement would have agreed to such a programme; and their programme of a self-managed republic became an artefact of history.

****

The period of socialism in Poland and CEE brought some real, although limited development. The socialist economy in Poland was able to rebuild a country ruined by war and overcome the developmental block that suppressed capitalist expansion in the country, instigating a process of mammoth industrial growth. The share of national income devoted to industry grew from 22% in 1947 to 49% in 1988 and that assigned to agriculture declined from 70% to 12.6%. Social inequalities declined, poverty significantly reduced and millions of people moved from the countryside to the cities. Between 1945 and 1988 eight million homes (170,000 a year) were built and in the 1980s only 1.5% of society received no formal education (compared for example with 19% in Italy) (Szumlewicz, 2005). However, the process of industrial development had reached its limit by the 1970s and the ruling parties in CEE were unable to implement the necessary mechanisms to instigate intensive economic growth based upon the production of high quality consumer goods and expanding the countries' consumption base. Also, the official party line that the working class was the leading class rang increasingly hollow, as the party bureaucracy rejected all demands by the working class for self-management and real political power. Economic growth began to slow and the social structures built during this time became frozen and appeared outdated in relation to those in WE. The Socialist Bloc was unable to overtake the world's most advanced capitalist economies, despite continuing predictions by Soviet propagandists, and contradictions within the CEE economies grew as they became financially indebted to the West. It was in such a situation that the process of capitalist restoration was embarked upon from the end of the 1980s.

3

THE SOCIO-ECONOMIC EFFECTS OF THE TRANSITION TO CAPITALISM

When examining the socio-economic development of a post-socialist country, we are dealing with the negation of one mode of production by another. Capitalism historically emerged out of and surpassed feudalism, creating a superior economic and social system. This was a sublation of feudalism, with feudal elements remaining within the capitalist system and steadily decaying as capitalism grew. In EE, capitalism did not fully go beyond feudalism, whose methods of production and social structures remained dominant. Socialism, in EE, was a negation of both capitalism and feudalism, with elements of both preserved within the socialist socio-economic systems. The transition from socialism to capitalism stands as a new historical stage in this process. Unlike during feudalism, a strong and organised bourgeoisie did not grow within the socialist system and the socialist economy was not surpassed internally by a developing capitalist mode of production. Rather, what occurred is that capitalism, as a global system, showed itself to be more advanced than the regional version of socialism in EE. It was this external factor that proved to be the decisive element in the disintegration of socialism in EE and has shaped the subsequent transition in the region. The post-socialist transition has been characterised by the opening up of the socialist economies to global capitalism. There has been a transfer of capital and commodities to EE that has raised areas of socio-economic life to the level of that in the advanced capitalist nations. However, as capitalism has not grown organically out of the socialist systems, it has been limited in its scope and, as we shall see, has involved the buying up of large sections of the EE economies by sections of international capitalism, corresponding to the methods of primitive accumulation. Therefore, elements of the socialist system remain some of the most advanced social and economic constituents in the ex-socialist countries, although the aim of the transition has been to destroy them as rapidly as possible, which has tended to lead to economic decline and social degradation. Simultaneously, feudal aspects have remained and even strengthened in EE, as seen, for example, in the preservation of millions of small peasant holdings in Poland.

1

One of the unique features of the capitalist class is that it uses a large part of its accumulated capital for production, rather than consumption. Also, an increasing part of this capital goes into investment in the productive process, which increases in relation to the growth of wages. This allows for the expanded production of surplus value, although it begs the question where will the necessary increase in demand for commodities come from? According to Rosa Luxemburg this cannot come from the working class, as they simply refund the capitalist the amount that they spend on variable capital. She concluded that expanded production was only possible through access to non-capitalist strata and countries. These provide a market for the realisation of surplus value, open up access to new sources of material elements necessary for the production of surplus value, and make available cheap pools of labour for the bourgeoisie in the advanced capitalist states. A campaign is waged first against the natural economy and then against simple commodity production, seeking to separate the producer from the means of production.

Luxemburg created a synthesis between the realisation of surplus value and the relationship between advanced capitalism and pre-capitalism, incorporating the rise of monopoly capitalism and imperialism. Despite numerous and often justified criticisms of this model, as a general theory of capitalist breakdown, its influence on Marxist and socialist thought has been enormous, especially in CEE.[1] As well as instigating and adding to the growing debates around imperialism and socialist strategy it laid the way for the emergence of theories of capitalist development based upon the question of demand

and the realisation of surplus value. These proved to be particularly attractive in Luxemburg's native Poland. For example, the Polish economist, Michał Kalecki, developed many of the ideas of Keynesianism, before Keynes himself, using some of the research methods of Marxism. Concerned mainly with the situation in 1930s Poland, Kalecki sought to create a theory of effective demand to counter the recessionary tendencies of capitalism (Kowalik, 2002). He supported the implementation of planned elements into the economy, including the fixing of prices. This was in contrast to Keynes, who, emerging from British liberalism, sought a compromise with the bourgeoisie in the more favourable conditions of an advanced capitalist economy.

The internal economic logic of the CEE socialist states was distinct from that of a capitalist economy, with the absence of cycles of slump and boom and mass unemployment.[2] However, as shown in the previous chapter, the socialist economies were stricken by imbalances between investment in heavy industry and investment in consumption, light industry and services, which lay behind the economies of shortage. During the socialist period a school of CEE reformists, influenced among others by the work of Luxemburg and Kalecki, analysed the existing planned economies. Economists such as Włodzimierz Brus, Kazimierz Łaski, Otta Sik, Oscar Lange and Tadeusz Kowalik promoted the implementation of the market mechanism into the planned economy, which they believed would help rationalise enterprises, facilitate the creation of the consumer sector and instigate technological innovation and growth. They also urged the implementation of measures to raise the population's consumptional capacity, with attention focussed on the supply side, as the lack of consumer goods meant that raising wages was insufficient to boost demand. They believed that the isolated socialist economies should seek to import technology from the capitalist world and begin a policy of export-oriented growth. They also advocated policies of self-management and autonomy of the enterprises and a reduction of centralised bureaucratic planning. Such economic thinking never gained a lasting prominence in any of the ruling parties in CEE and rather than opening up the planned economies to elements of market regulation, self-management and international integration, the socialist aspects of the CEE economies were dismantled by the neo-liberal reforms from the beginning of the 1990s.[3] State planning, the suppression of private property, the state monopoly of foreign trade, the collectivisation of land, price controls and the policy of full employment were totally abandoned.

2

The Round-Table talks, that negotiated Poland's transfer of power at the end of the 1980s, did not include any economic proposals similar to those included in the shock-therapy reforms introduced at the beginning of transition. On the contrary, the negotiations concluded that the aim of the economic reforms was to build a social-market economy based upon the social-welfarist model of WE capitalism (Bugaj, 2002). This was in line with the policies being proposed, at least in theory, by Gorbachev in Russia, and was one of the last expressions of the belief that the two world historical blocs were converging. However, the wheels of history were turning in the opposite direction and once there had been a political transfer of power in Poland, neo-liberalism gained a supremacy over other alternatives. The blueprint for the shock-therapy reforms was derived from the Chicago school in the USA and brought, literally, to the Polish parliament by the economist Jeffery Sachs. Any debate that took place about the course of economic reform centred on whether there should be a rapid leap towards a capitalist economy or whether this should be a more gradual evolutionary process. A political consensus emerged, in Poland and CEE from the mid-1980s, that the socialist economy was unreformable and that a decisive break from this system needed to be made. This was articulated by part of the CEE intelligentsia, who had previously sought a reform of the socialist economies.

The most famous exponent of such thinking is the Hungarian economist Janos Kornai, who constructed a theory of 'soft budget constraints' after experiencing more than a decade of reform in Kadar's Hungary. Kornai (1992; 1993) concentrated on the relationship between publicly owned firms and the state. The state relied on the firm to produce goods, employ workers, fund social services and pay taxes. Concurrently, the firm depended on the state for such things as investments and favourable tax and loan rates. There was constant pressure placed on the state to redistribute revenue from the most profitable firms to the least profitable ones, which was compounded by a disproportionate flow of investment and resources towards heavy industry, and an under-investment in consumer goods and services. Kornai reasoned that any partial reform of the socialist economies would be undermined by these firms' 'soft-budget constraints' and that a programme of mass privatisation had to be instigated to cut the reciprocal dependency between firms and the state. Such rationale guided the transition from socialism in Poland. The first 'non-communist' government inherited an economy burdened by large international debt, with social services worsening and the consumer sector depressed, creating an overwhelming sense of social dissatisfaction and apathy. The failure of successive reforms, in the latter years of the socialist period, helped to strengthen the belief in society that the system was unreformable and that there needed to be a clean political and economic break from the past. It was such a situation that created the opportunity for the introduction of the shock-therapy reforms in 1990. The architect of the shock-therapy package, Leszek Balcerowicz, termed the early transition period as being one of 'extraordinary politics'.

> In the interval between the discrediting of the old political elite and the coalescing of new interest groups, conditions are especially favourable for technocrats to assume positions of political responsibility. There is also a greatly increased probability that the population will accept difficult, normally controversial economic policy measures as necessary sacrifices for the common good. But the experience of Eastern Europe suggests that this period of 'extraordinary politics' usually lasts no more than one or two years (Balcerowicz and Gelb, 1995: 209).

The *shock-therapists* seized the political opening and exploited it to the full, with Tadeusz Mazowiecki's government introducing a package of neo-liberal reforms from January 1st 1990. The philosophy guiding the shock-therapy reforms was that if it had not been for socialism Poland would have a modern WE economy and therefore the constraints of this system should be removed as rapidly as possible. The logic behind this was one of *neo-Schumpeterian* 'creative destruction', whereby elements of the old productive system were consciously dissolved in order for more 'rational' economic agents to grow. Enterprises were subjected to 'hard budget' constraints, determined by the market, with the belief held that the old inefficient and wasteful industries would perish, while profitable and market orientated ones would replace them and flourish.[4]

3

At the beginning of transition the Polish political class and population harboured illusions that they would become recipients of large inflows of capital from the West, after breaking from the protectionist arrangements of socialism. Lech Wałęsa predicted that Poland would become the 'next Japan' and Poles expected, understandably, that the West would repay them for their efforts in helping to destroy socialism in terms similar to the Marshall Aid they had been denied in 1947. The strategic importance of Poland, as the first and one of the largest countries to restore capitalism in CEE, meant that it did receive some direct help from the West, most notably when 50% of its external debt to the Paris Club was written off in 1991. However, it soon emerged that there was no gigantic sum of money awaiting the newly 'liberated' countries and that the West was most interested in extending its own economic interests into the lands beyond the rubble of the Berlin Wall.

The first act of the transition in CEE was to break up the Comecon and open up its economies to trade with the West. The newly elected Polish government reasoned that, in order to reap the benefits of the global economy, Poland should immerse itself, as swiftly as possible, into the world market. The rapid removal of trade barriers to the West was not accompanied by the government developing any coherent export strategy, which may have enabled it to compete in this market. This was in line with neo-liberal thinking that the state should remove itself from the economy in order for market forces to freely develop.

In such circumstances the strong unsurprisingly prospered. Table 3.1 shows how in 1990 Poland's two major trading partners were Germany and the USSR. By 1997 trade with Russia had fallen considerably and by 2003 the amount of exports going to Russia was minimal, with the share of imports coming the other way well under a half of what it had been in 1990.[5] This collapse of the Soviet/Russian market for Poland was caused by the general recession throughout the former Eastern Bloc and was then magnified by the Russian financial crisis in 1998. Trade has therefore been conducted mainly with the countries from WE, with Germany remaining Poland's major trading partner. Throughout the majority of the transition period Poland has borne a sizeable trade deficit. Twice during transition the trade deficit has neared $20bn and in 2000/01 it amounted to 8% of Poland's total GDP and the value of imports per capita was 40% higher than that of exports per capita. However, since EU entry, revenues from exports denominated in euro have grown by nearly 20% annually. This growth has been driven by favourable currency conditions, leading to the trade deficit declining from 4.3% of GDP in 2004 to 1.5% in 2005.[6] Despite this improvement in Poland, large trade deficits have become a feature of the CEE states as they have entered an enlarged EU, threatening them with a Latin American type of economic development.[7]

The rapid opening up of the CEE economies to the world economy after the collapse of socialism created the conditions for the growth of a dual economy and society. On the one hand shops filled with goods, usually of a far superior quality to those commonly available during socialism. The economy of shortage was destroyed and steadily the availability of high-quality products reached the level of that in the West. However, this was combined with the degradation of these countries' domestic productive sphere and the instigation of a process of mass privatisation, which was tantamount to the selling off of national companies to foreign capital (see below). Foreign owned companies have become the engine for economic growth in the region, but large swathes of their income is transferred abroad, creating large social and economic imbalances.[8]

TABLE 3.1
Imports and Exports to Poland 1990-2003 (%)[9]

Import 1990	Export 1990	Import 1997	Export 1997	Import 2003	Export 2003
Germany 20.1	Germany 25.1	Germany 24.1	Germany 32.9	Germany 24.4	Germany 32.3
USSR 19.8	USSR 15.3	Russia 6.3	Russia 8.4	Italy 8.5	France 6.1
Italy 7.5	UK 7.1	UK 5.5	Holland 4.7	Russia 7.7	Italy 5.7
UK 5.7	Switzerland 4.7	Italy 9.9	Italy 5.9	China 4.5	UK 5.0
Austria 5.7	Czechoslovakia 4.1	France 5.9	Ukraine 4.7	Holland 3.4	Holland 4.5

4

One of the main problems for the ex-socialist countries has been how to build capitalism without capital. In contrast to feudalism, socialism did not create a class, which had accumulated sufficient capital to become a bourgeois class in the newly restored capitalist economies. Where then was this capital to come from? It has often been suggested that the old party nomenclature used its political connections and influence to transform itself into a capitalist class (a 'red bourgeoisie'). Certainly, a part of this bureaucracy has prospered, especially in areas of the ex-Soviet Union, where the rich sources of raw materials were monopolised by a semi-criminal element, with connections to part of the old nomenclature. However, in the majority of the CEE countries the bureaucracy was not able to amass sufficient capital to privately take over and/or develop the major sectors of the economy. Also, individual savings during socialism were relatively low and therefore there was no basis for the creation of a 'mass capitalism'. Rather, the source of capital was to come from abroad and a major strategic aim of the transition has been to attract Foreign Direct Investment (FDI).

The large size of Poland's population makes it difficult for it to develop economically through foreign investment. Poland presently obtains 14% of all FDI coming into EE (the second largest share after Russia, which receives 27%). This outstrips neighbouring countries such as Hungary, the Czech Republic and Slovakia, yet Poland trails these countries in terms of FDI per capita.[10] 74% of FDI coming to Poland is from EU countries, with France the largest single contributor (20.1%); followed by the USA (18.2%) and Germany (15%).[11] Therefore, the investment coming into Poland is tied strongly to nation states, with only 16.6% classified as being international (i.e. from multinational firms). Table 3.2 shows the quantity of FDI and income from privatisation since 1989. As we can see, the amount of FDI soared at the beginning of transition, growing steadily until it exceeded $9bn in 2000. Thereafter, there was a dramatic slump in the size of FDI received by Poland, standing at around $4bn in both 2002 and 2003 and rising to $6bn in 2004, as FDI has risen after EU accession. A general drop in FDI internationally can partly explain this decline, falling by $570bn in 2001, following the global slowdown at the turn of the century. However, FDI coming into CEE was not affected by this slump, which actually rose by over $3bn between 2000 and 2002. So why was there such a huge fall in FDI in Poland after 2000? The reason for this can be found in the type of FDI that Poland has attracted. Between 1997 and 2002 FDI Greenfield investments equalled €10,514bn euro, while those connected to privatisation amounted to €27,553bn (Symański, 2005). At the beginning of transition the amount of income from privatisations increased steadily and then began to rise sharply from 1997, increasing fourfold to ZŁ27bn in 2000. However, once the country's most desirable assets had been sold, the amount of capital flowing into the country subsided too. By this time the ownership structure of the Polish economy had been transformed, with large sections of the economy falling into foreign hands, creating a dependent form of capitalism, with the country's fiscal and monetary policies distorted in favour of foreign investors.

The majority of the CEE economies are characterised by their large concentrations of foreign ownership. At the turn of the century foreign ownership in WE equalled 15% in the industrial sector and 13% in banking, while in CEE it reached 33% and 52.5% respectively (Poznański, 1999). Foreign capital has gained control of some essential elements of the Polish economy and between 1997 and 2000 (i.e. when FDI and privatisations were at their height) the level of foreign ownership in banks went up from 20% to 70% and in industry from 15% to 35% (Symański, 2005). The sale of national assets to foreign buyers was justified by the hope that it would bring much needed capital into the country and the necessary technology to improve productivity. However, throughout the transition in EE there has actually been an inverse correlation between FDI and economic growth (Mencinger, 2003).

As FDI has usually been linked to privatisation and the sale of domestic assets to foreign buyers, it has often been accompanied by a decline in production and employment.[12] Also, privatisations carried out with direct or indirect foreign capital have generally not involved the expansion of exports and those companies taken over by foreign investors have regularly been used to sell foreign goods on the domestic market. The share of imports coming into Poland, linked to investment, has averaged around 20% during transition, while that connected to the import of goods has exceeded 60% (Szymański, 2005). It is estimated that the proportion of sales devoted to exports, in Polish firms with foreign capital involvement, stands at barely 13%.[13] (Nieckarz, 2002) However, the prospective large inflows of capital in the form of direct subsidies and funds from the EU is qualitatively different to FDI, as they are often directed towards the poorest areas of the country and regularly involve the development of infrastructure, if not industry (see below).

From the beginning of transition the Polish economy was opened up to foreign capital, with the aim of selling off state property as quickly as possible. Poland has been particularly attractive to foreign investors, due mainly to the fact that it has sold its industrial and banking property at a very cheap rate (estimated in some cases to be as low as 10% of its value) and has offered foreign investors favourable tax rates (Poznański, 1999). The banking sector has been especially attractive to foreign investors due to the fluid nature of finance capital, which moves more freely than industrial capital settling where it can guarantee the greatest profit. By 2003 the percentage of Polish banks, with a majority foreign ownership, stood at 78%, up from 12% in 1993 (Table 3.3). The sale of Polish banks to foreign investors increased sharply from 1997, when the law was liberalised to facilitate an inflow of foreign capital into the banking sector. By the end of 2003 foreign banks controlled over 70% of all bank assets in Poland and two-thirds of the country's credit market. Poland therefore lacks a stable domestic capital base, from which investments in the country's infrastructure and businesses can be made.

TABLE 3.2
FDI and Privatisation in Poland 1989-2004

Year	FDI (million $)	Privatisation (million Zł)
1989	11	-
1990	89	-
1991	291	170.9
1992	678	484.5
1993	1715	780.4
1994	1875	1594.8
1995	3659	2641.6
1996	4498	3749.8
1997	4908	6537.7
1998	6365	7068.7
1999	7270	13347.5
2000	9341	27181.8
2001	5713	6813.8
2002	4131	2859.7
2003	4225	4143.5
2004	6159	10254.0

TABLE 3.3
Ownership Structure of Polish Banks 1993-2003 (%)

	1993	1995	1997	1999	2001	2003
Foreign Capital Holds Majority Share	12	22	35	51	67	78
Owned Directly by State Treasury	18	16	7	4	4	5
State Owns Majority Share	15	12	11	5	6	7
Polish Private Capital Owns Majority Share	55	45	47	40	23	10

Source: Szelągowska, 2004.

5

In early 1990, 90% of all prices in Poland were liberalised; whilst industrial subsidies dropped from 15% of GDP in 1989 to 6% in 1990, which led to industrial output falling by 26.8% in 1990/91 (Glynn, 1997; Slay, 1994). The fall in production occurred across the whole industrial sector; declining by 37.8% in the machinery sector, 40.7% in light industry and 25% in the production of consumption goods (Szumelewicz, 2005). Therefore, along with the sudden over exposure of the economy to international competition, the development of new domestic industries and businesses was suppressed. One outcome of the introduction of market commodity relations into the Polish economy was spiralling inflation, which exceeded 650% in 1990. In response, the government sought to reduce domestic demand. This was achieved through its so-called stabilisation programme, which included retaining a low credit supply, through the maintenance of extremely high base interest rates, which were set at 60% in 1991and remained in double figures until 2003(Table 3.5). The result of this policy was successful, in the sense that by 1991 inflation had fallen sharply to just over 70% and then continued to decline steadily until it stood at only around 1% in 2003. However, this fall in inflation was accompanied by the growth of mass unemployment, suppressed internal demand and a decimated domestic productive sphere.

The claim that the reform programme in Poland was designed to introduce 'fair' and 'neutral' market mechanisms, within which the different economic sectors would compete, is far from the truth. From the beginning of the transition, state industries were deliberately discriminated against, markedly through the introduction of the *Popiwek* tax in the early 1990s. This tax, which private firms were exempt from paying, was imposed on state sector wages, taking up to 91% of state sector profits in 1991 (Poznański, 1996). Such measures were used to encourage firms to privatise, although the pace of privatisation was slow in the early years of transition, with the mass privatisation programme not really taking off until the mid-1990s. However, the unfavourable fiscal and monetary policies, sudden withdrawal of subsidies, rapid opening up to foreign competition and general atmosphere of uncertainty meant that the state sector slumped in the first two years of transition, which was also accompanied by a downturn in the private sector (Table 3.4).

A huge process of de-industrialisation has occurred during transition, with industrial employment declining by a half, from 5.2m in the mid-1980s to 2.8m in 2002 (Szymański, 2005). The number of steelworks in Poland has reduced by 50% since the beginning of transition, with employment in this sector falling from 126,000 in 1991 to only 32,000 in 2002. Similarly, employment in the mining sector fell from 388,000 in 1990 to 147,000 in 2002. The inability of the transition to facilitate the growth of alternative modern industries has meant that large swathes of these workers remain unemployed and the industrial advance that was made during socialism has been wasted.[14] Another feature of the shock-therapy reforms was the closure of state farms. Subsidies were withdrawn from state farms in 1990, which, along with the opening of the Polish market to imports, caused the bankruptcy of hundreds of state farms, pushing agriculture into a prolonged recession. Agricultural output fell by 15% between 1989 and 1993, and only crossed its 1990 level in 1999.[15] (Franciszek, 2005; Poznański, 1999). This recession deepened the underdevelopment of Polish agriculture, which is now dominated by small peasant holdings of a 'pre-capitalist' nature. Over 55% of Poland's two million farms are less than five hectares in size and 75% of all the farms in Poland are individual private farms, with commercial farms only making up 15% of the total number (Czykier-Wierzba, 1995).

In the two years after the shock-therapy reforms were launched, Poland's GDP fell by 24% and unemployment rose from 1.5% in 1989 to 16.4% in 1993. Despite its severity, the fall in GDP was relatively mild in relation to many other countries in CEE.[16] Another feature of the Polish transition was that growth returned quicker than in any other CEE economy; and Poland, in 1996, was the first post-socialist country to cross its pre-transition level of GDP. Table 3.4 shows how the recovery in the Polish economy was accompanied by a growth in both the private and state sectors. From 1993 the state sector began to grow, helping to pull the Polish economy out of recession and into a period of steady growth. The beginning of economic growth actually coincided with the return of the state as a more active socio-economic agent. By 1992 the government had begun introducing counter-measures, to offset the socio-economic effects of the shock-therapy reforms, including protecting bankrupt industries and raising tariffs on some imported goods. The period of 'extraordinary politics' had been exhausted and attempts to speed up reforms by the Prime-Ministers Jan Bielecki (1991) and Hanna Suchocka (1992) proved politically impossible to implement.

The return of interventionism was furthered once the Democratic Left Alliance (SLD) formed a government with the Polish Peasants' Party (PSL) in 1993. This government believed in building a national capital base and that the level of foreign capital ownership in finance and industry should not exceed 30% (see chapter 5) (Poznański, 1999; Szelągowska, 2004). The government continued the privatisation process, with privatisation actually speeding up during the years of this government.[17] However, it generally favoured gradual change, reducing the social costs of the transition and accelerating investments through providing lower interest rates (which fell from 32% in 1992 to 23% in 1996) and tax incentives. The uncertainty caused in the state sector by the shock-therapy reforms was lessened, as the government restored assistance to state industries, reintroduced some tariffs and eased the *Popiwek* tax. As a result state enterprises began to increase production, helping to instigate growth in the economy as a whole. Between 1993 and 1997 economic growth averaged nearly 6% and unemployment fell from 16.4% to 10.3%. However, by 1998, the state sector had slid back into recession and with growth in the private sector receding, the economy slowed sharply.

When the Solidarity Electoral Alliance (AWS)-Freedom Union (UW) government was formed in 1997 it promised that the economy would grow by around 7% and that unemployment would be virtually eliminated. The reality was the absolute reverse. Poland's economy began to slow significantly in 1998, barely surpassing 1% growth by the end of the AWS-UW's term in office in 2001. Neo-liberalism is based upon the ideological belief that the influence of the state in the economy should be reduced in order to instigate socio-economic development. Until 1997 the share of the state in the Polish economy stood at over 50%, but by 2000 this had fallen to below 45%. During the same period economic growth reduced to barely 1%, there was a huge rise in unemployment (from 10.3% to 17.4%) and a large widening of social inequalities. The transformation of Poland into a dependent capitalist country left the economy susceptible to a financial crisis, similar to the capital flight that occurred in Hungary in 1998. The majority of this outflow of capital in Hungary resulted from the repatriation of income by foreign owners, which could not be compensated for by an increase in privatisation, as the most profitable assets had already been sold (Poznański, 1999). When Poland faced a similar situation at the turn of the century, the AWS-UW government, with Balcerowicz installed first as Finance Minister and then head of the National Bank of Poland (NBP), reasoned that domestic demand had to be decreased in order to reduce the spiralling trade deficit. The government adopted a strategy of *cooling down* the economy, in order to reduce domestic demand, so that the flow of imported goods into the country would decline, thus maintaining external financial stability, whilst also pushing down the inflation rate.

TABLE 3.4
Financial Result of Public and Private Sector 1992-2003
(Million ZŁ)

Year	Public Sector	Private Sector
1992	-3252.4	-367.3
1993	-1889.9	323.5
1994	3057.1	1839.5
1995	3972.4	4578.3
1996	2309.0	7577.9
1997	4002.4	9909.4
1998	-3700.0	9375.9
1999	5518.9	6726.0
2000	-738.6	7282.2
2001	-5813.6	3284.4
2002	-6940.4	2810.3
2003	7063.7	19157.5

This was driven by a monetary policy of maintaining high interest rates, which repressed growth in Poland's industrial and agricultural sectors. It was in these conditions that the second SLD-led government took Poland into the EU in 2004. As it entered the Union a dependent form of capitalism had been established; with its corresponding imbalances, diminished domestic productive base and mass unemployment.

TABLE 3.5
Basic Economic Indicators in Poland 1989-2005

	GDP Growth	Unemployment (%)	Inflation	Interest Rate (%)
1989	-0.6	1.5	251.1	26.0
1990	-17.0	6.5	658.8	49.0
1991	-7.0	12.2	70.3	60.0
1992	2.6	14.3	43.0	32.0
1993	3.8	16.4	35.0	29.0
1994	5.2	16.0	32.2	28.0
1995	7.0	14.9	27.8	31.0
1996	6.0	13.2	19.9	23.0
1997	6.8	10.3	14.8	26.1
1998	4.8	10.4	11.5	25.0
1999	4.1	13.1	7.4	16.1
2000	4.0	15.0	10.4	20.0
2001	1.0	17.4	5.5	20.5
2002	1.4	18.0	1.8	12.0
2003	3.8	18.0	1.1	7.25
2004	5.3	19.1	4.3	6.25
2005	3.4	17.6	2.4	-

6

The dismantling of the social welfare system is postponed during the early stage of transition, but becomes its major focus as the wave of privatisation descends. Kornai (1992) has described the post-socialist countries as 'pre-mature Welfare States', meaning that these countries' welfare systems are over-mature for their general level of development and increasingly become a burden on their budgets. Certainly, it is hard to imagine how these countries could have created such extensive welfare systems if they had developed along capitalist lines; and the question is directly posed as to whether they can be maintained after capitalism has been restored.

The introduction of the shock-therapy reforms was accompanied by an economic slump and a huge rise in unemployment. During the first three years of transition five million Poles (26% of the labour force) moved from the productive to the redistributive and social spheres (Cook, 1999; Kabaj, & Kowalik, 1995). This led to a sharp rise in the level of social expenditures, with social security and pension/retirement payments growing from nearly 8.5% of GDP in 1989 to almost 21% in 1992 (Table 3.6). The elimination of subsidies and closure of large enterprises eroded the enterprise based benefit system and created the need for large-scale income support and unemployment benefit. One of the effects of this policy was a growing budget deficit, which, after initially recording a surplus in 1990, ballooned into a deficit of over 6% of GDP in 1992. During the early years of transition the government was primarily concerned with maintaining the course of privatisation and liberalisation and was therefore prepared to increase social spending in order to uphold social and political stability.

The first SLD government could maintain social spending, due to economic growth and the decline in unemployment during its term in office. Between 1993 and 1997 social expenditures, as a percentage of GDP, fell from 28.6% to 25.5% and its overall expenditures decreased from 49.9% to 45.5% (Bugaj, 2005; Ringold, 1999). Yet, the government was able to increase its social expenditures in real terms and the budget deficit declined to 1.26% of GDP; international debt reduced from 63% of GDP to 21% and public debt from 86% of GDP to 43.1% (Bugaj, 2005). However, the economic downturn from the late 1990s created further compulsion for the government to cut social expenditures. The AWS-UW government could initially hold down its budget deficit, as there was a surge of proceeds from privatisations. Once this subsided, in 2001, the budget deficit doubled to 4.25%.

The economic downturn and rising unemployment in the late 1990s meant that social security spending soared, after decreasing during the mid-1990s.[18] Another area of government spending that has been maintained since 1993, is that allocated to subsidies and allocations, which stands at nearly 13% of GDP. Despite the course of privatisation and de-industrialisation, many of the industrial and agricultural subsidies and payments, which survived the shock-therapy reforms, remain intact. The Polish government provides subsidies to sectors such as the railways (€250m a year) and mines (€350m a year). Also, some workers in heavy industry, who had a privileged status during the socialist period, still receive certain social security payments. Attempts to remove these benefits have met with fierce opposition from the workers in these industries, and is an example of how certain social classes defend elements of the socialist, enterprise based, social security system.

The logic of the post-socialist transition in Poland means that the government is compelled to speed up privatisations in order to fill the budget gap. As the country's most attractive assets are sold so governments then increasingly look to curtail their spending. Therefore, as the transition progresses, attention moves from dismantling the productive base of socialism towards removing the social guarantees of this system. It becomes increasingly harder for capitalism, in the post-socialist reality, to maintain the infrastructure (such as housing and transport) and social-welfare system that was left after the collapse of socialism. The Polish railways are in debt up to ZŁ10bn and are only able to service this through selling off some of their assets and closing many regional lines.[19] The number of train passengers fell by 70% between 1990 and 2004; while those using the roads increased by 170%. However, there has been no corresponding investment in roads by the Polish governments. Between 1990 and 2004 only 340km of motorways were built, which is ten times less than the EU average. Only 1% of Polish roads met EU standards in 2004, creating the conditions for thousands of fatal road accidents each year.[20] The lack of government spending has also created a housing shortage in Poland. Between 1945 and 1970, 28.7% of all present housing was built and from 1971 to 1988 30.2% was constructed. In comparison, between 1989 and 2006, only 13% (620,000) of houses and flats in the country have been built.[21] The success of Poland's entry into the EU will be largely judged by the extent to which funds are made available and utilised to develop the country's infrastructure.

The curtailment of government spending also further erodes public services. The major decline in government spending, from the end of the 1990s, has occurred in areas such as health-care and education (Table 3.6)[22] The current level of health spending in Poland is the lowest of any country in the OECD, trailing far behind not only countries such as Germany (who spend 11%) but also other post-socialist countries in the region (Slovakia – 5%, Hungary – 5.46%, Czech Republic – 6.7%). Government spending on health was reduced to around 3% of GDP in 1999 and has since remained at this level. The health service now faces a drastic situation, with 600 of the 750 main

Polish hospitals in serious debt (amounting to ZŁ8bn).[23] The reality of a free and comprehensive health care system, which is enshrined in the country's constitution, increasingly becomes a fiction as individuals are expected to pay for more and more services and products. Similarly, although education is nominally free, it is the norm that parents are expected to pay for things such as textbooks. Also, only 1/3 of children aged 3-5 attend nursery school, falling to 1/8 in the countryside. During the past decade over 30% of nursery schools in the country have closed and this situation is again worst in the country's poorest rural areas. In the district of Podlaskie only 4% of children have access to a nursery school and 5% in Warmińsko-Mazurskie and Zachodniopomorskie.[24]

The other major focus of the latter transition period, after the mass privatisations recede, is the increasing rate of labour exploitation, brought about through a reduction in the protections of workers in the workplace. The transition from socialism has not been a progression towards the social-welfare capitalism existent in post-war WE. The levels of exploitation and working conditions, for millions of Polish workers, are more akin to those under nineteenth century capitalism and signify an historical regression. Polish workers work the longest hours in Europe (1,984 hours annually), which is more than in any other country in the OECD apart from South Korea, even surpassing Japan (Łepik, 2006). Despite the fact that trade unions were the central organisational structure of the opposition movement during socialism they have since found themselves marginalized, especially in the private sector (see next chapter). In areas where the trade unions are absent, the level of exploitation is the highest. For example, the Polish Work Inspection Organisation has found that over half of employees in supermarkets work more than eight hours a day and that they regularly receive no overtime pay for this. Research has shown that the working day of an increasing number of factory workers (around 30%) is extended beyond their contracted hours.[25] A large section of the workforce, estimated at around 700,000 people, is also not paid regularly on time. Furthermore, over a quarter of Polish workers, over 2.4m people, are employed on temporary contracts (with this number doubling between 2002 and 2005) and 27% of workers are classified as self-employed, thus essentially placing the burden of social security payments onto the shoulders of the employee. In this way, Polish employers are exempt from providing at least part of the social protection afforded to full-time workers. Increasingly, governments are attempting to liberalise the labour law and reduce the remaining benefits afforded to workers such as sickness benefits, maternity leave, workplace training, etc. The most extreme result of the lack of protection in the workplace is the more than 500 deaths that occur each year due to accidents at work.[26]

TABLE 3.6
Budget Spending 1989-2003 (% GDP)

	Budget Deficit/ Surplus	Health Care	Education	Pensions and Sickness Retirement	Social Security	Subsidies and Allocations
1989	-3.03	3.39	2.96	6.5	1.98	n/a
1990	0.44	5.83	3.93	8.6	2.95	n/a
1991	-3.83	4.80	4.34	12.59	4.50	12.1
1992	-6.01	4.94	4.49	14.60	6.39	n/a
1993	-2.91	4.78	4.55	15.55	6.99	n/a
1994	-2.79	4.63	4.20	16.16	6.94	n/a
1995	-2.26	3.98	4.14	13.46	4.65	9.61
1996	-2.38	4.30	4.27	14.26	4.56	10.38
1997	-1.26	4.00	4.37	14.30	4.52	9.93
1998	-2.38	–	4.24	14.02	5.10	9.20
1999	-2.03	5.70	4.23	14.05	4.78	11.84
2000	-2.13	3.60	4.36	12.80	5.07	11.53
2001	-4.25	3.30	4.59	13.42	6.06	12.92
2002	-5.04	3.10	4.37	13.81	6.77	13.36
2003	-4.55	3.10	4.13	13.86	6.66	12.91
2004	-4.49	3.10	4.13	12.80	5.26	–
2005	-2.89	3.20	4.10	-	4.58	–

7

The transition in Poland has created what we may term a dual society. The city centres of Poland's major cities now resemble those in WE and large sections of Polish society have access to products, services and cultural activities, which were denied them during socialism. Part of Polish society has enjoyed new opportunities to travel, consume high quality goods, shop in comfortable well-stocked shops and socialise in new restaurants, bars and cafes. This diversity of consumer choice contrasts with the staid, depressive reality of shortage, so prevalent in Poland during the 1980s. Capitalism, by its nature, attempts to expand the consumption base for its products and Poland's absorption into the world market, particularly after entering the EU, means that its population increasingly enjoys access to consumer products from abroad. The innovation of the Polish population, developed through necessity during the years of shortage, has helped individuals and communities to survive in the harsh climate of a capitalist economy. However, the destruction of Poland's productive base has also led to the impoverishment of millions of people and the creation of large structural social inequalities.

The major failing of the transition in Poland has been the deactivation of millions of people. In 1988 there were 21.8m people of working age and 18.2m of these, 83.5%, were in paid employment. Fourteen years later the number of Poles of working age had increased to 23.6m people, although the number of these working had decreased to 10.4m people, i.e. 56%. About 1.2m of these are students, whose number has increased sharply during transition, leaving around 9m Poles who are neither studying nor working (Kabaj, 2005)[27] Unemployment soared, during the first three years of transition, growing from 1.5% in 1989 to 16.4% in 1993 (Table 3.6). Then, between 1994 and 1998, unemployment fell to 10.4%, with over 1m people returning to the labour market. Unemployment began to rise again from 1999, as the country re-embarked on a liberal economic course, reaching 19.1% in 2004, with around 1.5 million Poles once again becoming redundant. After joining the EU unemployment has begun to reduce, with the mass emigration of Poles to WE contributing to this decline. However, long-term unemployment (defined as unemployment for more than twelve months) has remained at a stable level of above 10% and the rate of very long-term unemployment (more than two years) has increased from 5.0% in 2004 to 5.3% in 2005. The problem of unemployment is compounded by extremely low government expenditures on labour market policies, which equal just 1% of GDP.[28]

The vast majority of those leaving Poland are young people, which is the result of the huge level of youth unemployment in the country. The number of those under twenty-five, who are unemployed, grew from 567,000 (1998) to 938,000 (2002). Likewise, the amount of people aged between twenty-five and thirty-five without work rose from 496,000 to 892,000 during these years. In the regions of Małopolska and Wielkopolska one-third of the unemployed are under twenty-five, while in Lubelskie and Podkarpackie 32% and 30% of the unemployed, respectively, are younger than twenty-five.[29] This has also affected some of the most dynamic and educated Polish youth, with young graduates making up 30% of the country's unemployed.[30]

This deactivation of the Polish population has inevitably led to a surge in poverty in the country. Table 3.7 shows how poverty, in terms of minimum existence and social minimum measures, has grown significantly during transition.[31] For example, while around 3m Poles (8.4%) had an income below the social minimum level in 1981, by 2002 this had escalated to 22.7m (58.7%). Once again the growth of poverty during transition has been dependent on the extent to which the state has withdrawn from socio-economic activity. The shock-therapy reforms brought a sharp rise in poverty, as millions exited the workforce. However, between 1994 and 1998 poverty fell from 57.3% to 49.8% (social minimum) and from 6.4% to 5.6% (minimum existence). After this, poverty once again began to grow rapidly, up to 58.7% (social minimum) and 11.1% (minimum existence) in 2002. The largest section of society affected by poverty is the unemployed and those dependent upon social security payments; and the areas most hit by poverty are those where the withdrawal of the state has been most severe.[32] This is particularly the case in those regions where state farms were situated. The closure of state farms not only resulted in a loss of jobs but also removed a vital source of social assistance. The Polish state farms owned around 500,000 houses and flats, housing over 2 million people and making up 9% of housing in the countryside in general. They also possessed nursery schools, health centres, sports centres and various clubs, with around 23% of the total value of Polish state farms' fixed assets assigned to this social sector (Despiney-Zachowska, 1999).

The rise of poverty in Poland has invariably hit children and youth the hardest. In 2000, 16.2% of 14 year olds went to sleep hungry, compared to 2.9% in 1988. 31.7% of 14 year olds did not possess a second pair of shoes in 2000, up from 11.6% in 1988. Also while 0.9% of 14 year olds did not have a warm blanket in 1988, this had risen to 7.9% in 2000 (Domański, 2002). The Polish Humanitarian Organisation has discovered that 30% (0.5m) of Polish children aged between 7-16 are undernourished. Child poverty is exacerbated by the deterioration of public services. For example, 65% of all state schools in Poland lack the facilities to provide their pupils with a warm meal. In 2002, 26% of Polish schoolchildren did not receive a school meal, rising by 5.5% from 1998.[33] The growth of poverty and deterioration in the public health system has led to the return of diseases, such as tuberculosis, which had been eradicated after WW2.[34] Another result of the growth in poverty has been the social and cultural degradation of a section of Polish society. In 1990 there were 10,200 libraries and 17,500 library points, but by 2003 this had declined to 9,500 and 4,400 respectively. This situation has particularly hit the countryside, where the number of libraries fell to only 1,100 in 2003. In turn there has been a sharp decline in the number of books read in the country. Between 1990 and 2002 the number of people who did not read even one book a year had grown by 15% (up from 29% to 44%) and those who read more than seven books a year had declined by 19% (Szumlewicz, 2005).

TABLE 3.7
Poverty in Poland 1989-2002

	Social Minimum		Minimum Existence	
	%	Million People	%	Million People
1989	14.8	5.6	n/a	n/a
1990	31.2	11.9	n/a	n/a
1993	n/a	n/a	n/a	n/a
1994	57.3	22.1	6.4	2.5
1995	n/a	n/a	n/a	n/a
1996	47.7	18.4	4.3	1.7
1997	50.4	19.5	5.4	2.1
1998	49.8	19.3	5.6	2.2
1999	52.2	20.2	6.9	2.7
2000	53.8	20.8	8.1	3.1
2001	57.2	22.1	9.5	3.7
2002	58.7	22.7	11.1	4.3

8

The transition in Poland has also brought about a large rise in social inequalities. Table 3.8 reveals how the largest losers of the transition have been those working in agriculture. The incomes of both agricultural workers and farmers were above the national average in 1990, yet had declined to 77% and 70% of this level by 2003. The relative decline in the income of those working in agriculture has increased as transition has progressed. In 2002 farmers' real incomes stood at around 40% of those outside of agriculture, while in 1997 this figure stood at 80% (i.e. a fall of 50%).[35] The greatest winners of the transition have been the self-employed whose income is over a quarter of the national average. Along with the decline in the position of those working in agriculture there has been a relative growth in the wages of pensioners and wage earners. However, this disguises the large inequalities existent within these groups. For example, between 1995 and 2001, the minimum wage fell from 41% of the average wage in Poland to 37%. Also, the share of income owned by the top 10% of Polish society increased from 21% in 1990 to 26% in 2002, while that of the lowest 10% declined from 4% to 2.4% during this period. Between 1990 and 1997 the Gini coefficient, which measures income inequality, rose from 24 to 33. This was not only higher than in WE but also greater than in Poland's neighbouring countries Hungary (25), the Czech Republic (24) and Slovakia (25).[36]

Table 3.9 divulges the differences between private and state wages in Poland. As we can see state sector wages remain around 10% higher than the national average, while domestic private sector jobs are around 22% lower than the average income. This shows how workers in state companies, which are more trade-unionised than in the private sector, have been able to defend their wages to a greater extent than those in the private sector. However, the wages of public sector workers, including those working in health and education, are amongst the lowest in society. Doctors salaries in Poland are ten times below the EU average, with a monthly salary of around ZŁ1,500 and many doctors are compelled to take on more than one contract, with some working up to 400 hours a month. Teachers face a similar situation, with their monthly salary averaging around ZŁ1,200.[37] The sector paying the highest wages is that encompassing foreign owned private companies, which, however, makes up a tiny minority of employment in Poland. Salaries of workers in this sector grew from 316% of the national average in 1995 to 385% in 2003. The wages of the managers and directors in the international corporations now rival those in the world's most advanced economies. In the 10 largest corporations in Poland the salaries of the members of the management board are 218 times greater than the minimum salary and 82 times greater than the average salary. In the 43 largest corporations they are 100 times larger than the minimum salary and 37 times greater than the country's average salary (Kabaj, 2005).

The reintroduction of capitalism has also exaggerated regional and gender inequalities, with the majority of FDI directed towards the most wealthy areas of the country. GDP per-capita in Mazowieckie, the region around Warsaw, is 52% higher than the national average, with the next richest region, Dolnośląskie, only 3% greater than the national average. The four regions in the east of Poland (Warmińsko-Mazurskie, Podlaskie, Lubelskie, and Podkarpackie) have GDP per capita levels ranging from 70% to 76% the national average.[38] There are also huge income differentials between men and women. Women in high managerial positions and/or with a higher education earn over 30% less than men; and women in manual work receive salaries that are more than 40% below male wages. Also only 2-3% of company directors and presidents in Poland are women. This is despite the fact that women are better educated than men (10.4% of women have a higher education, compared to 9.3% of men.)[39]

TABLE 3.8
Social Groups' Income as a Percentage of National Average Income 1990-2003

Year	Wage Earners	Farm Workers	Farmers	Self Employed	Pensioners and Retirees
1990	100.00	105.66	102.49	n/a	87.57
1991	100.00	94.99	84.17	n/a	95.61
1992	n/a	n/a	n/a	n/a	n/a
1993	101.72	83.73	90.84	126.05	106.96
1994	101.63	84.25	88.85	128.91	106.47
1995	100.23	86.77	93.94	128.47	106.36
1996	103.08	83.92	89.50	127.22	106.94
1997	102.66	83.95	92.72	130.52	104.40
1998	104.48	80.19	77.79	125.28	105.47
1999	105.69	78.22	73.40	127.76	106.43
2000	107.66	79.12	74.69	130.16	101.11
2001	105.99	79.09	77.20	125.41	104.56
2002	105.10	76.95	86.09	126.95	105.24
2003	107.25	76.60	69.70	126.41	105.80

The increase of poverty and decline in the living standards of large sections of Polish society has once again ensured that the major structural obstacle to sustained economic growth in the country has been the lack of domestic demand. Neo-liberal protagonists have consistently identified reducing labour costs and nurturing the growth of a middle class as the key elements for maintaining socio-economic growth. Labour costs in Poland are already over four times below the average in the EU15 countries, which, along with long working hours, makes the country an attractive destination for foreign capital. Workers employed in foreign firms make up society's most dynamic consumer group and a large part of the new middle class in Poland. However, as this group is only a small minority of the workforce it cannot compensate for the low level of consumption in other sections of society. Alongside the existence of mass unemployment one of the major causes of low consumer demand and poverty is the extremely low minimum wage. In 1998, this stood at 40.2% of the average wage, more or less the same as it had been in 1993. However, it then fell to 38.5% in 1999 and declined to 35.9% in 2004, which, after deducting social security payments, equals around ZŁ600 per month and is below the social minimum level of existence. In the majority of EU countries the minimum wage equals at least 50% of the average wage.

TABLE 3.9
Incomes in Economic Sectors as a Percentage of National Average Income 1995-2003

Year	State Sector	Domestic Private	Foreign Private
1995	109.05	78.89	315.55
1996	109.95	77.94	329.62
1997	110.45	79.20	335.25
1998	110.33	79.80	333.52
1999	108.04	81.00	365.39
2000	109.08	80.25	392.66
2001	109.20	78.91	386.00
2002	110.82	77.36	400.53
2003	110.89	78.35	384.88

9

The latest stage of Poland's socio-economic transition began after it joined the EU in 2004. From 2003 economic growth began to increase and by the end of 2006 the economy was growing by more than 6%. This growth was being driven by a huge inflow of capital into the country, primarily in the form of direct EU subsidies. We have previously seen how the CEE states, after the collapse of socialism, received no significant aid from the advanced capitalist world. However, once inside the Union, new CEE EU states (herein referred to as the Accession Eight (A8) countries) have the opportunity to receive large amounts of EU funds. These funds, which are designed to foster the development of the EU's poorest regions, are essentially a form of direct (multi) state investment and economic redistribution. Poland poses the greatest challenge for the EU's eastward expansion, as its population and number of farmers are larger than the seven A8 countries combined and the six poorest regions in the enlarged EU (before Romania and Bulgaria joined) are situated in Poland.[40] In turn, this means that Poland has the opportunity to obtain large amounts of EU funds.

Poland's entry into the EU opens up another stage in its attempt to close the developmental gap with WE. Poland's GDP per head stands at less than 40% of the EU15 average, far behind its closest neighbours the Czech Republic, Hungary and Slovakia, meaning it would take Poland 34 years to reach the EU15 GDP per person average (assuming that it registered an average growth rate of 5%, while the EU15 recorded one of 2%).[41] From the beginning of transition, European institutions set a framework for EU integration that served as an impetus for the liberal market reforms in CEE. Also, the major WE capitalist economies have greatly profited from the opening of the CEE economies to global capital. However, the prospect of the A8 states receiving large EU funds, offers a potential counterweight to the further liberalisation of the CEE economies. Essentially, the question is raised as to whether the CEE economies, their living standards and social security systems will rise to the position of those in WE; or whether EU expansion will further erode these countries' productive bases and help to further deepen neo-liberalism within the whole of the EU.

There was no immediate economic shock connected with Poland's EU entry, as the country's economy had largely been opened up before accession. The assimilation of Poland into the EU market provides many of its businesses and farmers with new opportunities for exports. Helped by the relative strength of the euro, Polish exports to the EU increased from €59.7bn in 2004 to €87.5bn in 2006, which led to a rapid increase in the profitability of many of Poland's leading firms. There was no significant increase in inflation connected with EU accession, and Polish consumers have been able to enjoy the benefits of the enlarged EU market, including the arrival of some cheaper consumer goods, services and communications. Consumer demand has also been boosted by the decline in the country's interest rates.[42]

The major impetus for the improved economic performance of the Polish economy was provided by EU funds and subsidies. Up until the end of the first quarter of 2007, Poland had received over ZŁ13,02bn from the EU, funding more than 56,000 projects.[43] Also, Polish farmers, which include some of the country's most impoverished citizens, have obtained billions in subsidies. However, the major prospective source of money for the A8 countries is included in the EU budget from 2007 to 2013, from which Poland could potentially receive over €59bn.[44] From this sum, over €21bn is intended for investment in infrastructure, such as roads, railways, airports, gas pipelines, etc.[45]

The other major export, to have grown since Poland's EU accession, has been labour; despite the fact that citizens from the A8 states are restricted in their freedom to live and work in some EU15 countries.[46] Around 1.2m Poles have emigrated since EU accession and a large number of these have declared that they intend to settle permanently in their destination country.[47] The major reason for this large exodus of people is the exceptionally high unemployment rate and low wages in Poland. Poland has the lowest level of employment in the EU and its minimum wage is over ten times less than that in the EU's richest states. This large-scale emigration brings some relief to the country's massive unemployment rate, as there were around 300,000 less jobseekers in 2006 than in 2005. It has also led to the appearance of labour shortages in a number of sectors, with many of the country's youngest, most educated and dynamic citizens leaving the country. For example, two years after joining the EU, over 5% of Polish health workers had already left the country.[48] It has also meant that wages have begun to grow in areas where there are labour shortages (particularly construction). The return of economic growth, labour shortages and years of pent up frustration over suppressed wages, have led to a rise in labour protests demanding salary increases. This has been particularly evident in the public sector (e.g. health workers and teachers), many of who survive on wages close to the social minimum level of existence.

After nearly two decades of neo-liberal reform, there has been no significant investment in the country's crumbling infrastructure. While the economic dictum of the transition has been to withdraw the state from economic activity and allow for the invisible hand of the market to extend its reach, the recipe for economic development now seems to be a package of huge state induced investment. The majority of this funding comes through the EU, via a process of redistribution from the Union's richest states that contradicts all accepted neo-liberal wisdom. Also, this demands large investment from the Polish state. In order for a country to receive structural and cohesion funds the national government needs to first supply at least 25% of the cost of any investment. However, the possibility of fully utilising these funds is restricted by the tight monetary policy that it is obliged to comply with as a member of the EU, as well as having to find funds for its own payments to the EU. In compliance with EU expectations, the government plans to reduce the budget deficit to 3% by the end of the decade, which will require further spending cuts. Pressure for the government to reduce its budget deficit is also connected to the new EU states' obligation to move towards entry of the *eurozone*, through adjusting its currency and monetary policy to meet the Maastricht convergence criteria. These criteria, institutionalised in the Growth and Stability Pact, include, among others, reducing budget deficits to 3% of GDP as a first step towards having a balanced budget. These tight budgetary conditions could seriously hinder the government's ability to fully utilise EU funds and invest in the country's economy. Also, the impoverishment and financial debt of the country's public services (and employees) is increasing, with governments seeking methods to further privatise these services.

A decade and a half of neo-liberal reform, in post-socialist Poland, has created a dual economy, labour market and society. EU entry is undoubtedly beneficial for the country's burgeoning middle class and also provides opportunities for those frustrated with their prospects at home to seek work in WE. The issue at hand, however, is whether Poland will receive and be able to utilise sufficient EU funds that would allow it to modernise its infrastructure and support its existing industries and develop new competitive ones. However, EU entry also brings the possibility that a new wave of liberal reforms will have to be introduced. After joining the EU the government is not allowed to give subsidies to businesses without an agreement from Brussels and will only be allowed to support those companies that are predicted to make a profit in 3 to 5 years. The further opening of the Polish economy to foreign competition and withdrawal of subsidies threatens another wave of closures and redundancies. Despite the economic improvement connected with EU entry the country's inherent economic imbalances and huge social problems of unemployment, poverty and inequality remain. Excepting gaining EU funds, the proposed solutions to these problems are further IMF type stabilisation packages, which attempt to solve the economic imbalances by cutting social spending, privatising public services and liberalising labour markets.

****

Poland has once again been immersed into the world capitalist economy and its development is determined by its relationship with the more developed capitalist states to its west. While areas of Polish socio-economic life have been elevated to those in the West others have undergone a process of regression and impoverishment. The major structural block in the economy, similar to during the inter-war period, has been the lack of domestic demand. The expansion of capitalism into Poland and CEE has been driven mainly through the destruction of the socialist elements of the economy and the monopolisation of large areas of these countries' financial and industrial sectors. This has coincided with the disintegration of the country's existing industrial base and the failure to create other modern industries and services that would allow the country to compete in the world economy. It has also reinforced the pre-capitalist elements of the economy, with the small, subsistence farms growing alongside the process of de-industrialisation. As the process of ownership transformation is completed then the destruction of the inherited social welfare system accelerates. During this later transition period the form of capitalism in Poland is established. The system is far less fluid and while it inevitably undergoes periods of growth and decline, as in any capitalist system, these occur within certain limits. The large social inequalities, low wages, areas of poverty and structural unemployment are all now established features of Polish capitalism. This socio-economic course of the transition is reflected socially, ideologically and politically; with the liberal consensus, prevalent at the beginning of transition, disintegrating and allowing for the emergence of an alternative conservative paradigm and the weakening of the liberal-democratic institutions of the state.

4

POLAND'S FRAGMENTING CONSENSUS

What's Missing in the project of building a liberal democratic market economy is the hegemonic bourgeois class that can plausibly present its own interests as the general interest. (Ost, 1993).

Any hegemonic system is broadly built upon an acceptance of ideas, which are supported by material resources and institutions (Bieler and Morton, 2004; Cox, 1987). The material capabilities of a system are formed out of productive relations, which create the social forces that become bases of power. When there is a change in the social relations of production, such as happened when capitalism was restored in EE, a new configuration of social forces is fashioned. The establishment of a dominant position by leading social forces, over contending social forces, is created through the state and its specific relationship with civil society. Leading social forces attempt to integrate a variety of class interests economically, politically and ideologically, transcending particular corporate interests. Therefore, states, and their relationship with civil society, are formed on a universal plane and rest upon a set of ideas which permeate society. The most political and idealistic phase of an historical bloc is during its creation, when new social forces are establishing their dominant position.

In the previous chapter we examined how the transition in Poland can be understood through the inter-relationship between pre-capitalist,

capitalist and socialist forces. One of the characteristics of the post-socialist transition has been the lack of a strong bourgeoisie, which did not develop during the socialist system as it had during feudalism. The transition from socialism has involved the opening up of the ex-socialist economies to global capitalism, creating a dependent form of capitalism in CEE. This corresponds to the methods of primitive accumulation; i.e. the destruction of socialist socio-economic structures, to allow for the development of a capitalist economy. Whilst areas of socio-economic life have risen to the level of those in the advanced capitalist countries, others have undergone a process of decline and impoverishment. Therefore, some of the inherited socialist structures are amongst the most advanced elements of socio-economic life; while pre-capitalist elements, particularly in agriculture, have been enforced. Neo-liberalism grew as the hegemonic ideology of transition, facilitating the rapid demolition of the socialist economy; a dominant position which has been short-lived.

1

Despite the imposed character of socialism in Poland and the hostility felt by substantial sections of the population towards Soviet domination, the system managed to secure a large degree of social and political legitimacy (Tarkowski, 1994). Above all this came from the post-war global reality, and the participation of millions of citizens, regardless of their feelings towards the PRL, in the reconstruction of the country. This combined with a genuine process of social advancement for millions of the poorest sections of society, via the growth and advancement of the proletariat; agricultural reform and ubiquitous access to education and many cultural activities (Wiatr, 2003). The construction of this new system was formally based upon the universal ideals associated with Marxism. The ideal of socialism/communism 'clothed' the entire system, justifying its activities throughout the fifty years of its existence. This was supplemented by other universal values such as such as equality, national independence, internationalism and democracy. These ideals were then replicated through particular notions such as the leading role of the working class and party; the nationalisation of industry and a global alliance with other socialist nations.

From the outset, the actualisation of some of these notions conflicted, at least in part, with the wishes of the Polish population. For example the ideal of national independence was commonly perceived to contradict the dominant position of the USSR within the Warsaw Pact and Comecon. Similarly, the ideal of a peoples' democracy was at variance with the one-party state and bureaucratisation of the ruling party.[1] In contrast, the socialist ideal of equality was partly realised during the first decades after WW2, through the socio-economic advancement of millions of people. Also, the notion of the leading role of the working class could be maintained, despite episodic workers' protests, through economic cooption; ensuring that an oppositional alliance between the intelligentsia and the working class was not cemented. However, once the process of industrial expansion had exhausted itself by the mid-1970s, leading to a region wide economic slowdown, the distance between the system's universal ideals and living reality widened. Some particular notions associated with the early period industrialisation, such as the priority given to heavy industry, then gained a fixed persistence and were presented as universal values of the system.

The essential difference between the *Solidarność* movement in the early 1980s and previous uprisings (e.g. in 1956 and 1970) was the alliance formed between the working class and the intelligentsia. From the mid-1970s the intelligentsia had orientated itself towards the working class. At its height *Solidarność* claimed ten million members and evolved from a trade union into a mass political organisation, representing the whole of society. Initially it put forward demands for independent trade union activity and workers' self-management of enterprises, which then broadened into a general programme for society as a whole. Self-management of the workplace referred to the direct control of production by producers and the distribution of the goods produced amongst society. The autonomy created in the workplace would guarantee the democratic self-governing of the state, thus leading to a self-managed republic. *Solidarność*'s economic programme concentrated on social ownership, which literally meant ownership by society rather than by the state, and is a prime historical example of the universal and potentially hegemonic quality of the working class. Furthermore, *Solidarność* did not seek the destruction of socialism, but rather sought its true realisation. In effect, it aimed to socialise and democratise the system, by gaining economic and political control from the party bureaucracy.

Economic stagnation, combined with the defeat and atomisation of the *Solidarność* movement after the imposition of Martial Law from 1981, ensured that disillusionment with the socialist system and its ideals increased. In 1986 58% of young people believed that it was worth continuing with socialism, which declined to 43.3% in 1988 and to 28.8% in 1989. Also, in 1980, 89.7 percent of society supported limiting high incomes, declining to 53% in 1989. Similarly 77.8 percent of Poles agreed with the principle of full-employment in 1980, which had reduced to 49.3 percent by 1989 (Przeworski, 1993). As the *Solidarność* movement was pushed underground the opposition movement withdrew from competing with the state for political power and instead assumed the tactics of 'anti-politics', which sought to by-pass the state, believing that change would not occur in the realm of politics but through a change in consciousness. The concept of living outside the system has a long history in Poland, with Polish society defining itself as living alongside or in opposition to the state during the years of partition and Nazi occupation (Kurczewska, 1995). Whilst in the advanced capitalist states the bourgeoisie managed to absorb social layers economically and culturally, through a strong civil society, the state during socialism operated as the 'sole existing reality' (Bielasiak, 1992). This meant that any feelings of dissatisfaction in social, political or economic life were directed against the state, with the opposition identifying civil society as an alternative to this state (Morawski, 1992; Wesołowski, 1994).

2

The notion of civil society and its relationship to the state had previously been deployed as a way of understanding capitalist societies. Marx saw civil society as being an inherently modern phenomenon and one specifically related to the capitalist mode of production. We have seen how Gramsci took up the question of civil society, through his analysis of the differences between capitalism in Eastern and Western Europe. In contrast to the East, where the state is dominant and coercive, in the West a developed civil society formed to help maintain consent, without the direct coercive rule of the state. This dichotomy, between Eastern and Western Europe, was not resolved during the Cold War and in many respects it became even more crystallised (Lester, 2000). Capitalism needs a separation of the state and civil society in order for a space to exist where independent business interests can operate. This obviously has its limits as both the market (especially through monopolisation) and the state can and do encroach upon the independence of civil society. Marx understood civil society in capitalism as being reflective of the fragmented nature of bourgeois society and that this diversity of interests would be superseded during socialism, due to the universal nature of the proletariat, which would de-differentiate the state and civil society (Ost, 1990) In addition,

Gramsci envisioned the development of a 'regulated' society that could exist without the state. The Stalinisation of CEE societies, and the level of socio-economic development achieved during the socialist period, did not create unified societies growing beyond the differentiated societies in the West, but rather societies suffocated by the overwhelming power of the state. The early *Solidarność* movement may be viewed as an attempt by the working class to universalise society in its own image. Sections of the opposition movements in CEE began to consider whether it would be possible to create a 'socialist civil society'. For example, the Hungarian intellectual Ivan Szelenyi believed that this could occur through an expansion of democratic rights and workers' self-management (Konrad and Szelenyi, 1979).

Civil society, which had come to be associated with individualism and the market in the West, emerged in Poland and CEE as a concept connected with the democratisation of the socialised economy and an extension of the aspirations of the working class. This collective understanding of civil society also has its roots in the historical weakness of capitalism in the region and the continued existence of pre-capitalist social structures. As we have seen, there was no inherent tendency within the CEE socialist systems to create a bourgeois class that could articulate its own ideology and hegemonic project. Therefore, intermingled with the socialist ideological expressions of the working class, were communitarian ideals connected to the family, Church and nation. However, the defeat of *Solidarność* in the early 1980s and continued existence of the seemingly insurmountable obstacle of Soviet domination in CEE, led the opposition movement to look for help from external forces. This view had been strengthened by the appointment of the Polish Pope John Paul II in 1978. It was also spurred by the relative economic decline in CEE vis-à-vis the major capitalist economies; the decline of the post-war consensus in WE and the election of more aggressively anti-communist governments in the West. In turn, the opposition intelligentsia increasingly advocated the integration of Poland into the global capitalist economy, placing more emphasis on bourgeois ideals such as the market and private property. Once Gorbachev had made clear that the USSR would not interfere in the internal matters of the CEE states then the material and ideological forces that gained supremacy were those associated with international capitalism.

3

The collapse of socialism in Poland and CEE did not come about through an 'existential revolution', as some opposition leaders had envisioned, but through a negotiated political transfer of power. This negotiated transition, precipitated by Gorbachev's reforms in the USSR, was initially portrayed as being part of the historical convergence between socialism and capitalism. Precisely, this was represented as a preservation of the positive aspects of socialism, whilst adopting the dynamic economic system existent in the West. Therefore, at the round-table talks, the *Solidarność* movement maintained its formal position of building a self-managed republic; no plans for implementing the radical shock-therapy economic reforms were passed and it was agreed to build a social market economy in Poland. So, how was it that neo-liberalism was able to achieve such a dominant position in Poland once the political transfer of power had been completed in 1989?

Neo-liberal ideology propagated the allegory that socialism had restricted society's natural development and that after the removal of this 'straightjacket' society's natural forces would develop. It was argued that the socialist period represented 'fifty wasted years' and that Poland could reach the living standards of the advanced western capitalist states by opening up its economy to the world market. A set of concepts, negating socialism, accompanied the reintroduction of capitalism in Poland. Neo-liberalism became the embodiment of 'anti-politics', seeking the removal of the state and politics from socio-economic life. The market came to be seen as a fair and objective criterion for determining the distribution of social goods, in contrast to the corrupt practices of the state. The concept of civil society was stripped of its collective meaning and became an ideological tool used to roll back the state and promote neo-liberal economics. Ideals of the individual counter-posed the collective; an open and free society stood against a closed and regulated society and private ownership superseded state ownership. The transition was purported to be Poland's 'return to Europe', which stood, without any seeming contradiction, alongside the ideals of becoming part of 'the West' and a 'global' economy.

The growth of neo-liberalism, as a hegemonic ideology in Poland and CEE, was part of a global trend accompanying the collapse of socialism. For the previous century the socialist project had claimed the mantle of the enlightenment and the project of social progress and advancement. However, the collapse of socialism in EE and the combined retreat of welfare reformism in WE, reversed this point of reference. The left was now seen as conservative, authoritarian and regressive, while the right was viewed as liberal, democratic and progressive. Neo-liberalism evolved into the organic formula of the post-socialist age, through fusing economic liberalism with civil and political liberalism. In Poland and EE neo-liberalism achieved such dominance that it came to be seen as non-ideological. Its precepts and procedures were purportedly fair and objective and offered a proven path of development whose only obstacle was the interference of the state. Neo-liberalism's zenith was reached in EE during the early years of transition creating an organic composition within which all social and political forces, including the left, Church, media and intelligentsia, were incorporated.

Despite its purported objectivity, the ideological package associated with the post-socialist transition correlates with the methods of primitive accumulation and the opening up of the ex-socialist economies to international capital. As shown in the previous chapter, the reality of the shock-therapy reforms in Poland was far removed from the idealised version presented at the beginning of transition. While the tenets of neo-liberalism initially gained widespread support, this rapidly declined as the socio-economic effects of the transition were felt. Neo-liberal hegemony breaks in two main areas, which are symptomatic of the weakness of the international historical bloc. Firstly, neo-liberalism, particularly within the ex-socialist states, creates large socio-economic inequalities and areas of poverty. Secondly, the unity of the West or globalised economy, into which the ex-socialist states were submerged, fragments as the divisions between the main global powers have grown after the disintegration of socialism in CEE. Both of these factors determine how the ideological unity, built at the beginning of transition, breaks up in the post-socialist states.[2]

The population's assessment of the transition is a subjective reproduction of its material reality and the dual society it created. The living standards of a section of Polish society have been raised to a level similar to those in the West. Alongside an increased access to goods and services came an inflow of new ideas and lifestyles. Becoming submerged into the global economy ensured that a plurality and openness to a new range of ideas and opinions grew. This has not been simply confined to the new urban middle-class but has, to some degree, permeated all sections of society. However, just as the material benefits of the reform have been limited in scope, so too have its corresponding subjective expressions. The strict connection of economic liberalism with political and civil liberalism has meant that as support for the former has declined so the base of the latter has eroded. Also, as support for neo-liberalism has reduced, then ideologies relating to the pre-capitalist or socialist systems have grown. As we shall see, this process has been most pronounced when the economic reforms have speeded up and most reduced when they have slowed.

4

The historical development of citizenship within modern capitalist society, identified by Marshall in the 1950s, from civil, through political to social rights, is reversed in the post-socialist states. The socialist systems in CEE granted its citizens a range of social rights, while certain civil and political rights were restricted. After the collapse of socialism, various civil and political rights were granted, while many social rights began to be eroded. This has entailed the rapid and acute withdrawal of the state from socio-economic life and the removal of numerous social protections.

The erosion of the protective elements of the state has meant that both civil and political rights are weakened and the need for the return of more repressive elements of the state grows. For example, there were around 852,000 cases of reported crime in 1993, which fell to about 600,000 in 1999. However, the number of reported cases had soared to 1,404,000 by 2002, after the speeding up of the neo-liberal reforms. Concurrently, the number of people in prison fell from over 61,000 in 1995 to around 50,000 in 1998 and then grew to over 82,000 in 2002.[3] We can also measure how the effects of the neo-liberal reform restrict some of the civil and political gains of the transition. At this point we shall focus on civil rights, with the question of political rights considered below. Many of the civil gains of transition have been undermined, primarily due to falling living standards, ensuring that millions of citizens are unable to take advantage of some of the freedoms previously denied them during socialism. Most obviously, the growth of mass unemployment and large pockets of poverty mean that many are denied the basic means for ensuring a healthy and dignified life. One of the main frustrations felt during socialism was connected with the economy of shortage and the harsh day-to-day task of purchasing consumer goods. Although, from the beginning of transition shops began to fill with previously unavailable products, many of these have been unavailable to large sections of society.

The decline in the livings-standards of millions of Poles has eroded civil freedoms in a number of areas. For example, the decline in the quantity of books read in the country, as shown in chapter three, conflicts with the freedom to write and publish without restraint. A similar example regards the right to travel freely abroad. Although Poles enjoyed a greater freedom to travel abroad than many other citizens inside the Socialist Bloc, there were still large restrictions placed on the freedom to travel outside of Poland. Conversely, during socialism, the vast majority of Poles had guaranteed holiday breaks and could afford to take vacations within Poland, which were often subsidised by their workplace. However, each year, since the early 1990s, around three-quarters of Polish society have not taken a holiday lasting at least one week. After peaking at 79% in 1992, this fell to 71% in 1997 and then rose to 74% in 2002, after the pace of the neo-liberal reforms was increased. Furthermore, of the minority of society who took a holiday in 2002, only 25% travelled abroad; of the rest over 80% of respondents cited a lack of money as being the reason for not taking a holiday. Therefore, the limit of domestic demand not only hampers socio-economic development, but also constricts the civil and political freedoms gained after the fall of socialism.

5

The neo-liberal consensus, created at the beginning of transition, disintegrates as the negative effects of transition grow and this is generally more pronounced when the reforms are speeded up. This is most evident when examining attitudes to the economic aspects of transition. Table 4.1 describes the attitudes to the presence of foreign capital in the country and to privatisation. Four years after the introduction of the shock-therapy reforms, a large majority of society believed that the presence of foreign capital was too great. By 1997, after the SLD government had slowed the reforms, this had fallen to a small majority. However, in 2004, after the reforms had been accelerated again, 61% agreed that the presence of foreign capital was too large, with only 22% disagreeing. Support for privatisation has also steadily declined as the transition has progressed. By 1994 a majority of society still believed that privatisation was beneficial for the Polish economy (33% for, 20% against). By 1997 this had reversed with 21% agreeing that it is beneficial and 35% disagreeing, which had increased by 2004, with 25% agreeing and 40% disagreeing.

As shown in the previous chapter, the programme of privatisation and liberalisation combines with the erosion of inherited welfare guarantees. However, there is wide social support within Polish society for the maintenance of this welfare system. In 1997, 75% of society agreed that a social Welfare State should be constructed in Poland, which had grown to over 90% by 2001. Also, in 2005, 85% of society, up from 74% in 1996, believed that the state should provide comprehensive social services such as health care and education. Only 7% of Poles, down from 15% in 1996, thought that individuals should be responsible for their own healthcare and the education of children. However, there is general dissatisfaction with the reality of public social services. For example, only 18% of society agrees that the health system works well, with 76% disagreeing. Also, just 30% of Poles agree that the health system is in reality free, while 68% disagree. There is also large resistance to social spending cuts in Poland. Table 4.2 shows how large majorities are against cuts in areas such as sickness benefits, pre-retirement benefits and subsidies for the disabled. Also, most people are against reducing the benefits received exclusively by certain social sectors, such as farmers and miners.

This decline in support for the policies of neo-liberalism has been accompanied by a corresponding rise in support for government intervention in the economy. As shown in Table 4.3, those believing that the government should intervene in the economy, using a range of methods, have increased as transition has advanced. Huge majorities support the government providing finance, training and loans to boost employment. There are also significant majorities believing that the government should cover some of the costs for businesses creating jobs and even support industries that are facing collapse in order to protect existing jobs. A small majority believes that taxes ought to be raised in order to finance the creation of new jobs. Large majorities of society believe that the state should fix prices for healthcare (85%), housing (75%), electric energy production (64%) and basic food products (59%). A similar trend can be observed regarding the opinions of Poles towards the ideals of egalitarianism (Table 4.4). Once again a clear trend can be seen whereby support for the principles of egalitarianism has increased over the years, especially after 1997 when the pace of reform was increased. Presently 93% of society considers that the divide between the rich and the poor is too large; 89% that differences in wages are too great; 80% that one of the tasks of the government should be to reduce the gap between high and low earners and 75% that wealth and income should, to a large degree, be divided amongst workers.

As support for the methods of neo-liberalism has declined and backing for government intervention and egalitarianism has risen, how has the population's attitude to the transition changed? In Table 4.5 we can see that in 1994 a large majority felt that the transition had brought more losses than benefits, but that this had reversed by 1998 with more people believing that it had brought more benefits than losses. However, by 2001 this had once again switched, with only 15% of society believing that the transition had brought more benefits and 55% thinking that it had brought more losses, although this gap had narrowed by 2004. These trends are further accentuated when we consider the opinions of the social groups, which hitherto have been most supportive of the reform process. Between 1998 and 2001 the percentage of the intelligentsia and managers who believed that the transition had affected them more positively than negatively declined from 58% to 32%, with those assessing the transition negatively growing from 12% to 40%. Also, while 69% of these social groups believed that privatisation brought positive results in 1998, this had declined to only 25% in 2000 (Kolarska-Bobińska, 2002).

Despite the increase in negative opinions about the effects of the reforms, a majority of society has maintained the opinion that Poland has changed for the better since 1989 and that the transition was worth it (Table 4.5). Although these majorities were smallest following the speeding up of reforms at the end of the 1990s, one can still see that the Polish population preserves a commitment to the transition. However, as the transition has progressed society's view of the socialist period has become more positive. For the first time, in 1999, more people believed that the socialist system had brought more benefits than losses, which had increased by 2004 (Table 4.5). There has also been a large change in the perception of society towards the former governments of the former PZPR. In 1998, over 50% of society negatively assessed these governments, with 37% regarding them positively. However, by 2002, 40% gauged these governments positively and 34% negatively. The period of modern history, which is consistently remembered in a positive light, is the time of the Gierek government, in the 1970s, when living standards rose. 73% of those who were at least eighteen years old during this time look at this period positively, with only 6% viewing it negatively.[4]

Another result of the decline in support for the principles of neo-liberalism has been a fall in trust for the democratic system and its institutions. Table 4.6 reveals the attitudes of Poles to the country's democratic chambers. We can see how the Polish population holds very negative opinions about the parliament and senate, although local governments are generally seen positively. Once again this increased after the reforms were speeded up, with those negatively assessing parliament, for example, growing from 31% in 1997 to 79% in 2005.[5] Simultaneously, there has been a large rise in the number of people who believe that the political system is corrupt. In 2004, 95% of society believed that corruption was a problem, with 75% thinking that it was a very big problem. Although a majority of society still believes that democracy is a system that has advantages over all other forms of government, this reached a nadir in 2005 when 45% agreed with this statement, compared to 40% who thought that a strong individual holding power could result in a better government (Table 4.7). Also, the percentage of respondents who believe that democracy above all brings chaos and disorder grew from 19% in 1995 to 31% in 2005. Therefore, although a majority still believes in the democratic system, a sizeable and growing minority have become disillusioned with democracy and would support a more authoritarian style of government.

The democratic systems, formed in CEE in 1989, replicated those in the West, which partially included the principle of the separation of the Church and state. The implementation of such a policy has obvious difficulties in Poland, due to the historical weakness of liberal capitalism and the contemporary lack of a hegemonic bourgeois class. Catholicism has remained dominant, with over 95% of Polish society declaring themselves as believers and more than half affirming that they practice their religion at least once a week. During transition, the religiosity of Poles has marginally increased, with those described as believers and regular practitioners growing from 50% in 1988 to 58% in 1999.[6] Although, the separation of the Church and the state was partly formulised in the constitution in 1997, the Church has exerted an increasing influence on social and political life (see below). This has led to an increase in those who believe the Church should not express its opinions on political matters and in those who feel that the Church should have less influence (see Table 4.8). The socialist system also enshrined a number of civil rights, such as the right of a woman to an abortion, which are opposed by the Church. Table 4.9 reveals how large majorities continue to believe that abortion should be legal, at least within certain limits. Polish society is less liberal when it comes to the rights of Lesbians and Gays. Large majorities are opposed to the right of same sex couples to marry (72%/22%); believe that same sex couples should not publicly express their relationship (78%/16%) and that lesbian and gay organisations should not have the right to organise public demonstrations (74%/20%). This is an example of how civil rights, gained throughout the socialist period, retain a high level of support during the post-socialist period; while those rights that did not exist during socialism, such as lesbian and gay rights, lack roots in social consciousness and have not been instilled during the transition to capitalism.

Another feature of the consensus, formed after the collapse of socialism, concerned Poland's integration with the West. As shown above, the West was seen as one united entity at the beginning of transition. Therefore, the Polish governments have sought to integrate Poland into the institutions of the West and ally both with the EU and the USA. Throughout transition, support for Poland's entry into the EU and NATO has remained strong. Table 4.10 shows how a large majority supported EU entry and although this ebbed in the years preceding expansion, since Poland's entry into the Union support for accession has grown to around three quarters of society. Also, support for Poland's membership of NATO has remained strong, although the level of support has declined slightly in recent years. As divisions between some European states and the USA have grown, especially following the war in Iraq, Poland has increasingly been seen as an ally of the USA (see chapter six). Poland was one of the countries, along with India and the Philippines, whose population positively assessed the re-election of George Bush in 2004 (44%/27%).[7] Despite this, one can observe how the positive perception of Poles towards America has declined. For example, while in 2006 62% of the Polish population believed that America had a positive influence in the world, this had fallen to just 38% in 2007.[8] Also, large sections of Polish society oppose the practicalities of Poland's alliance with the USA. For instance, around 70% of society does not support the participation of Polish troops in Iraq and believe that they should be withdrawn. Furthermore, the US proposal to extend its National Missile Defence system (NMD) into Poland (see chapter 6) is opposed by 55% of the population, in contrast to the more than 50% who supported it in 2005.

TABLE 4.1
Opinions about Foreign Capital and Privatisation

	Yes (%)			No (%)		
	1994	1997	2004	1994	1997	2004
Is the presence of foreign capital in Poland too large?	59	44	61	27	36	22
Is privatisation beneficial for the Polish economy?	33	21	25	20	35	40

TABLE 4.2
Attitudes to Government Spending

Should savings be made in the following areas in order to improve public finances?	Yes (%)	No (%)
Leaving pensions on the same level if price rises are minimal	44	47
Decreasing miners' subsidies	36	45
Restricting preferential credit for farmers	16	66
Decreasing subsidies for businesses with disabled employees	14	76
Restricting pre-retirement benefits	12	77
Decreasing sick benefits.	10	83

TABLE 4.3
Attitudes to Government Intervention

The government can intervene economically using a number of methods. In your opinion the government should:	Yes (%)			No (%)		
	1994	1997	2004	1994	1997	2004
Finance new investments to create new jobs	89	91	95	2	2	1
Organise professional training for the unemployed	90	94	92	3	1	3
Provide the unemployed with loans to create companies	72	79	81	9	6	6
Cover some of the costs for businesses to create workplaces e.g. tax relief	58	61	73	16	14	9
Support collapsing branches of industry with the aim of maintaining existing jobs	58	57	64	19	22	17
Increase taxes in order to pay for financing new jobs	22	19	24	16	14	15

TABLE 4.4
Opinions Concerning Egalitarianism

	Agree (%)			Disagree (%)		
	1994	1997	2004	1994	1997	2004
The divide between the rich and poor is too large in Poland	89	89	93	6	5	2
The differences in wages are too large in Poland	83	82	89	8	8	4
It should be the duty of the government to decrease the difference between high and low earners	71	70	80	11	12	8
The majority of Income and wealth should, be divided amongst workers	69	70	75	14	13	10

TABLE 4.5
Opinions about the Transition

Have the changes in Poland since 1989 brought more benefits than losses?	1994 (%)	1998 (%)	2001 (%)	2004 (%)
More benefits than losses	15	32	15	22
More losses than benefits	42	27	55	37
In your opinion since 1989 Poland has:	1991	1996	1999	2004
Changed for the better	49	64	50	45
Changed for the worse	10	24	36	37
With the perspective of time do you think that it was worth changing the system 15 years ago?	1994	1999	2001	2004
Yes, it was worth it	64	63	56	65
No, it wasn't worth it.	28	24	30	21
Did the socialist system bring the majority of people in Poland more benefits than losses?	1994	1998	1999	2004
More benefits than losses	28	30	28	28
More losses than benefits	27	32	29	30

TABLE 4.6
Attitudes towards Public Institutions (2005)

	Positive (%)	Negative (%)
Parliament	11	79
Senate	18	61
Local Government	51	35

TABLE 4.7
Opinions about Democracy

	1995 (%)	1997 (%)	2005 (%)
Democracy is a system that has advantages over all other forms of government	53	51	45
A strong individual in power can result in a better government than a democratic government	31	32	40

TABLE 4.8
Attitudes towards the Church

Should the Church Express its Opinions on political matters?	1988 (%)	2004 (%)
Yes	21	11
No	57	85
Should the Church have more or less influence in Poland?	1998 (%)	2004 (%)
More	30	12
Less	14	45

TABLE 4.9
Attitudes towards Abortion

In your opinion abortion should be:	1994 (%)	1998 (%)	2005 (%)
Legal without limits	22	15	13
Legal with certain limits	37	38	42
Illegal with certain exceptions	22	30	32
Completely illegal	9	10	10

TABLE 4.10
Attitudes towards EU and NATO Membership

Attitude towards EU Integration	1996 (%)	2001 (%)	2005 (%)
For	80	53	74
Against	12	30	15
Attitude towards Polish membership of NATO	1999 (%)	2002 (%)	2005 (%)
For	60	73	62
Against	23	6	6

6

The socio-economic effects of the transition have eroded the material capabilities for preserving neo-liberalism's ideological hegemony in Poland. We shall now examine how this has replicated itself institutionally. In 1997 a new constitution of the Third Republic was approved in a referendum, which amounted to a compromise between capitalist, pre-capitalist and socialist forces.[9] The constitution includes a commitment to building a social market economy. A number of social rights are included, with the state obliged to guarantee such things as free health care and education and introduce policies to guarantee full employment. Simultaneously, a collection of monetarist policies is enshrined in the constitution. Public debt must not cross three-fifths of GDP; parliament cannot increase the level of public debt set in a government's programme and the budget deficit cannot be financed directly by the Central Bank. Most importantly, the constitution guarantees the independence of the Central Bank, granting it the autonomous right to set the country's monetary policy. The constitution also reflects the changing relationship between the Church and the state. Representatives of the Catholic Church, who took part in the work of the Constitutional Committee on equal terms with Members of Parliament, blocked a provision guaranteeing the separation of the Church and state, replacing it with a clause providing for their 'mutual impartiality'. The constitution also obliges the government to regulate relations with the Church according to an international law concluded with the Vatican (Concordat). Whilst the Church, failed to win an amendment outlawing abortion they managed to block a provision that citizens should not be discriminated against on the basis of sexual orientation. The contradictions present in the constitution were a result of the compromise outcome of the round-table talks in 1989. The reintroduction of capitalism in Poland was established through a negotiated transition of power at these talks. By the end of 1990, after Jaruzelski had resigned as President, political forces derived from the *Solidarność* movement held total political power. Despite this transfer of power, the level of 'de-communisation' in the country was relatively small. The first 'non-communist' government adopted the policy of drawing a 'thick line' between the past and present. There are no restrictions on participating in public life for those who held high positions of power in the communist system; nor for ex-political police functionaries, intelligence officers or their informants. Political and trade union organisations, originating from the PZPR, became established players on the political scene. Also, in many spheres of economic and social life, ex-members of the PZPR have retained or gained dominant positions. It is no accident that the countries where 'de-communisation' has been most advanced are those nations, such as Germany and the Czech Republic, which have historically had a strong, independent bourgeoisie. In the majority of the EE states the lack of a bourgeois class, emerging from the ruins of socialism, meant that a compromise was sought with the ruling nomenclature, a significant section of which readily participated in and prospered from the restoration of capitalism. However, this layer did not possess the necessary capital to transform itself into a bourgeois class. As we have seen, this role was played by foreign capital, which has shaped Poland's political and economic institutions.

The policies of the shock-therapy reforms, designed to open up the Polish economy to foreign capital, have involved the restructuring of the state. National institutions have become the transmitters of policies from the global to the national level (Shields, 2003). This has first of all occurred through Poland's integration of global organisations such as NATO and the EU. Membership of these institutions has ensured that the liberal course of transition has continued and that Poland has not replicated the path taken by some countries to its east. It has also meant that the interests of global capital, and its competing national representatives, have gained supremacy within the Polish state and its institutions. For example, the American state has exerted its influence through NATO; and superstructural institutions, such as the legal system, are being transformed through EU membership. The institutions of the Polish state have also aided the flow of FDI into Poland and facilitated the sale of Polish assets to foreign buyers. As the Polish economy opened, representatives of international capital surged into the country, espousing the policies of neo-liberalism. The transnationalisation of Poland's institutions has primarily occurred in the area of finance. While the socialist system was drawing its final breath, a number of state owned banks were formed, which were used to restructure the economy and then sold to foreign buyers. This dominance also ensured that the Central Bank and Monetary Policy Committee became subordinated to the interests of foreign capital, often to the detriment of national interests.

The infusion of foreign capital into Poland's institutions has not been restricted to finance. Another striking example is the media, which plays a crucial role in the transmission of ideological values. From 1989, the PZPR's newspaper chain was dissolved and an independent media began to develop. Foreign media companies began investing in the Polish media market and by 2003 almost 80% of the press was in the hands of foreign capital. The Polish press is now dominated by German press giants such as Axel Springer Verlag, Passauer Neue Presse, Bauer and Gruner+Jahur, which hold over 50% of the colour magazine market and own numerous national and regional daily newspapers.[10] Although the spread of foreign capital into broadcasting has been less pronounced, due to the presence of public stations, foreign capital has begun to dominate the cable and satellite market. Poland has the largest cable market in CEE and the country's main cable operator, *UPC Telewizja Kablowa*, with over a million subscribers, was acquired by the Netherlands-based UPC in 1999, which in turn is owned by John Malone's US global media group Liberty Media.[11]

The rapid sale of state assets and the commercialisation of public life have supplied plentiful opportunities for corruption by politicians and civil servants. It has often been assumed that this is a hangover from the socialist system and the informal networks created in the economy of shortage. Whilst these have certainly had their effect, the level of corruption grew as privatisation increased. According to research, carried out by *Transparency International,* the level of corruption in Poland is the highest of any of the eight A8 states. In 1996 Poland was ranked 26th in the world in the list of corrupt states, but by 2005 it had slumped to 70th.[12] Also, while in 1997 55% of society believed that government officials derived illegitimate benefits from their positions, by 2001 this had risen to 70% (Castle and Taras, 2002). The absence of an efficient protectionist state has allowed for the market and private property to exert an overbearing influence over individual and public life. The infusion of private capital into the state's institutions and the growing pathology of corruption has led to a decline in public participation and scrutiny of public policy.[13] In such conditions the space for an independent civil society to flourish has diminished. The concept of civil society has been reduced to the atomisation and individualisation of society and its segregation into niche consumer groups, which in itself has been restricted by the limit of consumer demand. Also, the imbalance in favour of international capital has meant that the economy has become monopolised, thus suppressing diversity and innovation in socio-economic life.

The main counterbalance to the incursion of private property and the market into the public sphere has come from those institutions formed during the socialist period. The existence of national trade union federations has ensured that attempts by employers to increase their rate of exploitation has met some collective resistance.[14] However, trade union membership has declined as the transition has progressed and is virtually non-existent in the new private companies. In 1991, 18% of the adult population was trade-unionised, which had fallen to 11% in 1999 and slumped to just 6% in 2002. Trade Unions are present in all large state enterprises (over 250 employees); 75% of medium state enterprises (50-250 employees) and 50% of small state enterprises (under 50 employees). Although these trade unions have retained a presence in the privatised large enterprises, they have virtually disappeared from the small and medium ones. Also, trade unions are only present in 5% of the new private companies.[15]

Public services, such as the health service and education, also provide an institutional counterweight to the commercialisation of public life. They both provide some protection for society's most vulnerable and act as social levellers, forming common public spaces and facilities for diverse social classes. However, these institutions come under increasing attack, with the dual nature of the transition, described in chapter three, involving attempts to break up and privatise these services. In these circumstances it becomes harder for them to fulfil their universal welfare role, with the holes in the system's safety net widening. Concurrently, the country's middle class bemoan the fact that they must contribute to a system that they frequently opt out of in favour of the private sector. Therefore, the social cohesion and stability that these institutions supply is corroded by the neo-liberal reforms.

The other major social institutions in Poland have their roots in the historical underdevelopment of capitalism in the region and the predominance of alternative institutions to the state, including the family and the Catholic Church. Despite the fact that two-thirds of society claim that family and children are the most important things in their lives, there has been a dramatic fall in the country's birth rate. The fertility rate in Poland is presently 1.23, which is among the bottom five in Europe. Over the past five years the country's population has fallen by almost half a million and it is estimated that there will be four million less Poles by 2030. This can partly be attributed to the growth of individualism in society and the break up of traditional family ties that were frozen during the socialist period. However, for the majority of society, it is due to the fact that state assistance and full employment, existent during socialism, have since disappeared. Conversely, the family often fills the gap left by the receding state, with, for example, only 20% of working mothers sending their children to kindergartens and 40% relying on family members for support.[16]

The social institution that has evidently benefited from transition has been the Catholic Church. The destruction of socialism opened the way for the clericalisation of the state and society and the Church has prospered financially since capitalism was reintroduced. Firstly, it has received subsidies from the state, including help to build numerous Catholic institutions such as high schools and universities. Secondly, the Church has benefited from the return of land and property nationalised after WW2. The Catholic Church is now one of the country's largest property and landowners and absurdly receives gigantic subsidies from the EU, via the Common Agricultural Policy. The Church has used this weight to influence social and political life. In 1990, the teaching of religious education returned to Polish nurseries and schools. In 1992 a regulation was introduced that the public media must respect the 'Christian system of values'. In 1993 abortion was made illegal, after parliament had rejected a resolution a year earlier, signed by 1.5 million citizens, requesting a referendum be held on the issue. Finally, in 1998 parliament ratified the Concordat with the Vatican. The Concordat asserts that Catholicism is practiced by the majority of Polish society and formalises Catholic education in schools, giving church marriages the same status as civil ones. Controversially, it also includes clauses seeking the further restitution of church property, expropriated after WW2.

7

The cultural hegemony, that underlies consensual rule within a democratic capitalist state, is situated within the parliamentary democracy and the ideas of the 'representative state' and 'self government' (Anderson, 1976). Put another way, it is politics that provides the basis for the bourgeoisie's cultural hegemony and it was in recognition of this that Gramsci wrote that political activity is the first moment or level at which the superstructure mediates with the structure (Gramsci, 1991a). As such, in the post-socialist states, politics interacts with capitalist, socialist and pre-capitalist forces. Politics reflects the unfolding subjective logic of the transition and the initial support for and then decline of neo-liberalism is reproduced on the party political scene. We have already observed how liberal-democratic values have been weakened by their close connection with neo-liberal economics. The same is true on the political plane. The reduction of political choice to competing parties with near identical socio-economic programmes has led to a decline in the participation of citizens in the democratic process. Therefore, just as civil rights are eroded by neo-liberalism, so too are political rights. The right to vote and freely join a political party were two of the major democratic gains of the transition. However, turnout in Polish parliamentary elections has only exceeded 50% once (51% in 1993), reflecting dissatisfaction with and a separation of society from politics. A stable section of society consistently abstains from voting and is permanently disengaged from the democratic process (Markowski & Cześnik, 2003). The level of party membership is extremely low, with only around 1.5% of the Polish population belonging to a political party (Szczerbiak, 2001). Also, voter loyalty is exceptionally weak, with large sections of the electorate changing their allegiance from election to election (Markowski & Cześnik, 2003).

A feature of the political transition has been the failure of a strong independent liberal party to stabilise itself in Poland. The weakness of the domestic bourgeoisie and middle class has meant that the social space for such a political current has remained small.[17] Therefore, the neo-liberal course of transition was guaranteed through creating a cross-party consensus for the shock-therapy reforms. A defining feature of Polish politics, as in most CEE states, has been that political parties have not divided around immediate material issues. During the early years of transition the capital/labour and left/right political divides were viewed as outdated notions, bound up with the ideological package of socialism. It was believed that society had developed beyond these cleavages and that politics was becoming fluid, individualised and post-modern.[18] This was coupled with the opinion that economics and politics are distinct spheres and that economics should be separated from politics and state interference. Gramsci identified how such thinking justifies the distribution of wealth to particular social classes. The view that the state should not intervene in the economy is itself fundamentally political and those representing the interests of benefiting social classes promote the argument that parties are not connected to social classes. Within the post-socialist reality, this became another ideological tool employed to justify the practices of primitive accumulation.

The dominance of the historical cleavage can partly be understood by referring back to the classic work of Lipset and Rokkan (1967). They explained how long-standing social cleavages strongly structure partisan alignments and voting choice. In WE, macro developments such as the national-democratic revolution, the Protestant Reformation and the industrial revolution produced enduring structures of conflict that shape the development of political parties and divisions. Regardless of the problems and disputes concerning this theory, it can usefully be applied to the post-socialist states. The transformation of society, politics, the economy and culture, during the socialist period, was so extensive that it generated social divisions that have shaped Polish politics during the post-socialist era (Grabowska, 2004). The socialist transformation created a social layer, tied to the party-state, with up to 150,000 people working for the state and party apparatus. By 1948, 1.4 million Poles belonged to the PZPR and millions of others participated in the building of the socialist system out of the devastation of Nazi occupation and war (Ibid.). Simultaneously, the high level of resistance to the socialist system, throughout the PRL's existence, culminated in the creation of *Solidarność*, which stood as the largest alternative political camp in the Eastern Bloc. Therefore, after the political transition from socialism had been completed, politics divided into these two political blocs.

Another major cleavage in Polish politics has been the liberal/conservative divide. This is not primarily driven by economic interests but by attitudes towards cultural and moral values; such as religion, sexual rights and ethnicity. Above all, this has taken the form of secularism versus religion. As we have seen, after the collapse of socialism, the Catholic Church flexed its muscles, seeking to de-secularise areas of social and political life. Secularism had been guaranteed via socialist policies and institutions and the weakness of the liberal bourgeoisie in post-socialist Poland has meant that the post-communist left has become the principal political guardian of a secular society. The close connection between the Catholic Church and *Solidarność* continued in the post-socialist period. The Church filled an ideological void for the post-*Solidarność* parties, with the programme of self-management becoming obsolete and liberalism unable to command a dominant ideological foothold. Therefore, the historical and liberal/conservative cleavages overlapped, and a left-right political divide was crafted.

For a decade and a half these party divisions allowed for the uninterrupted transition to a capitalist economy and Poland's assimilation into the West; with parties opposed to this course isolated to the margins of politics. These 'non-material' cleavages were not artificial constructions, but reflected the continued existence of socialist and pre-capitalist forces in contemporary Polish society. However, the superseding of immediate material and class interests could only be an intermediate phase. For the continued influence of the socialist system upon Polish politics corresponds with material class interests and is not purely connected to previous partisan alignments. For example, industrial workers in state industries or health-workers in public hospitals have an interest in defending elements of the socialist economy. However, governments from both sides of the political spectrum have participated in the dismantling of these structures, which helped to shake the foundations of the party political system.

8

The dominance and unity of the *Solidarność* movement in Polish politics, around the liberal consensus, lasted little over a year; and the first break in the post-socialist political consensus occurred just six months after the introduction of the shock-therapy reforms. A wave of dissatisfaction with the neo-liberal course of transition grew within society. The political imitative was taken by the Centre Alliance party (PC), led by Jarosław and Lech Kaczyński, who had been involved in creating the Mazowiecki government but then sought to stand at the head of the opposition movement against this administration. By the end of 1991, Jan Olszewski had formed a government, supported by the Kaczyński twins. Olszewski questioned the fundamentals of the reform process and in particular the alliance between liberals and communists formed at the round table negotiations. He began a process of lustration (vetting whether someone had worked for the secret services) and de-communisation and questioned the manner in which property was being privatised. Despite this, Olszewski essentially continued the country's economic course, after appointing the staunch neo-liberal, Andrzej Olechowski, as Finance Minister. President Wałęsa, who was accused by the government as having with the secret police, managed to help defeat the government and form a new administration dominated by liberals (Kowalik, 2006).

The next political consequence of the shock-therapy reforms was the unexpected election of the SLD at the 1993 elections; followed two years later by the election of its presidential candidate, Aleksander Kwaśniewski. The hypothesis that there would be no room for the left in the post-socialist states had been decisively invalidated. The historical cleavage came to dominate Polish politics, reaching its acme at the 1997 elections when the two political blocs, AWS and SLD, monopolised the political scene. They together attracted the support of a range of social classes, encompassing both the *winners* and *losers* of the transition.[19] However, their implementation of the neo-liberal reforms led to the disintegration of these parties'/blocs' electoral bases and even to their own organisational implosion. To date, no political party, having formed a government, has managed to retain power in the succeeding elections. This was most evident in the case of AWS and UW, who formed a coalition government in 1997. At the following parliamentary elections, in 2001, both failed to enter parliament, and have since disappeared from the political scene. In contrast, despite losing the 1997 election, the SLD became the only ruling party to increase its share of the vote after a term in office. It achieved this through slowing the pace of reform, thus maintaining its electoral base. However, it was unable to repeat this feat in 2005, losing three-quarters of the vote it had gained in 2001. The SLD had paid the political price for its adoption of neo-liberal policies, under the ideological guise of the Blairite *Third Way* (see next chapter).

The collapse of AWS at the 2001 elections signalled the beginning of the end for the dominance of the historical divide in Polish politics. Opposition to socialism and the post-communists was no longer enough to unite the right, which splintered organisationally and politically. Three main parties of the right emerged out of the disintegration of AWS (and the decline of UW): the Citizens' Platform (PO), the Law and Justice Party (PiS) and the League of Polish Families (LPR). PO adopted the mantle of neo-liberalism, whilst assuming more conservative social policies than previous liberal parties had done. PiS presented itself as a conservative, anti-communist party, promoting strong law and order and anti-corruption policies. LPR advocated an anti-EU programme along with nationalist and socially conservative policies. The situation for the Polish right has been made particularly difficult due to the underdeveloped nature of the Polish countryside and the existence of millions of small private farmers. In WE a wealthy rural strata makes up a large part of the electorate for the Christian Democratic parties. However, in Poland, the underdevelopment of the countryside, not only in relation to WE but also compared to neighbouring countries like the Czech Republic and Hungary, hampers the development of a strong Christian Democratic party. The countryside vote has been dominated in Poland by parties who have almost exclusively represented this electorate: the Peasants' Party (PSL) and also, from 2001, Self Defence (Samoobrona). At the 2001 elections these parties won over 60% of the countryside vote, with the rise of the more radical Self Defence party reflective of the huge impoverishment which had taken place in the countryside during the AWS-UW's term in office.[20] At the same time, the left remained united and won over 40% of the vote in 2001, gaining a large vote in the countryside and then forming a government with the PSL. However, by 2005 the SLD's vote had declined to just 11%; it had no serious contender for the presidential elections and the party had split.

9

Along with the dramatic decline in support for the SLD, two other major events occurred between the 2001 and 2005 elections. Firstly, Poland entered the EU, with 77% voting 'yes' in a referendum with a 59% turnout. The goal of EU membership had been a major component of the liberal consensus, with anti-EU parties consigned to the fringes of politics. It also provided an impetus for the reforms and helped maintain societal support for the transition. After joining the EU, a major pillar of the liberal consensus was removed and new political divisions opened up on the political scene. Secondly, in April 2005, Pope John Paul II died. The Polish Pope had provided a powerful source of national unity and in many ways personified the compromise formed at the beginning of transition. Whilst advocating strong conservative policies, on issues such as reproductive rights, he sought reconciliation with the post-communists and spoke out strongly against poverty and unemployment in the country. Shortly before the EU referendum he gave his unequivocal support for Poland's EU accession, which was a decisive factor in ensuring that turnout was above the required 50%.[21] Both of these events, along with the country's socio-economic problems, contributed to the dramatic change that occurred in Polish politics at the 2005 parliamentary and presidential elections.

The slump in support for the SLD paved the way for the return of the parties from the right. The SLD government had become increasingly embroiled in corruption scandals (see next chapter), which the right used as ammunition to launch an attack against the government. Both PO and PiS claimed that elements of the socialist state, including the secret services, had maintained a power base within Poland and that a business and political elite (*układ*) was unfairly maintaining a privileged position in society. The idea emerged, out of conservative intellectual circles, of building a new Fourth Republic.[22] All the parties of the right endorsed this, with conservativism and strong anti-communism uniting PO-PiS. They formed a de-facto opposition alliance, with PO seemingly set to become the majority party in a future governing coalition. It therefore appeared as though the historical divide was once again becoming the common point of reference for the Polish political right. However, during the 2005 elections, a new political division emerged between these parties.

With the left isolated, relations between PO and PiS dominated the election campaigns. PiS, created by the Kaczyńskis after the demise of PC, campaigned against PO's neo-liberal economic programme, particularly its support for a flat-tax rate, and sought to gain support from those who were frustrated with the transition.[23] PiS claimed that it stood for a social and united Poland (*solidarny* – which is the adjective from the word solidarity), whilst PO's liberal program (*liberalny*) only represented a small, privileged elite. PiS advocated policies such as building three million homes, halting the sale of state assets to foreigners, investing in health and education, and actively reducing unemployment. They combined this with a strong law and order policy, anti-communism, social conservatism and a foreign policy that was sceptical of the EU and hostile to Russia. The parliamentary and presidential elections, with record low turnouts (40.6 % and 49.7 % respectively), resulted in PiS becoming the largest party in parliament and its candidate, Lech Kaczyński, winning the presidency. PO's vote was restricted primarily to a wealthy, urban electorate. PiS, on the other hand, won the votes of a broad section of society, including gaining a strong vote in the countryside. However, the majority of those who voted for either PO or PiS did so in the expectation that the two parties would form a coalition government.

With PiS installed as the dominant political party a new chapter opened in Polish politics. It soon became clear that a PiS-PO coalition government would not be formed, with both parties blaming the other for the breakdown in negotiations. Buoyed by its electoral successes,

PiS looked to hegemonise the right and build a large conservative party in Poland. It did this not by appealing to the liberal centre and middle class, but through seeking an alliance with the nationalist and peasant parties and winning the support of the peasantry and poor in the countryside. After months of political wrangling, PiS eventually formed a majority government with Self Defence and LPR, i.e. with parties that had previously been ostracised and opposed to the course of transition. For the first time in post-socialist Poland, a party representing the countryside (Self Defence) had joined a coalition government with a party from the right. Combined with PiS gaining a strong vote in the countryside, one of the major features of the 2005 elections was the move of the rural vote/parties to the right.[24]

The entry of LPR into the governing coalition, with its leader Roman Giertych gaining the post of Education Minister, also meant that a far right party had entered a government in Poland for the first time since the National Democrats participated in the Witos administration in 1923. LPR claims the heritage of the *Endecja* and Roman Giertych's grandfather, Jędrzej Giertych, was a close associate of Dmowski's before the War. Therefore, while the left and liberal right have looked for support from the urban middle class and intelligentsia, the conservative right has sought the votes from a larger section of society, in order to win a governing majority for its conservative political agenda.

The coalition government, of PiS with Self Defence and LPR, is extremely unstable and has undergone a number of convulsions.[25] It is a transitional government, as Poland's political scene undergoes an extensive restructuring. The presence of the LPR and Self Defence in government is unacceptable to both domestic and international capital and does not provide a stable political platform for continuing Poland's economic transition. The aim of PiS is to marginalise and divide these parties and to become the hegemonic party of the conservative-nationalist right. This would assist in the creation of a new two party system. A centre-left party, grouped around the liberal wing of PO and parts of the left (especially that grouped around Kwaśniewski) would stand against the conservative right, with the conservative faction of PO forming an alliance with PiS. Much depends on whether PO decides to challenge PiS as a liberal party defending the Third Republic, or as a competitor to lead the conservative right in its aim to build a Fourth Republic. Divisions remain within all the major political parties, including PiS. The alliance of the anti-communists (former PC members) with the Catholic Nationalists (former members of the

Christian-National Union (ZCHN)) that makes up PiS has its own internal contradictions and divisions that threaten the stability of the party. Polish political life is also dominated by the historically unique situation whereby the positions of President and Prime Minister are held by identical twins. This extraordinary state of affairs concentrates power in a way that is democratically legitimate but above the standard regulations and norms of political accountability. The Kaczyńskis are inherently suspicious of any individual and grouping that maintains a degree of autonomy within their party, coalition, or government, meaning their government takes on an increasingly autocratic form.

10

After the collapse of socialism a liberal ideology gained hegemony in Poland, claiming the historical mantle of the *Solidarność* movement. Proponents of this liberal creed promulgated the idea that everything remaining from the socialist system held back the modernisation of the country. This included social classes, primarily the working class, who had contributed more than any other section of society to the overthrow of the socialist system. Therefore, the worsening situation of this class and the dismantling of its rights and benefits were viewed as a regrettable yet inevitable part of the country's development. This permeated political and social consciousness to such an extent that even the majority of the left (whether from the communist or *Solidarność* traditions) accepted such wisdom (Ost, 2005). This ideological framework was underpinned by Poland's integration into the 'international community'; the prising open of its economy by international capital and the subjective limitations of the neo-liberal historical bloc, which disqualified alternative paths of development.

The social realities of the neo-liberal reforms created a growing sense of isolation, dissatisfaction and anger within society. However, with the left weakened and disorientated, the main alternative to the liberal consensus emerged from the right. The right in particular has looked to harness the support of the peasantry and poor in the countryside. This alternative outlook assumed a strong anti-communist stance, blaming the problems in Poland on the continued dominance of ex-communists in political and economic life. Furthermore, it is claimed, ex-communists maintained this position through allying with a section of the *Solidarność* leadership, around a liberal ideological framework. Jarosław Kaczyński, has described the Third Republic as being a 'post-communist monstrosity' and argued that the state should be 'cleansed, reformed and consolidated' in order to rebuild its authority.[26] The leaders of PiS have regularly referred to Piłsudski as their historical inspiration and they assert they are attempting to emulate his policy of 'cleansing' the state and public life (*Sanacja*). This is also combined with an alliance with political forces who lay claim to the *Endecja* tradition and the close connection with the Catholic Church.[27] PiS's anti-communism and anti-liberalism is merged with catholic-nationalism and the dominance of foreign capital is criticised for having destroyed the country's domestic capital base.

The Polish conservative-right not only criticise the socialist period but also the liberal transition of the past seventeen years. They argue that the 'cleansing' of the state of ex-communists should be combined with a strengthening of the state. This can be understood through referring back to the ideas of Gramsci, who grasped how the lack of a protectionist state leads to the return of coercive elements of that state. The primacy given by PiS and its allies to law and order reflects the reality of a society that has been atomised and partly impoverished by the neo-liberal reforms. Since 1989, the country has been governed according to the principles of individualism and personal freedom. Poland's conservative-nationalists argue that such values are incompatible with building a strong nation-state and that liberalism's cultural relativism has failed to provide a system of values around which the population can congregate. They also claim that the weakness of the state has allowed for the rise in crime and dishonesty and criticise the conception of the neutral state, which allows for a plurality of ideas and life-styles in society (i.e. civil society).

The transition in Poland and CEE has been based upon an idea of modernity, through replicating the political and economic systems of the West. It is this 'proven' model of development that the conservative-right is questioning, along with the moral and cultural norms that it brings. A central feature of conservative intellectual thought is the strategy of 'historical politics'. Accordingly, the state must direct historical policy, seeking the rehabilitation of the national community through promoting a new interpretation of Polish history. The conservative-right criticise the policy of unquestionably imitating the systems to the West and they endorse the promotion of patriotism and traditional values connected to the family and Catholic Church. Essentially, the right are querying the concept of a neutral, secular state and advocating the politicisation of the public sphere. The Polish government is attempting to introduce a series of reforms aimed at irreversibly changing the country's political, social and cultural life; ultimately leading to the creation of a new republic. The strategy of the conservative right is to harness social dissatisfaction and create a new cultural and moral climate, through utilising and reforming the institutions of the state. What we are observing is the exhaustion of the liberal phase of capitalism, after the collapse of socialism, and the strengthening of more authoritarian and pre-capitalist structures. Also, the fact that this conservative turn began almost simultaneously with Poland's accession into the EU is not coincidental. The lure of EU entry pulled the country through an intense political and economic transition. However, once inside the EU this compulsion is removed and the country adjusts itself to the realities of EU membership. This is reflective of developments within the world historical bloc, which include the general conservative turn in world politics and the growing divisions between the major global powers. The present conservative turn in Polish politics is a constituent part of these wider global changes. These issues and the practices of the PiS-led government will be considered in chapter six. Before this we shall turn our attention to the question of the left and the role that it has played during the Polish transition.

5

FROM STALINISM TO SOCIAL DEMOCRACY

It may be said that to write the history of a party means nothing less than to write the general history of a country (Gramsci).

The events of 1989-1991 closed the period of history, began in 1917, signifying a gigantic defeat for the international left. The gains of the left, not least in post-war WE, were intrinsically tied to the Russian Revolution and its advance into EE after the liberation of Europe from Nazi tyranny. However, the Soviet model had long ceased to be a source of inspiration for the international left that, especially after the invasions of Budapest and Prague, was repulsed by the undemocratic practices of the Stalinist bureaucracy. The majority of the left initially misunderstood the historical significance of the events of 1989-91. It was commonly believed (or hoped) that these 'democratic revolutions' would democratise the socialist systems; or at least lead to the extension of a social democratic form of capitalism into EE. Social democrats and euro-communists became convinced that the European continent could be unified through the development of socially orientated market economies. Likewise, many prominent Marxist thinkers heralded the fall of the Berlin Wall as signalling the return of the EE socialist systems to their democratic socialist roots; an event that would have had huge progressive repercussions in WE and beyond.

These delusions were short-lived; as the left adjusted itself to the global neo-liberal hegemony, gained after the reintroduction of capitalism in EE. The triumphant declarations, in the early 1990s, that the historical division between capital and labour had been overcome, were co-joined with the belief that the historical role of the left had been exhausted. Such thinking resonated most strongly in the post-socialist states. The left was portrayed as a relic of socialism, which would be consigned to the annuls of history, along with the system's outdated industry. If a left were to survive, it would be of a new kind and would have to break decisively from the past. One thing seemed clear; there would be no room, in the post-socialist reality, for that part of the left, which was connected to the former ruling parties during socialism. However, in the vast majority of the post-socialist states, the main parties of the left have been those derived from the former ruling parties. Some of these successor parties have retained their communist heritage, such as in Russia and the Czech Republic. Others, such as in Poland and Hungary, reformed themselves in a social democratic direction and became important political players in the transition to capitalism. The Polish successor party became the first in the region to achieve electoral success and form a government. Despite its social democratic conversion, the successes and failures of the Polish successor party have been greatly shaped by the continued influence of the socialist system in contemporary Polish life.

1

The 1917 Russian Revolution saw the country leap, within a few months, from a semi-feudal monarchy to a socialist government. Immediately this government faced civil war and foreign intervention; along with the unemployment and poverty of an under-developed rural economy. The ebbing of the revolutionary wave in Europe, from the early 1920s, and the internal social tensions and weariness of Russian society, laid the way for the growth of a bureaucratic caste. A common historical feature, of most revolutions, has been an ensuing reaction, or even counter-revolution. This reaction devours the leaders and pioneers of the revolution, bringing those from the second line to the front (Trotsky, 2004) The victory of Stalin(ism) in Russia, is an example of such a reaction. It represented the distancing of a bureaucratic caste from the working class and peasantry; and opened up a period of repression and historical falsification. The Soviet bureaucracy rejected the international extension of the revolution and instead sought the building of 'socialism in one country'. This entailed the internal development of the country's productive forces, beyond those of international capitalism, meaning that over-riding attention was given to heavy industry, at the expense of other sectors such as services and consumption goods. After WW2, the Stalinist bureaucracy could extend its influence westwards, buoyed by the military and moral authority it had gained from the defeat of the Nazi Army on the Eastern Front and the liberation of much of CEE from fascism.

The socialist governments, formed throughout EE from 1945, were, with the partial exception of Yugoslavia, created in the image of the Soviet bureaucracy. The wave of revolutionary optimism was shallower and shorter than it had been in Russia and the crucial factor in the creation of the socialist governments was not the revolutionary party but the Red Army. However, the socialist systems were greeted with a degree of optimism and popular support, which differed from country to country. For example, in Czechoslovakia the Communist Party had acquired authority in the resistance movement and, by the end of the war, had broad worker/peasant support. Czechoslovakia had close relations with the USSR, due to Soviet support for Czechoslovakian independence before the war, which was strengthened by the withdrawal of Soviet troops in November 1945. In contrast to Czechoslovakia, where there was a strong indigenous communist movement, the pro-Soviet left in Poland was weak.

Polish socialism was historically linked to the ideas of independence and the creation of a Polish state. Early socialist thinkers shared a vision of re-creating an independent Poland, along similar lines to the Narodniks in Russia. This idealistic vision of socialism, which thrived during the years of partition, was only partly challenged by a reformist left, which was hampered by the weakness of capitalism and the bourgeoisie. A Marxist left formed in Poland, from the beginning of the 1880s, with the party, *Proletariat,* adopting an internationalist and anti-nationalist programme.[1] In the 1890s, the Social Democracy of the Kingdom of Poland and Lithuania (SDKPiL) was established. This was built in opposition to the main party of the left, the Polish Socialist Party (PPS), whom they regarded as social patriots and saw their struggle for Polish independence as being utopian.[2] The PPS was also divided, prior to WW1, between a faction organised around Józef Piłsudski, who sought a national uprising against Russian rule and a left faction that believed the party should form an alliance with Russian revolutionaries. Such thinking was given impetus by the fact that some of the largest strikes and demonstrations, connected with the Russian 1905 revolution, took place in the Polish lands. It would be wrong to suggest, therefore, that Marxism has no social or ideological roots in Poland. After all, the Polish nation has spawned Marxists of the calibre of Rosa Luxemburg and Isaac Deutscher. However, a strong pro-Soviet left was not able to mature in the country, as relations between Soviet Russia and Poland worsened and Stalinism gained a stronghold.

The independent Polish state, formed after WW1, was created under the leadership of Piłsudski, who came out of the PPS. As shown in chapter two, Piłsudski saw Russia, and then the USSR, as Poland's major threat and he allied with armies from the West in seeking the creation of 'independent' states between Poland and Russia. The defeat of the Bolshevik army, at the gates of Warsaw in 1920, stirred the patriotic sentiments of Poles, who opposed the presence of the Russian army in Poland. Throughout the inter-war years, the Polish Communist Party (KPP) was a small, although not insignificant party, with around 4,000 members. However, the party suffered a crushing blow, after the division of Poland by Nazi Germany and Soviet Russia. The KPP became caught up in the purges sweeping the USSR; with a number of its members accused of being agents of the Polish government. Virtually its entire leadership was arrested and murdered and finally Stalin, who accused it of being run by fascists and Trotskyists, dissolved the party.[3] Therefore, the indigenous communist movement was extremely weak when the Red Army gained control of Poland in 1944. A Polish Communist Party was re-formed after the German invasion of the USSR in 1941, leading to the establishment of the Polish Workers' Party (PPR). The PPR forced a merger with the PPS to form the PZPR and consolidated its position as the sole party of the left and the undisputed leading party in society. However because of the historical weakness of pro-Soviet communists in Poland the period of Stalinism was relatively 'mild' and short-lived, with some other parties allowed some limited freedom of existence.[4] The inability of Polish communists to create a substantial mass base created internal divisions, with the leadership of the PZPR divided into 'pro-Moscow' and 'National Communist' factions. Throughout the socialist period, the leaders of the PZPR sought to reconcile Polish patriotism, with the official communist ideology sent down from Moscow.

2

Due to the weakness of the indigenous communist movement, the bureaucracy of the PZPR was, from its conception, removed from its political base and historical roots. Pragmatism reigned supreme, whereby the party bureaucracy would switch its positions at ease, free from the constraints of political conviction and ideological belief. This did not mean that the PZPR was ranked solely with matter-of-fact foot-soldiers and administrators. As shown in the last chapter, the PZPR achieved a level of mass support and popular participation, particularly in the early period of socialist industrialisation. Large numbers of pre-war socialists, peasant activists and trade unionists critically supported the activities of the PZPR. Millions perceived the international reality that they were living in as meaning that the PZPR represented the most progressive option for society and that the party stood as a more palatable alternative to the *Endecja* forces who had gained ascendancy in the years before WW2. However, the feeling that Poland was under the domination of Russia and that the government and system were imposed upon society, existed and grew throughout the socialist period. As the working class protested against bureaucratic privilege and lamented the distance between the realities and ideals of the system, so too it rallied around the patriotic ideals of independence. The Catholic Church, unique in the region in its size and social weight, gained a level of social prestige beyond anything it had enjoyed before, or since, as it, and Pope John Paul II, became rallying symbols for the opposition.

The rise of *Solidarność*, along with the worsening domestic economic situation, had severely weakened and demoralised the PZPR's membership. The imposition of Martial Law further shifted the axis of power away from the party towards the state and the military (Poznański, 1988) The PZPR introduced a series of reforms, designed to move the system in a capitalist direction and the party became a training ground for the future architects of shock-therapy reform, including Balcerowicz himself. Despite declarations by party leaders that the 'socialist nature' of the system would remain intact, the reforms being introduced by the government were pushing the country further away from this reality (Bugaj, 2002). The severe defeat of the PZPR, in the first semi-free parliamentary election in 1989, convinced a section of the leadership that a new party needed to be formed.

> A group of very young individuals in the party, the most influential being Aleksander Kwaśniewski, understood that leftist ideas would remain in Poland but that a new social democratic party had to separate itself from the old party.[5]

The last General Secretary of the PZPR, Mieczysław Rakowski, argues that a young liberal current emerged in the PZPR, from the late 1960s, encompassing individuals who had studied abroad and were open to different ways of life. Because the PZPR was an 'amalgamation' of the PPR and PPS, it is claimed that a clandestine social democratic tradition had always existed within the party.[6] The worsening economic situation during the 1980s, and the weakening of Soviet authority in CEE, meant that a section of the party's liberal wing began seeking the complete transformation of the party and the system; believing that the course of socialist development had been exhausted.[7] In 1989, this social democratic current linked with a new social democratic party platform, *8th July movement*, which had been formed by activists in the party's Warsaw University student organisation. At the XI congress of the PZPR (January 1990) the party was dissolved and it was decided to create a new social democratic party: Social Democratic Party of the Republic of Poland (SdRP). When the PZPR metamorphosed into the SdRP it declined from a membership of around 2.1 million to about 60,000, with all the new members having to reapply for membership of the reformed party (Machejek & Machejek, 2001) This still constituted one of the largest parties on the Polish political scene (after the other successor party PSL) and was seen as a blueprint in the region of how to 'social democratise' a communist party in an ex-socialist state.[8]

At the beginning of the transition to capitalism, the Polish post-communist left was fighting to maintain its presence on the political scene. It retained the legal right to operate freely at the round-table negotiations and then via the policy of drawing a 'thick line' on events from the past. The left was concerned with proving its democratic and pro-market credentials and was encompassed into the expanding neo-liberal hegemony. This was shown most strikingly when the PZPR voted in parliament for the shock-therapy reforms in December 1989. The leadership had calculated that this could give the party some legitimacy in the new system and that it could simultaneously avoid the negative political consequences of implementing the neo-liberal reforms. The excesses of the shock-therapy reforms would then lead to the population seeking a political force, which could offer an alternative to liberal economic policy.[9]

The first leadership of the SdRP was filled with younger elements of the PZPR's bureaucracy who had no ideological commitment to socialism. The party's first leader, Aleksander Kwaśniewski, was the most prominent member of a group of young PZPR activists, who faced an uncertain future after the transfer of power. The initial aim of this pragmatic leadership was simply to avoid the elimination of the left, or at least of itself, from political life. In the first years of its existence, the SdRP was politically isolated and became a haven for individuals and groups, connected to the PZPR, who felt threatened by the prospect of a process of 'de-communisation' being instigated by the government. Conversely, this isolation created a solidarity, political network and organisation for these different parts of the post-communist left to organise themselves into a new political party.

The creation of the SdRP was occurring at a time when the Cold War international order had not yet been fully usurped, with the USSR yet to fall. On the one hand, along with accepting the radical market reforms, the SdRP abandoned concepts such as the vanguard party, the leading role of the working class and central planning. However, it still laid claim to the traditions of the reformist current within the PZPR and remained ambivalent in its attitude to the PRL. It also formally held the idea that market reforms were being introduced into a system, which would retain some of its socialist characteristics, making the bitter pill of reform easier for some of the party's members to swallow. In the documents of the First Congress of the SdRP (1992), references were made to the ideal of building a democratic socialist system. The SdRP was also sceptical about joining NATO, maintaining that Poland should secure its safety through the building of joint European structures, and no mention of the EU was made in the party's manifesto. One distinct feature of Polish social democracy was its commitment to secular liberal ideals such as the separation of the Church and state and the legal right to have an abortion. The post-communist left's acceptance of the economic course of the transition was the decisive factor in the division of party politics around issues concerning the past and liberalism/conservatism. These factors, which have their roots in the continued existence of pre-capitalist and socialist forces in contemporary capitalism, were instrumental in shaping the Polish left.

3

The initial isolation of the post-communist left was amplified by the overwhelming support given by society to *Solidarność*. However, this support collapsed, as the social effects of the shock-therapy reforms were felt, with the *Solidarność* camp splintering into a range of political parties and organisations. The SdRP stood in the 1993 parliamentary elections as the dominant participant in the electoral coalition: the Democratic Left Alliance (SLD), which included the General Association of Trade Unions (OPZZ). The left made a dramatic return in the 1993 parliamentary elections, with the SLD wining 20.4% of the vote and the Labour Union (UP) 7.3%. The SLD proposed forming a coalition government with the main liberal party UW, which had come third in the parliamentary elections. Such a government would have continued the neo-liberal course of reform, as the left/liberal government in Hungary did from 1994. However, UW refused this offer, unwilling to cross the historical divide and enter a government with a post-communist party. Instead, the SLD established a majority government with the Polish Peasants' Party (PSL), a party that had grown out of the PZPR's satellite party, the United Peasants' Party (ZSL), who represented an electorate at the opposite end of the social scale from UW. UP did not enter this government, citing the SdRP's liberal economic programme and communist past as reasons for not joining the coalition (see below) The balance of forces within the SLD-PSL coalition was very even, with the SLD gaining 171 seats compared to the PSL's 131. By forming a government with the PSL the historical divide was strengthened and the SLD's pro-market tendencies restrained. By the second round of post-socialist elections in Poland, the two parties with roots in the socialist system had won the largest share of the votes and formed a government.

The SLD's parliamentary success was followed two years later by the election of its presidential candidate, Aleksander Kwaśniewski. The importance of Kwaśniewski's presidential victory in 1995 was that it both confirmed the SLD's legitimacy on the Polish political scene, whilst, paradoxically, strengthening Kwaśniewski's independent status. Despite being the most obvious candidate for PM in 1993, Kwaśniewski did not take up the post, so that he had the freedom to stand for President in 1995. He beat Lech Wałęsa, winning 35.1 % of the votes in the second round, in a contest split along historical lines. Once in power, Kwaśniewski resigned from the SdRP, presenting himself as being above party political and historical schisms and as a President for 'all Poles'. Kwaśniewski won support from the left, due to his ability to legitimise its existence on the political scene and stave off any radical lustration proposals that could have excluded 'ex-communists' from political activity. Also, during his election campaign, Kwasniewski stressed that he stood on the side of workers and that he would not support cutting social spending (Piławski, 2005) Despite these pledges Kwaśniewski came to represent the most liberal section of the SLD.

These electoral successes paved the way for the post-communist left's acceptance into the structures of international social democracy, which was accompanied by the SdRP fully accepting Poland's integration into NATO and the EU. By the end of 1993 (i.e. after it had entered government) the SdRP's policy had begun to soften towards NATO and by 1997 (the year Poland joined NATO) the party's programme clearly stated that 'Poland's membership of NATO is the surest guarantee of our external security'.[10] In the SdRP's 1991 and 1993 programmes the question of the EU was not mentioned, although from its conception the party underlined its orientation towards the WE social democratic tradition. During the party's term in office it began to adopt a more openly positive attitude towards the EU, and the 1997 party programme stated that accession negotiations should be opened with the view to Poland joining the EU as quickly as possible (Sokół, 2001). The Socialist International (SI) and the Party of European Socialists (PSE) were initially reluctant to accept the SdRP as a member, due to the party's historical roots. It was widely believed, within the SI and PSE, that parties arising out of the opposition movements would form the main social democratic parties of the region. However, the SLD's victory in 1993, followed by a wave of similar victories for successor parties throughout the region, opened the way for the SdRP's membership of these organisations. In 1994, the SdRP was invited to have observer status in the SI and in 1996 the SdRP (along with UP) were admitted as full members of the SI and in 1999 the PSE.[11]

4

The electoral victories of the SLD and Kwaśniewski not only signalled that the left would remain an important political player in Poland, but also that the main representatives of this left would be those who had previously been part of the PZPR. It would not have been unreasonable to have expected that an opposition movement organised around a trade union, *Solidarność*, could have provided fertile ground for the creation of a strong left party in Poland. However, the majority of this movement adopted neo-liberal and/or socially conservative policies as the system transformed. This was partly the result of the period of Martial Law, when *Solidarność* was severely weakened and all hopes of transforming the PRL in a democratic socialist direction were quashed. Therefore, by the end of the 1980s, *Solidarność* was more resolutely anti-socialist and heavily influenced by the Catholic Church and pro-market ideology. The left of *Solidarność* understood this situation too late, underestimating the conservative role of the Church. In fact, the *Solidarność* left often relied on the anti-liberal economic policies of the Church as a counter-weight to the growth of neo-liberalism in the early transition period and it only belatedly began to organise itself independently.[12] Meanwhile, the leadership of *Solidarność*, including Lech

Wałesa, were taking up governmental positions and using the trade unions as a vehicle to help push through the shock-therapy reforms.

Despite these difficulties, a post-*Solidarność* left emerged in the early 1990s, attempting to position itself to the left of the SdRP. Labour *Solidarność* (SP) was organised around the renowned *Solidarność* figures of Karol Modzelewski, Ryszard Bugaj and Tadeusz Kowalik, who accused the *Solidarność* leadership of betraying the values and ideals of the movement by supporting the Balcerowicz plan (Strabowski, 2002). Simultaneously, a left arose from the *Solidarność* citizens' committees, which opposed Wałesa's presidential candidacy in 1990. These activists formed ROAD (Citizens' Movement Democratic Action), the majority of whom then entered the Democratic Union UD, with a minority joining the Social Democratic Movement (RDS), in 1992.[13] Both SP and RDS were humiliated in the 1991 elections, receiving 2.06% and 0.46% of the votes respectively. These currents were brought together in 1992, through the formation of the Labour Union (UP). Significantly, this party also incorporated some former activists from the PZPR, including prominent activists from the *July 8th Movement*. The party stressed that it was building a party above 'historical divisions' and looked to the social democratic parties of WE as a model for inspiration and emulation (Ibid.). The party had a genuinely left social democratic programme and was active in campaigns around social issues such as abortion. Despite their proclamations of neutrality on the historical question, the party was still struggling to define itself vis-à-vis the post-communist left. The leader of UP, Ryszard Bugaj, was hostile to the SdRP/SLD, arguing that it was an extension of the communist elite, which had accepted the neo-liberal agenda.[14]

The 1993 parliamentary elections represented a significant breakthrough for UP, which was qualified, however, by the fact that the SLD's vote was nearly three times higher. The party had only managed to extend its support into the post-*Solidarność* electorate and failed to make inroads into the post-communist vote (Strabowski, 2002). Also, UP's vote was mainly restricted to white-collar voters and the party was unable to appeal to the working class and poor; with the most secular and liberal part of this group also sympathetic to the previous socialist system. Quite simply, UP was unable to create a social democratic party based purely on socio-economic policies; as was clearly shown in its failure to win a significant trade-union base, due to the two main trade union movements being divided along historical lines. Divisions began to emerge within UP, with some activists, especially ex-members of the PZPR, questioning UP's decision not to enter the SLD-PSL coalition government. These divisions were laid bare when UP (and ex-PZPR) member, Marek Pol, accepted the post of Minister of Industry, in a 'personal capacity'. These discords were further confirmed when three UP MPs (all ex-members of the PZPR) decided to form their own parliamentary group (*New Democracy*) in 1995. An alternative course to UP was taken by the reformed PPS, which had been re-founded in the late 1980s, incorporating part of the *Solidarność* left, under the leadership of Piotr Ikonowicz.[15] The PPS stood on the SLD slate, in the 1993 and 1997 parliamentary elections, although their MPs had an independent parliamentary caucus. The participation of the PPS gave the SLD a level of credibility as it included a party, which had partially grown out of the *Solidarność* movement.

5

Despite claims by the right that the election of the SLD would mean a return to the PRL, the SLD-PSL government continued Poland's transition to capitalism. The government embraced the concept of the free-market economy and pushed through a privatisation programme, which was often only tempered by the protests of its coalition partner. The SLD also continued Poland's integration with the West and deepened the country's close alliance with the USA. At the same time, the left was elected on a pro-social platform; promising to reduce the social costs of the transition. Rising unemployment and growing social inequalities meant that millions of citizens looked to the SLD as a party connected with the social guarantees of socialism. As we have seen in chapter three, the term of the first SLD-PSL government coincided with a period of rapid economic growth and falling unemployment. This was achieved primarily through slowing the neo-liberal reforms, thus reducing their social costs and strengthening the state sector. The strong presence of the PSL meant that the social weight of an impoverished peasantry weighed heavily on the government. The PSL aimed to retain subsidies in the countryside and blocked those initiatives of the government, which they felt went against the interests of their electorate/party. The decline in unemployment and protection of some of the poorest members of society contributed to the economic recovery. A period of classic social democratic, demand-led growth occurred, through drawing upon resources from the socialist system.

The party's economic programme was formulated by Finance Minister Grzegorz Kołodko and approved by the coalition government in June 1994.[16] This programme continued the process of liberalisation and privatisation, whilst placing more emphasis on the social dimension of the reforms. One of the first acts of the government was to increase the minimum wage and minimum pensions and raise the pension indexation. The government created a 'partnership system of labour relations', by establishing the Tripartite Commission on Socio-Economic Issues and successfully reformed the economic administration of the state, through merging the different economic ministries into the new Ministries of Treasury and Economy (Cook and Orenstein, 1999). Social spending was raised in real terms, boosted by increased government revenue, although the public sector decreased as a share of the whole economy.

The major public spending issue for the government concerned pensions, which accounted for 15% of the country's GDP in 1993. The government attempted a radical reform of the pension system in 1995-1997, based upon the Chilean model of pension reform. Kołodko had initially proposed a more radical reform, linking pensions to prices rather than wages and including a mandatory private insurance system to supplement the state pay-as-you-earn system (Ibid.). This was opposed by the Labour Minister Leszek Miller, who became regarded as the defender of the SLD's pro-social programme. Finally, a reform was implemented that guaranteed a minimum pension, whilst setting up a second mandatory pillar, whereby contributions were channelled to private pension funds. The other major controversial law, introduced by the first SLD led government, was that allowing for the eviction of residents (including pregnant women). from re-privatised flats. This law was subsequently withdrawn and its introduction declared a mistake by the SLD's leadership.

The government also sought to introduce policies in line with its liberal, secular programme. The SLD parliamentary club, in alliance with UP, sought the liberalisation of the abortion law, a proposal that was rejected by the Constitutional Tribunal. The SLD strongly criticised the Concordat signed with the Vatican. During negotiations around the new constitution, the SLD argued for the separation of the Church and state and against the banning of abortion. It also helped to win the inclusion of articles into the new constitution, such as that stating that a social market economy should be built in Poland and that governments should aim to secure full employment (Piławski, 2005).

6

Although the SLD lost the 1997 parliamentary elections, it made the notable achievement of increasing its vote to 27.13%, from 20.4% in 1993 (a net increase of 700,000 votes). The major factor in the 1997 parliamentary elections was the unification of the post-*Solidarność* parties, leading to the formation of the AWS-UW coalition government. However, the left had emerged from its term in office generally united and strengthened and it was in this atmosphere that the Polish successor party sought to assert is hegemony over the Polish left, by transforming the SLD from an electoral coalition into a single political party. The developments within the Polish successor party, were influenced by changes within European social democracy in the 1990s. The most coherent and forceful expression of neo-liberalism was embodied in the governments of Thatcher and Reagan. However, from the early 1990s, centre-left governments gained power in the USA, UK and throughout most of WE, which continued the neo-liberal course of financial and labour de-regulation, but combined these with elements of social conciliation (Anderson, 2002). This shift in social democratic thinking was formulised into the theory of the *third way*, materialising from within British social democracy (taking inspiration from the American Democrat theories of *Clintonomics* and *triangulation*) and theoretically developed by the British sociologist Anthony Giddens.

As discussed in chapter one, the *third way* was built upon the idea that capitalism has entered a post-materialist era, characterised by the downsizing of the working class and the growth of a large middle-class and a political 'radical centre' *Third Way* social democratic thinking reached its peak in 1999, when the leader of the German SPD, Gerhard Schroeder, published a joint manifesto with Tony Blair. This theory gained no lasting popularity within German or European social democratic circles, and the economic downturn at the turn of the century, along with the defeat of a number of centre-left governments in WE, left it redundant.[17] However, its lingering influence was enough to inspire the SLD leadership in its attempts to create a new party and change its political direction

> We are trying to do what the Labour Party has done in Britain. Blair is often criticised by members of the Labour Party but he explains that they are moving to power and that only a centre party can gain a majority, whether left or right (....) It is not true that the majority of the workers support the SLD, as it is a national party, with votes from workers, entrepreneurs, intelligentsia and

pensioners (....) The SLD has continued with the tradition from the past and therefore there are some within the party who have liberal opinions, but are isolated from other parties because of their historical connections. The SLD is very broad and I do not know of anyone who could not be in the SLD.[18]

The broad nature of the SLD membership, with disparate elements attracted to the sanctuary of the successor party after the collapse of socialism, was used as a political justification for moving the party to the political centre and adopting more market orientated policies. The SLD looked to situate itself as a party of the centre-left, which could attract support from a range of political traditions. The SLD electoral coalition had been largely successful because of its ability to unify different political currents on the left, who would not have been prepared to join the SdRP. However, this pluralism was becoming strained, with the leadership of the SdRP wishing to assert a disciplined unity within the SLD and thus generally over the Polish left. It began by disconnecting the new SLD party from the left wing inside the electoral coalition and reducing the influence of the trade unions.

The latter was achieved by formally separating the trade unions from the newly formed SLD party. The OPZZ, which was instrumental in the creation of the SdRP and the SLD electoral coalition, retained a close relationship with the new SLD party, but was formally disconnected from its structures. The second pillar of this transformation (the isolation of the left-wing opposition in the SLD electoral coalition) focussed on the exclusion of the PPS from the new party. The SLD leadership argued that the programme of the PPS would restrict the left to a narrow electoral base, with the left permanently reduced to the status of a minority opposition.[19] Therefore, when the SLD was formed as a political party in April 1999, the PPS was left isolated.[20] On the other hand, UP, now led by ex-PZPR members such as Marek Pol and Tomasz Nałęcz, began to co-operate closely with the SLD, although UP retained its status as an independent party. This was accompanied with UP moving towards the political centre.

Another source of left criticism had come from the main newspaper of the left, *Trybuna*, under the editorship of Janusz Rolicki.[21] Rolicki was critical of the leadership of the SLD and its political project, arguing that they were avoiding discussion on the format of the new party; that it lacked a programme to tackle poverty and that they were only interested in gaining power.[22] Divisions between the leadership of the

SLD and Rolicki grew during the NATO bombardment of Yugoslavia. The SLD leadership's support for this action was a significant turning point, as it came shortly after the country's entry into NATO and showed how the SLD were prepared to support it in a war against another EE country. It also underlined the SLD's alliance with the centre-left governments in Washington and London. A small but vocal opposition expressed its discontent within the SLD and *Trybuna*, ran a campaign against the war. [23] The SLD, under the leadership of Leszek Miller, sought to exert its control over the newspaper. Rolicki was removed as editor of *Trybuna*, and the paper brought in line with the SLD's project.

The new SLD party was trying to simultaneously reach out beyond the post-communist camp and towards the political centre. The most significant breakthrough came when ex-*Solidarność* leader and UW member, Andrzej Celiński, joined the new SLD party. Celiński was appointed to help write the party's new programme and, although critical of some of Balcerowicz's neo-liberal policies, he openly described himself as being 'liberal'.[24] Conjointly, the SLD made an attempt to supersede the liberal-conservative divide by reducing its conflict with the Catholic Church. The new party was to be one of 'believers' and 'non-believers', which endeavoured to find an understanding with the Church.[25]

These developments in the Polish left were accompanied by the growing strength of Kwaśniewski, who had gained a large degree of political independence since becoming President and leaving the SLD. Kwaśniewski became associated with the most pro-market elements of the SLD and with those who sought to make a clearer break from the socialist past. Kwaśniewski, as leader of the party's parliamentary club, apologised for the socialist period at a parliamentary tribunal, after the SLD had formed its first government in 1993. He later stated that he believed that Miller should do the same, after he had become leader of the SLD (Machejek and Machejek, 2001). Kwaśniewski had consistently attempted to create a left-liberal political alliance, in what he believed would be a 'historical compromise'. He formed a close political relationship with the main liberal party UW and with the influential liberal newspaper, *Gazeta Wyborcza* and its editor and renowned opposition leader Adam Michnik. Along with influencing the PZPR's acceptance of the shock-therapy reforms in the early 1990s, Kwaśniewski also nominated Balcerowicz as head of the NBP in 2000 (after he had resigned from his post as Finance Minister), acquiring Leszek Miller's support. However, the SLD parliamentary club refused to back this nomination, which was won through the combined votes of the AWS and UW. Despite some internal opposition, the new SLD party was concurrently adopting pro-market economic policies and attempting to further break from its historical connection to the PRL/PZPR. It is this combination, which brought the Polish successor party into line with *third way* social democratic thinking, in the run up to the 2001 parliamentary elections. Kwaśniewski and his supporters pursued this most vehemently, with the most pro-liberal members of the SLD leadership coming out of the presidential office.

7

The 2001 elections were marked by the disintegration of the post-*Solidarność* vote and no party, directly associated with the *Solidarność* movement, entered parliament. The AWS-UW coalition government had lurched from crisis to crisis, with the tensions caused by the results of its economic policy eventually leading to its break up. In the run up to the elections a financial crisis gripped the government, with the Finance Minister, Jarosław Bauc, sacked just three weeks before the parliamentary elections, after warning that the budget deficit could rise to as much as 11% of GDP if an austerity package was not introduced.

A sizeable section of society believed that the SLD would manage the reform process better and ensure that their social effects would be less harsh. The SLD's election slogan, 'A return to Normality', appealed directly to the achievements of the first SLD-PSL government. The party's 2001 manifesto included a commitment to continuing the economic transition and taking Poland into the EU, whilst remaining committed to the principle of a Welfare State. The manifesto promised such things as increasing education spending and standards; reconstructing a modern and efficient health care system for which the state is responsible; helping to finance school meals and trips for children from poor families and providing a system of support for the disabled.[26]

Kwaśniewski was re-elected in 2000, winning over 50% of the vote from a broad cross-section of the electorate, managing to distance himself from the growing unpopularity of the AWS-UW government. At the 2001 parliamentary elections, the SLD (in coalition with UP) won 40.1% of the vote, increasing its share by 13% from 1997 (a net increase of 700,000 votes). The SLD had managed to expand beyond its core 15-20% electoral base, which identifies strongly with the left and is favourable in its attitude to the PRL, thus increasing its share of the vote across the social spectrum. It won most votes from pensioners, manual and non-manual workers and the unemployed; whilst also winning large support from managers and businesspeople. The SLD was the largest party both in the cities (with 50% of all urban votes) and in the countryside (gaining 35.4% of all rural votes).[27] Shortly before the 2001 elections the SLD's membership swelled to 150,000, of which about 20,000 joined shortly before the parliamentary elections and the majority of whom had never been a member of a political party before.[28]

One of the principle differences between the second SLD-led government and the first one, was that although it was once again formed in alliance with the PSL, this time the SLD was by far the largest coalition party. This meant that the SLD was in a stronger position to carry out its own programme and shape the policies of the government. However, when the SLD came to power in 2001, in contrast to 1993, the Polish economy was stagnating, unemployment was rising and the government had less resources to tackle these problems.

> We had a lot of state resources and also a lot of foreign investment that helped us to reduce unemployment, etc in 1993. However, now the Polish state is in a financial crisis.[29]

This inherited financial crisis meant that the potential problems for the new government were becoming apparent even before it had gained power. Principally, this involved solving the budget crisis, with the SLD's Finance Minister elect, Marek Belka, announcing shortly before the election that he would push through austerity measures to rebalance the budget; an action that many within the SLD claimed cost the party an overall majority. Belka, along with many of the most neo-liberal members of the government, had previously been employed in the President's office. The President exerted a strong influence over the government and a strained and competitive relationship between Kwaśniewski and Miller dominated the SLD's second term in office; despite there being little programmatic disagreement between them.[30]

The other major feature shaping the SLD's second term in office was the international situation. International capital exerted a strong influence over the Polish economy, due to the large amount of foreign ownership in the country. Also, Poland was in the final stages of EU negotiations, with the government having to complete some difficult and controversial reforms, whilst maintaining domestic support for accession. The SLD was also keen to prove to the EU that it was a pro-

European formation and was not bound to its past. Finally, the SLD was governing during a period when the divisions between the world's major powers, principally between the USA and the EU, were widening.

8

Facing a possible financial crisis the new government introduced a budget, which included freezing the pay of some government officials and blocking a range of budget expenditures.[31] It adopted a 'Safety Anchor' policy, whereby yearly government expenditure would only grow by the predicted inflation rate plus 1%. The government was therefore attempting to implement a *third way* style economic programme with the market creating the conditions for economic growth, which would provide the means for growing social expenditure and a stable balanced budget.[32] A series of measures to ease the demands and controls of the state on businesses was proposed, which was seen as the key for bringing economic growth and a decline in unemployment. However, from the beginning of its second term in office the SLD faced a number of obstacles. The first few months of Miller's government were dominated by its conflict with the NBP and the Monetary Policy Council (RPP). The tight monetary policy, being pursued by these institutions, restricted the government's ability to adopt pro-growth monetary policies as Poland had the highest real interest rates in Europe and a highly valued currency. The government was urging a significant reduction in interest rates, combined with intervention to devalue the złoty.[33] The country's weak national capital base, with its financial institutions overwhelmingly in the hands of foreign financial institutions, meant that the activities of the NBP/RPP were subordinated to the interests of international capital.[34] The result of this stalemate was that the government's aim of boosting domestic demand and the performance of small and medium businesses was restricted.

Simultaneously, the second SLD-led government was meeting difficulties in continuing the process of privatisation and fulfilling its pre-election pledge to 'finish the process of ownership transformation in the Polish economy' by 2005.[35] The government accused the previous administration of failing to negotiate favourable conditions when selling Polish assets and quickly announced that it would not be privatising the three largest remaining state banks. Most controversial was its decision to withdraw from an agreement to sell the further 21% of shares in the state insurance company, PZU, to the Dutch concern Eureko, who already had a 30% stake in the company. This decision led to widespread condemnation by the international financial community, the EU and opposition parties who accused the SLD of protecting interests inherited from the socialist period.[36] Concurrently, the government faced a potentially damaging political crisis, when in March 2002 work at the shipyard *Stocznia Szczecińska* ceased and its 6000 workers were sent on 'compulsory holiday' without pay. *Stocznia Szczecińska* had previously been considered one of the most efficient and profitable shipyards in Poland and accordingly had been privatised by the AWS-UW government. It was estimated that the knock-on effects of the shipyard going bankrupt would be the loss of between 55,000 and 60,000 jobs in other shipyards and related industries.[37] This inevitably led to rising levels of social discontent; with workers demanding that the government intervene to prevent the collapse of the now privately owned company. In response the government guaranteed ZŁ40bn worth of credits, which the banks could take to invest in the shipyard's production, whilst increasing its stake in the concern so that it had effective control over the shipyard. Therefore, the government's wish to further privatise the Polish economy and break its connection with the PRL, met sizeable structural obstructions.

The government's problems came to a head as it emerged that the budget deficit in 2002 would reach ZŁ43bn (5.5% GDP) although it had previously been assured that it would not rise above ZŁ40bn. Combined with the SLD suffering a steady decline in the opinion polls, Belka resigned as Finance Minister in July. After less than a year in office it had become clear that the government's *third way* economic programme was not providing the means for it to meet its social democratic election promises. Grzegorz Kołodko replaced Belka and he promised a return to economic growth, combined with a reduction of social inequalities. In the programme Kołodko presented before becoming Finance Minister, he argued that it was possible to resume growth of 5-7%, a level necessary for Poland to 'catch-up' with WE. Priority was to be a given to the formation of domestic capital, helped through a significant devaluation of the *złoty* and a subsequent reduction of interest rates. He added that there should be a shift in employment from low-technology branches to more advanced industries and services. This process should be driven by state intervention, including projects funded by public money. He argued that a policy of deliberately redistributing income in favour of the most privileged sections of society had been maintained and Kołodko supported increasing the level of taxation for society's richest. He added that too much inequality negatively affects economic growth and that the state should adopt active policies to reduce the scale of inequalities through the use of industrial, trade and fiscal policies, including an increase in education spending. He argued that the question in the post-socialist states is not about how to limit the role of the state but how to define its role and restructure its involvement in economic life (Kołodko, 2001).

The significance of Kołodko's programme was that it attempted to combine economic growth with a reduction in inequalities and an increase in public spending. Also, Kołodko was re-emphasising the role of the state in economic life and looking to return Poland to a similar path of economic growth as that taken during the first SLD-led government. Kołodko introduced an *anti-crisis* package, aimed at supporting endangered industries and preventing their collapse. However the second-SLD government faced a number of problems in introducing this programme and a policy of supporting industries was more difficult during the term of the second SLD-led government than the first. This was because the size of the state sector was now considerably smaller, with the most profitable industries already privatised. Also, the government now only had one state bank at its disposal, which could be used to support industries, a situation that was accentuated by the high level of foreign ownership of banks. Secondly, as EU entry neared, there was increasing pressure on the government to reduce government industrial and agricultural subsidies. Thirdly, Kołodko's programme faced political opposition, not least from the President. Kwaśniewski refused to sign one of Kołodko's major proposals on tax abolition for companies facing financial difficulties, which had been passed in parliament, sending it to the Constitutional Tribunal where it was eventually rejected. The return to the socio-economic programme of 1993-97 was therefore blocked and in turn the government drifted back towards its pro-market policies.

The second SLD-led government halted the economic decline and Kołodko's anti-crisis programme had some success in protecting industries threatened with bankruptcy. Exports were also growing, boosted by a strengthening euro. However, this improved economic performance did not result in a decrease in unemployment, which reached 20% and the budget deficit and public debt remained high. The government was also unable to provide any significant investment in the county's infrastructure or public services. At the beginning of its term in office the government had pledged to build 900km of motorways and 400km of express roads by 2005.[38] However, the government's road-building scheme stalled as it was unable to generate the necessary capital, either internally or through foreign investment, to carry out its programme. Also, despite the SLD's pre-election manifesto promising that government health spending would rise to 4.5% of GDP, it actually fell to 3.1% 2003. The Polish left was governing during the second period of transition, when attention turns to reducing the state's social spending and increasing the level of exploitation through removing the protections of workers.

The SLD was performing the role, assigned to *third way* social democracy internationally, of continuing the process of de-regulation and liberalisation (i.e. primitive accumulation). The government had proposed a reform of the labour code, including such measures as suspending collective agreements and working regulations where the existence of a firm is threatened; reducing the level of overtime pay; making it easier for employers to lay off workers and reducing sickness pay. With the road to a more interventionist economic policy obstructed, Kołodko responded with a series of public finance reform proposals; including abolishing the annual rise in pensions and public service pay and reducing business tax. These proposals were deemed insufficient and the establishment pushed for more radical spending cuts. Jerzy Hausner, who put forward a more radical set of reforms known as the 'Hausner Plan', replaced Kołodko as Finance Minister.[39] The proposed spending cuts included decreasing subsidies for mines and railways, reducing sickness allowances, cutting help for companies employing disabled workers, increasing the retirement age for women, and limiting public sector pay. Business tax was cut to 19% (down from 27% when the SLD came into power) and Hausner recommended a more fundamental reform of the labour code.

This liberal economic turn instigated the PSL to leave the coalition and left Miller at the head of a minority government. Under increased political pressure, he sought to defend his government from attack by adopting a clear liberal economic agenda. This culminated in his announcement, the day after the EU referendum, that he would be prepared to consider the implementation of a flat-income tax rate. Therefore, Miller, who had previously been regarded as the party's social guardian, had gone even further down the liberal road than that travelled by Kwaśniewski and was committing himself to a policy that no social democratic government had introduced anywhere else in the world.[40] The pragmatism of the SLD leadership, born out of the PZPRs bureaucracy, had reached unparalleled proportions. This created an unbridgeable schism between the government and its political base, contributing to the disintegration of the government and a collapse in the party's support. This was added to by the international and social policies of the government.

9

A priority for the second SLD-led government was the completion of EU accession talks, and they faced negotiations on controversial chapters such as farming, land ownership, labour movement and the budget. The Polish government displayed its determination to speed up negotiations with the EU, when it began discussions on the movement of labour and sale of land, shortly after coming into power. On the question of labour movement, the Polish negotiating team agreed to accept a seven-year transition period after accession, before Polish workers would be free to work throughout the EU. The chapter on the sale of land was a far more difficult one to negotiate for the government, especially with the euro-sceptic opposition pressuring the government not to make too many concessions. For historical reasons land remains an emotional issue in Poland and fears persist about the possibility of foreigners buying up large amounts of Polish land. Land in Poland is, for example, ten times cheaper than in Germany and twelve times cheaper than in Holland, while an average wage in these countries is a few fold higher. Agreement was reached between the EU and Poland, with the EU accepting Poland's compromise proposal that there would be a 12-year gap before citizens from other EU states could buy land in Poland; and that an EU citizen who already leases land in Poland would be able to buy land after 7 years in the north west of the country and 3 years in the south east. It was also agreed that there would be a 5-year period after EU entry before other EU citizens could buy 'second homes' in Poland.

The area of negotiations, which caused the most controversy, was that of agricultural subsidies, with the Polish government agreeing to subsidies that are below those received by the EU15 countries.[41] Despite making these concessions, for which they were heavily criticised by the euro-sceptic right, the government had the general backing of the left electorate, due to its overwhelming support for EU accession. The absence of a strong pro-European centre-right party, meant that the SLD was the only political party that could maintain political support for the project of EU accession, during the most difficult stage of negotiations. A similar situation existed in neighbouring countries such as the Czech Republic and Hungary.

The area of international policy that was causing the most controversy within the left, concerned Poland's relationship with the USA and the support it gave to the war in Iraq. The second SLD-led government was governing during a period when the divisions between the USA and the EU were growing. Following *9/11,* Kwaśniewski firmly placed Poland in the 'alliance against terrorism' and as a loyal ally of the USA. The Polish government began to consider its relationship with the USA and Europe, attempting to create a role for itself as a strong ally of the USA, within a new expanded Europe. Poland's Chief in the Office for National Defence, Marek Siwec, stated:

> In Europe there are two countries, which are very good models for developing a relationship with the United States: Great Britain and Spain. In our place, in our reality, with our aspirations, we can be the third such country.[42]

This strategic decision was demonstrated when Poland agreed to buy American *F-16* fighter planes, instead of choosing a European option, with some European countries claiming that this was a politically motivated decision. Behind this lay offers of American offset investments in Poland, which barely materialised, and the possibility was mentioned of Poland allowing the stationing of US military equipment and forces on Polish soil, with perhaps even the siting of bases connected to the *Star Wars II* programme.[43] The reality of a host of new pro-US states entering the EU was driven home when the signatures of Poland, Hungary and the Czech Republic were added to the UK-sponsored letter supporting a war against Iraq; and then Donald Rumsfeld's subsequent definition of 'old Europe' and 'new Europe'. What is noticeable is that apart from Britain, the only countries with social democratic governments to sign the letter were from CEE.

The CEE social democratic parties, with the SLD at the forefront, had moved outside of the mainstream of European social democratic thinking on an issue that caused a serious divide between the EU and the USA. Furthermore, this was not an alliance with a Democrat President talking about 'triangulation'; but with a right-wing Republican President, armed with the convictions of Neo-Conservatism. Significantly, the vast majority of the European social democratic parties, including the German SPD, opposed the war in Iraq. Speaking about this situation, before the outbreak of war or publication of the letter, Jerzy Wiatr argued:

> There would be a serious divide within Polish social democracy if the government followed the unilateral action of the United States

and the policy of Tony Blair. However, knowing the leaders of the SLD I think that they will keep Poland within the framework of the European social democratic response.[44]

Poland not only supported the US/UK position but sent 2000 troops to Iraq and became one of only three countries (after the USA and UK) to administer a security zone in the country; thus confirming itself as the USA's most loyal ally in the region.

As shown in chapter four, a major axis of political divide, throughout the transition period, has been around liberalism/ conservatism. Issues such as the relationship between the Church and the state; the right to abortion and the teaching of sex education in schools became issues around which the left could both define itself politically and win the support of a significant electoral constituency. The first SLD-led government attempted to liberalise the country's restrictive abortion laws; and such a policy was included in its 2001 election manifesto. However, the second SLD-led government did not endeavour to implement such reforms and formed a *de-facto* alliance with the Catholic Church over EU accession. The government made a compromise with the Church, promising not to liberalise the abortion law and to campaign for a reference to God to be made in a future EU constitution, in return for the Church's support for a 'yes' vote in the EU referendum. The government was not in a position of political strength that could have allowed it to deliver on its liberal secular programme. It thus failed to meet the expectations of a sizeable section of its electorate, on issues that have helped to define the left in post-socialist Poland.

10

The decline in support for the SLD and the severance of its bureaucracy from its political base occurred concurrently with a series of corruption scandals. These concerned the alleged use of political connections by the SLD during the sale of state assets, such as the insurance company PZU and the oil company PKN Orlen. A glut of corruption allegations surrounded the government, with a number of MPs and Ministers forced to resign. The most serious scandal involved an alleged request for a bribe of $17.5m by the film producer Lew Rywin to Adam Michnik, the editor of the newspaper *Gazeta Wyborcza*, in return for SLD MPs voting against a proposed anti-monopoly media bill in parliament. The owner of *Gazeta Wyborcza*, Agora, wanted to buy the TV station *Polsat* and the anti-monopoly law was designed to prevent a media corporation owning both press and television companies.⁴⁵ A number of senior political figures were implicated in the scandal, not least Leszek Miller. The *Rywingate* scandal touched the upper echelons of the state and concerned connections between politicians, business and the media. It has subsequently been used as one of the major justifications by the conservative right in its efforts to create a new Fourth Republic.

During the first SLD-led government, scandals tended to centre on connections between party leaders and the PRL (and/or the USSR). However, the party was embroiled in no serious economic scandals during its first term in office and could maintain support and credibility due to its government's positive economic performance. The Polish successor party was able to connect its newly proclaimed social democratic ideology with its actual ability to improve the country's socio-economic condition. It was during the AWS-UW government that the opinion that corruption was rife in the political system grew substantially, related to the rapid increase in privatisations, which created the conditions for corruption to grow. It was also during this period that connections between the state, political society and business grew. The collapse of the AWS-UW government left the SLD as the single stable political party capable of forming a government. In these conditions, a new wave of members entered the party, a section of which were only interested in gaining power and using this for their own self-interest.⁴⁶ During socialism it was common, especially towards the end of its existence, for people to join the PZPR, with no affiliation to the official ideology, but rather in order to further their own personal advancement. This increased as the reality of socialism further diverged from its projected ideals. A similar process reoccurred when the new SLD party ranks swelled as it regained power in 2001 and was then reinforced as the practice of the second SLD-led government converged from its proclaimed social democratic ideology and manifesto.

The views of the SLD's active membership differ greatly from the policies carried out by the second SLD-led administration. SLD activists are generally supportive of the free market and *third way* concepts such as meritocracy. However, they also very strongly believe in government intervention to reduce inequalities; the maintenance of a comprehensive Welfare State and free education and health care; progressive taxation to fund the Welfare State and the principle of public services remaining in state hands. The party's activists oppose further privatisation and believe that the existence of state-owned industries is beneficial for the economy. This latter point is connected to the party's intrinsic connection to the socialist system and the state sector, although the party's active membership is divided around questions concerning the benefits of transition. The membership base holds liberal opinions on a number of social questions, such as abortion and the separation of the church and state. On international issues, the SLD membership is generally in favour of Poland's entry into NATO and the EU, although a divide existed over whether Poland should have supported the military interventions in Afghanistan and Iraq. Where the policies of the government and opinions of the activists closely correlate is around the issue of EU accession. The party's active membership is very pro-European and fully backed the process of EU accession, seeing it as a means to improve the country's living standards and social rights.[47]

11

The inability of the government to meet its social democratic pledges, and the growth of corruption allegations, led to the break up of the government and a split in the SLD. After standing down as SLD leader, Miller resigned as PM on 2 May 2004, i.e. the day after Poland joined the EU. Kwaśniewski appointed Marek Belka (who returned from his post as financial advisor in Iraq) to form a government of 'experts', as the SLD-led administration fell apart.[48] The party opened up a process of verification of SLD members (whereby all members had to reapply for membership), as a public action against corruption in the party. Rather than clearing out a small, corrupt minority, the party initially lost over 35% of its membership.[49] This was followed by some leading members of the SLD leaving the party to form a new party: The Social Democratic Party of Poland (SdPL). The founders of the SdPl, including the then speaker of parliament Marek Borowski, declared that they were building a 'true' social democratic party, which involved breaking from the era of the PRL/ PZPR and the corruption scandals of the second SLD-led government. The single defining feature of the SdPL was to be its 'honesty', with the party having no significant programmatic differences from the SLD. The ranks of the SLD were further depleted when both Hausner and Belka announced that they would be joining the Democratic Party (PD), set up by UW as a new liberal party in Poland.

The SLD entered the 2005 parliamentary and presidential elections with a new leader, Wojciech Olejniczak. Olejniczak is in his thirties and was chosen as someone who has no connections with the PRL or PZPR or the corruption scandals of the second SLD-led government.

He had gained a reputation as an effective Minister of Agriculture and was promoted by Kwaśniewski as the best candidate to lead the party. Olejniczak has declared that his role model internationally is Tony Blair and, as a declared Catholic, has attempted to position the party in the political centre. The 2005 elections pushed the left back to the position it had been in before 1991. For the first time after losing an election, the left was not the largest opposition group in parliament and it was unable to win in any of the country's 41 constituencies (Piławski, 2005) Despite this defeat, the SLD still won nearly three times as many votes as the SdPL, who failed to enter parliament; and the new leadership greeted the SLD's result of 11% as a triumph. The SdPL had more success in the presidential elections, as the SLD's candidate, Włodzimerz Cimoszewicz, withdrew from the race after a concerted political and media campaign against him. However, the 10% vote for the SdPL's presidential candidate, Marek Borowski, was still 5% below the joint vote of the left in the parliamentary elections.[50]

Despite the defeat of the left, the SLD had maintained itself as the major party of the left. The elections saw a number of the party's leading figures, who had helped build the successor party out of the ashes of the PZPR, fail to retain their parliamentary seats (after being placed on unfavourable positions on the party list) and were removed from leading positions in the party. Meanwhile, alongside the new leadership in parliament, a section of the old bureaucracy, who had been closest to Kwaśnewski and his wing of the party, retained prominent positions.[51] The strategy of the SLD's new leadership has been to continue Kwaśniewski's strategy of forming an alliance with the liberals, against the PiS-led government.

12

Third Way style social democracy entails a simultaneous break from many of the ideological foundations of *classical* social democracy and an adoption of liberal economic policies. In post-socialist states, such a programme meets the obstacle of the structural connection of these countries to the previous system; their relative economic underdevelopment and the intrinsic nature of the post-communist successor parties. This was the case in Poland, where the attempted implementation of a *third way* style programme did not provide the basis for an extension, or even retention, of the party's electoral and membership base.

The second SLD-led government's attempt to implement liberal economic policies and continue the dismantling of the socialist system met a number of obstructions. Firstly, the existence of large industrial enterprises, inherited from the previous system, impeded the government's efforts to continue the transformation of the country's ownership structure. In fact, the second SLD-led government was forced to partly 're-nationalise' a large shipyard due to social pressure for government intervention to prevent its impending collapse. However, the party was unable to repeat the socio-economic successes of the first SLD-led government, through slowing the pace of reform. The SLD leadership therefore deepened its liberal economic policy, seeking to reform the labour code and introduce extensive social spending cuts. Despite there being an upturn in economic growth, this did not lead to a fall in unemployment or a reduction in social inequalities. It also did not provide the means for investing in the country's infrastructure or public services.

The second obstacle to carrying out of a *third way* programme came from the reality of the SLD as a successor party. On the one hand there exist large swathes of the party membership and electorate that retain a genuine affiliation to the PRL and the ideals of socialism, which block the party from moving too far away from its historical roots. Concurrently, the party membership of the SLD is quite diverse, due to the fact that a range of people entered the party ranks, simply due to their previous connections (if not ideological) to the PRL/PZPR. This includes those who have no ideological affiliations but retain business connections that reach back to the PRL. There is a blend of personal connections within the SLD, many of which surfaced during the corruption scandals that dogged the second SLD-led government. Despite proclamations by the new SLD-leadership that it represents a break from the past, the present leadership is reliant upon the SLD's traditional electorate, membership and, at least part of, its bureaucracy.[52]

The colossal decline in support for the left in Poland has opened the way for the rise of the conservative-nationalist right. The present government proposes a break from the 'thick-line' policy introduced at the beginning of transition and is intent on opening up a process of lustration and 'de-communisation'. PiS has identified a campaign against the SLD, and those connected to the PRL/PZPR, as being at the leading edge of its drive to push through a range of conservative reforms, which reach the core values of a democratic-secular state. Jarosław Kaczyński has previously stated that political formations connected to the PRL should be eliminated; and LPR leader Roman Giertych, since becoming Education Minister, has raised the issue of the government banning the SLD.[53] At the same time, the conservative-nationalist right has adopted some of the rhetoric, commonly associated with the left, claiming to represent those who have suffered the most during transition.

Facing this new situation a debate has opened up within the left as to what political and organisational strategy it should adopt. One idea to have emerged is that of creating a new centre-left alliance (*centrolew*), uniting the left and liberals against the project of the conservative nationalists.[54] Supporters of this project compare the present situation in Poland to the authoritarian turn that occurred in the 1930s and that the government is attempting to create a conservative-nationalist hegemony in Poland through gaining control of the cultural and educational apparatus and excluding alternative views from the public sphere. In order to counter this, the left is urged to build an alternative hegemonic project, through forming a strategic alliance with the liberal-centre around issues of civil rights, the neutrality of the state, equality between the sexes and European integration. Such thinking has been endorsed by the leaders of both the SLD and SdPL and is an adaptation of *third way* social democracy to present Polish conditions. It assumes that the left can win the support of a majority of society, through placing itself in the political centre and appealing to liberal-democratic values.

Previous approaches by the left, aimed at forming a political alliance with liberal parties, had been rejected by the liberals. However, for the first time a liberal party, PD, agreed to join an electoral slate, at the 2006 local elections, with the left parties SLD, SdPL and UP: *Left and Centre –* LiD. As previously shown, the socio-economic effects of capitalist restoration have reduced the liberal centre to a small and insignificant minority, with PD gaining barely 1% in most opinion polls. LiD won 14% of the vote at the 2006 local elections, which was less than the combined votes of the individual parties in the 2005 parliamentary elections. The strategy of the SLD leadership is to continue this alliance into the next parliamentary elections and form a permanent political alliance with the liberal centre. Also, Kwaśniewski returned to the political scene in 2007, placing himself at the forefront of the movement to forge a strong left-liberal alliance; with LiD announcing that he would become their candidate for Prime Minister at the next parliamentary elections and lead its programmatic council. Kwaśniewski's strategy is to widen the centre-left alliance to include all those forces wishing to defend the Third Republic (incorporating at least part of PO) against the project of the conservative nationalists.

However, in order for the Polish left to seriously challenge the conservative right it would have to re-connect with those social layers that have suffered the most during transition. By continuing to accept the reasoning and strategy of the *third way*, the left is succeeding in further isolating itself from the majority of society and is handing the political initiative over to the conservative-nationalist right. The danger is that the left will be regarded as a movement that defends the privileges of the Third Republic; in contrast to one that represents the concerns of labour and the wider interests of the majority of society.

6

BEYOND EUROPEAN UNION ACCESSION

After the collapse of socialism in EE the terms globalisation and transition became synonymous; with the theory that the nation state had been superseded and the conflict between countries overcome gaining ascendancy. The creation of a neo-liberal historical bloc, from the mid-1970s, was consolidated and expanded through the reintroduction of capitalist relations of production in EE. The practice of primitive accumulation, in the post-socialist states, involved destroying the socialist aspects of these economies and allowing for their monopolisation by international capital. This created new opportunities for the penetration of capital into previously untapped markets; where there could be an investment of surplus profits, sale of goods, acquirement of resources and access gained to a wide pool of relatively cheap and well-trained labour.

The economic collapse, that escorted the re-introduction of capitalism in EE, was deepest and longest in the majority of countries that had previously belonged to the USSR. These countries, which were at a lower level of economic development than those in CEE, responded to this collapse by closing parts of their economies to international capital from the mid-1990s. A new divide opened up within the former Socialist Bloc, with the CEE states furthering their assimilation into the world capitalist economy, not least through their entry into the structures of the EU. While the economic recession and its social consequences were less severe in CEE, they were still sufficient to erode liberalism's political hegemony.

A feature of the post-Cold War international order has been the widening of divisions between the major world powers. The role of the USA as a supplier of capital to the rest of the world reversed from the 1970s and the political consensus maintained during the Cold War disintegrated along with the fall of the Soviet Union. Therefore, the transition in EE, which was deemed to have heralded the era of globalisation, actually widened global divisions. In turn, post-Cold War politics has been marked by the growth of conservative and nationalist political ideologies and parties, including in both the USA and Europe. The present conservative government in Poland is part of this global trend and opens up a post-liberal phase of the transition.

1

When Poland broke away from the Socialist Bloc in 1989, it did so with the stated aim of a 'return to Europe'. The socialist period was defined as having been 50 wasted years and a time when the country had been artificially bound to Russia and the countries to its east. Ironically, the post-war agreements, that had placed Poland within the Socialist Bloc, also moved the country westwards. Poland has historically played its part in the development of Europe's cultural and scientific civilisation, producing eminent figures such as Copernicus, Marie-Curie and Chopin. However, the idea that Poland was returning to its natural home, after the fall of socialism, was an idealised version of history; with the country historically defined by its positioning between Eastern and Western Europe.

Alongside the unique nature of the region's socialist past, EU integration creates a new and distinct historical situation, as many of the structural and superstructural features of WE capitalism are being institutionalised in these CEE states. EU entry exerts a contradictory pressure upon the ex-socialist economies and also forces changes within the EU and WE. EU expansion has meant that a host of new countries have joined the Union; countries which generally have higher levels of social inequality, lower wages, more liberal labour laws, longer working hours, lower tax rates and less social welfare guarantees. This creates opportunities for the WE bourgeoisies to augment their rates of surplus value through shifting operations to CEE where labour costs are cheaper and to draw new pools of cheap labour from these countries. This, in turn, creates a greater pressure for wages to be driven down and working hours extended in the EU15 countries.[1] This is a contemporary example of the bourgeoisies, in the advanced WE states, seeking to increase their profits through an expansion to the east. The governments in Poland and CEE have generally embraced the deepening of neo-liberalism within the EU, believing that it is in their interests to further liberalise the continent's economy and attract investment as low cost economies. Poland, and some of the other CEE governments, have aligned themselves with the most pro neo-liberal forces in the EU, especially Britain, around issues such as supporting the liberalisation of services, rejecting restrictions on working hours and harmonising taxes. This is creating further pressure on the European social model, with the WE states induced to lower their tax rates and labour costs, thus placing further pressure on their welfare systems. It also brings into question the model of redistributing wealth, from the richest to the poorest states via EU funds and subsidies, upon which the A8 economies rely.[2] The expansion of the EU into CEE has opened up a debate about the future direction of the EU, facilitating new divisions within the Union. The political crisis, accompanying the French and Dutch rejections of the European Constitution, and the large disagreements between countries during the budget negotiations (especially around agricultural subsidies), were all partly products of the tensions caused by the EU's eastward expansion.

2

We have previously seen how the West, during the Cold War, was viewed from the Socialist Bloc as being one united entity, with divisions between Europe and the USA given little consideration.[3] Therefore, at the beginning of transition, the idea of a 'return to Europe' could be combined with that of being part of the 'Washington Consensus' and joining NATO was synonymous with becoming a member the EU. Such thinking was partly to do with the unity that existed between the major capitalist powers during the Cold War. The ending of the Cold War shook the basis upon which this unity was built and these divisions have become clearer as the EU expands eastwards and competes with the USA to secure its strategic interests in the region. Poland stands as the major counterweight to Russian influence in the region and therefore as the most important outpost for the expansion of western influence eastwards and the opening up of the EE economies to international capital. The USA also sees Poland as playing a crucial role in its attempt to prevent the EU from developing as a global economic and military rival. An interesting insight into such thinking comes from the former US National Security adviser Zbigniew Brzeziński. Referring to the USA's sole position as a global hegemon, Brzeziński describes WE and CEE as essentially being American protectorates and that the USA should encourage European unity along desirable lines. Poland is recognised as the country that could emerge as Europe's third major player, alongside France and Germany, and as the USA's key cohort in an expanded, although contained, Europe. (Brzeziński, 1997)

In recent years, Poland has increasingly adopted positions on major international issues that coincide with those of the USA, becoming its principle partner in CEE. Strong pro-US sentiments have deep historical roots in Poland for a number of reasons. Firstly, generations of emigrants to the USA have created a physical bond for millions of Polish families. Secondly, Poland has never engaged in a conflict with the USA, while it has been invaded by or involved in wars with most of its immediate European neighbours. Thirdly, as Poland looks for an external ally, there is presently no stronger military power in the world than the USA. Fourthly, the USA has been seen as the country that most strongly opposed socialism in EE, possessing huge political and military weight in the region after the fall of the Berlin Wall.

Following the collapse of socialism, Poland had seemed to be emerging as a nation favoured by Russia as an outlet to the West and by Europe and America as a gateway to the East. However, the growing schisms between the USA and Europe and the differing paths of development taken by countries in the former Socialist Bloc, meant that this position could not be maintained. Poland's support for and participation in the war in Iraq created a large and visible schism between itself and the major European powers such as France and Germany. The divisions between the USA and Europe should not be exaggerated, as the opposition of Germany and France to the war in Iraq was more of an anomaly than a consistent trend. The EU/USA alliance remains strong on a number of issues, and Brzeziński's opinion that CEE and WE are essentially American protectorates is not far wide of the mark. However, the close alliance between the largest EU Accession State and the USA is symptomatic of the changing relations between Europe and the USA since the end of the Cold War. Poland became more isolated in its pro-US position, as Spain and Italy elected governments that distanced themselves from the American policy in Iraq and the Middle East. The embroilment of Poland in allegations regarding CIA flights of prisoners to Europe, the suspected existence of secret CIA prisons in Poland and the possibility that the USA will situate its European defence shields in Poland have reinforced the perception of Poland as a country strongly allied to the USA.

3

Historically, Poland's foreign policy has been shaped by its geographical location between Germany and Russia. This has meant that Poland has either allied itself with, or been incorporated by, one of these powers (as during the Cold War); or it has sought to divide them and look for the support of an external power. The USA's policy of extending its influence into the former countries of the USSR, thus isolating and surrounding Russia, complies with Poland's foreign policy to its east. Reaching back to Piłsusdski's inter-war policy, Poland supports the creation of 'independent' states that are outside of Russia's sphere of influence. The Ukrainian 'orange revolution' in 2004 provided the opportunity for these policies to be advanced. The 'orange revolution' resonated strongly in Poland, being compared to the *Solidarność* movement of the 1980s, with prominent figures, including Lech Wałęsa, appearing at rallies in Ukraine. President Kwaśniewski intervened directly in the negotiations between the opposition and government in Ukraine, and representatives of the opposition movement spoke in the Polish parliament. Poland's intervention was advanced as a promotion of 'democracy' and 'national independence' into the eastern states and tied in with Washington's campaign to export 'freedom' and 'democracy' to the world. Poland became the leading protagonist of the 'orange revolution' inside the EU, pushing the EU to take a hard position on the Ukrainian crisis and directly support the opposition.

The 'orange revolution' was presented as being part of a wider 'democratic revolution' in EE. After the 'rose revolution' in Georgia, Ukraine was now showing the way to 'freedom' and it was hoped that other countries in the region would follow their example. Ukraine was believed to be developing into a free, democratic state, seeking entry into the EU and NATO. The new Ukrainian government and President committed themselves to speeding up privatisation and opening the country to foreign capital. These policies eroded support for the 'orange revolution', with its leaders dividing and losing political support and those favouring a closer relationship with Russia regaining ascendancy. Also, the road to integrating with the West was blocked, with the EU excluding the possibility of a swift Ukrainian accession. On the other hand, NATO membership was offered to Ukraine within five years, if the country continued its course of reform. Such an offer does not meet the aspirations of the Ukrainian population, which overwhelmingly opposes NATO entry, whilst favouring EU accession.[4]

The belief that entry into NATO and the EU were integrated stages leading towards incorporation into the West, that drove the transition in CEE, had disintegrated by the time of the 'orange revolution'. The overthrow of the Lukashenko government in Belarus was seen as the next phase of this 'democratic revolution'. American policy towards Belarus is formalised in the 2004 *Belarus Democracy Act*. This states that the USA supports the strengthening of Belarusian sovereignty and independence and actively supports opposition political parties, NGOs and the media; describing Lukasheko as Europe's 'last dictator'. Lukashenko came to power in 1994, emulating the Russian course of halting privatisation. Many of the inherited Soviet economic and social guarantees have been maintained and the sale of its financial and industrial assets to foreign buyers blocked. Belarus's success in reducing poverty (see chapter one) has allowed Lukashenko to maintain a high level of support within the poorest sections of society, which, combined with his authoritarian style of rule, has restricted the popularity of the 'pro-democracy' movement.

After the Ukrainian 'orange revolution' relations between Belarus and Poland worsened. It is estimated that there are around 400,000 Poles (4-5% of the population) living in Belarus, mainly in the western areas of the country that belonged to Poland before WW2. The Polish government actively supported the opposition movements and parties in the 2006 elections and Lukashenko claimed that Poland was promoting the overthrow of his government. It was in this atmosphere that Lukashenko began a crackdown on the Belarussian Union of Poles organisation (UoP), in the summer of 2005. The Belarusian authorities claimed that UoP was an organisation promoting the downfall of the government in Belarus, whilst the Polish government said it was an act of repression against a national minority. The re-election of Lukashenko in 2006, and the failure of any mass-scale opposition protests to emerge after his victory, showed how the fusion of liberal democracy and free-market economics could not gain a stronghold in Belarus. It also revealed how Poland, with its mass unemployment, high levels of poverty and political instability, does not stand as a credible model for emulation in the countries to its east.

Poland's pro-US foreign policy and its active intervention in events in EE have contributed to a worsening of relations with Russia. Following the 'orange revolution', Putin accused Poland of working with the West to isolate Russia, which was followed by a number of public diplomatic rows. This reached a peak in September 2005, when it was announced that Germany and Russia had agreed to build a gas pipeline under the Baltic Sea, bypassing Poland. President Kwaśniewski claimed that this decision had been made without consulting Poland or the EU; fearing that the pipeline could be used to divert energy away from Poland for political purposes. The loss of a major gas line passing through Poland was a serious blow to the country's regional and international standing. Warsaw's main strategic aim of preventing a German-Russian alliance was shown to have failed, and hopes that it could help to forge a coalition of 'independent states' to its east, proved to be over-optimistic. Since joining the EU, Poland has been campaigning for a common European policy towards Russia. The EU, however, has been reluctant to be drawn into a conflict with Russia, as it, along with Poland, is heavily reliant on Russian oil and gas supplies.

4

For a decade and a half successive Polish governments had pursued policies that were broadly designed to move Poland towards entry of the EU, which, it was believed, would help guarantee, its economic and political stability. By the time it had achieved this goal, the liberal consensus that had underpinned the Polish transition had corroded and a more conservative ideology had gained ascendancy. The conservative-nationalist government's foreign policy is essentially a continuation of that practised throughout the past decade and a half. However, it deepens the country's pro-US orientation; seeks a harder line against Russia, is more eurosceptic and enmeshes a conservative-moral agenda into the country's foreign policy. PiS has forged a close relationship with the most pro-US and socially conservative parties in Europe (such as the British Conservative Party and the Czech Civic Democratic Party (ODS)), who are against the EU developing in a federal direction. These parties strongly oppose the European constitution and believe that Europe should further expand economically but not integrate more politically.[5]

The rationale guiding the foreign policy of the conservative right, differs from that deployed by previous administrations in post-socialist Poland. For example, while the PiS-led government is in favour of Poland's membership of the EU, it fears the domination of the Union over Polish affairs and in particular seeks to restrict the power of Germany.[6] The government's foreign policy can be further understood by referring back to its ideas of 'historical politics' and its aim of extending its moral revolution beyond Poland's borders. It is argued that there is a need for Poland to carry out a campaign inside the EU to fight the huge ignorance about matters concerning Poland. This relates to the attitude of WE countries to the events during WW2 and its aftermath, explicitly the post-war relationship between Poland and the Soviet Union. It is argued that after the defeat of fascism in Europe, the countries of CEE were then occupied by another totalitarian state the USSR, after the West had betrayed Poland by allowing Stalin to assimilate it into the Eastern Bloc. Lech Kaczyński has argued that relations between Russia and Poland had normalised for a period following the collapse of socialism; but that Russia then returned to seeing Poland as part of its zone of influence, carrying out policies aimed at regaining its authority in the country and region.[7] PiS had criticised President Kwaśniewski for attending the 60th anniversary commemorations of the signing of the Yalta Treaty in Russia, asserting that it was an "acceptance of the Soviet point of view on the history of WW2 and its consequences."[8]

The formation of a conservative-nationalist government in Poland has contributed to the worsening relationship between Moscow and Warsaw. The PiS-led government has adopted a tough stance against Moscow and a strong anti-Soviet interpretation of historical events in the region. This is part of a wider political trend within the right-wing governments of CEE, that equates Nazi occupation with Soviet domination.[9] Shortly after PiS formed a government, the new Polish Defence Chief, Radosław Sikorski (who had previously worked for the rightwing American Enterprise Institute think-tank in Washington), published a Warsaw Pact map showing Soviet simulations of nuclear strikes against WE, which previous Polish governments had agreed not to reveal. Sikorski also compared the decision to build a gas pipeline by Germany and Russia, to the Molotov-Ribbentrop pact that partitioned Poland before WW2. Concurrently, the Russian government banned the import of a number of Polish products; including meat, fruit, vegetables and wood products.[10] Russia also threatened that it wanted to renegotiate the price of gas that it sells to Poland, which was part of Russia's attempt to increase the price of its energy exports to a number of EE countries. Growing tensions between Russia and Poland (along with some other CEE states) have also led to a worsening of relations between the EU and Russia. This has been most vividly shown through Warsaw vetoing the start of negotiations on creating a new EU-Russia strategic pact.

Such developments have also led to changing relations between Poland and some WE countries. This is particularly the case with Germany, with dealings between the two countries deteriorating after the announcement of the plans to construct the gas pipeline with

Russia, which then reached a low point after the election of the PiS-led government and President.[11] The conservative-nationalists are able to combine the historical fears of the Polish population with their real concerns about the consequences of EU integration and the experience of opening up the Polish economy to WE during the transition. This is given impetus when politicians from Germany talk about such things as compensation for land and property lost during WW2.[12] The conservative-nationalists are able to exploit the genuine fears within the A8 states that the major European economies will use EU expansion to further monopolise the CEE economies. Nevertheless, Poland has become a major player within the EU since its accession and the election of right-wing heads of state in Germany and France has given the Polish conservative-nationalists new allies inside the Union.

These developments are being driven by the PiS-led government's policy of deepening the country's pro-US stance. The new government announced that it planned to extend the stay of Polish troops in Iraq, despite the fact that the previous government had planned to withdraw them at the beginning of 2006. In the summer of 2006 the government agreed to send a further 1000 troops to Afghanistan, to bolster the NATO forces in the country. Most controversially, the new administration has given its support for the building of the American National Missile Defence system (NMD) on Polish soil; after the American Defence Department had placed Poland and the Czech Republic as its favoured location for the development of its European NMD project. This decision is viewed in Moscow as an aggressive act and destabilises the post Cold War military balance in Europe. It also means that foreign troops could once again be based in Poland, less than two decades after the last Soviet troops left the country.[13]

The conservative-nationalist government is also promoting a zealous anti-communist policy internationally and seeking to extend its moral revolution into the EU. A number of politicians connected to PiS have previously given their open support to Augusto Pinochet's actions against the left in Chile, and leading politicians from the conservative right have praised the former Spanish dictator Francisco Franco.[14] In its document 'A Catholic Poland in a Christian Europe' PiS lays out its strategy of advocating religious and family values within the EU.[15] The document argues that the EU does not have a strong moral base and that the priority of PiS is to promote the rights of the Church and family within the Union. PiS opposes the EU's liberal policies on such things as equality for lesbians and gays; the right of women to have an abortion; fighting AIDS through increased access to condoms and developing stem-cell research. They believe that Europe is defined by its Christian traditions and that it should expand into Christian countries such as Ukraine rather than into nations such as Turkey. PiS also recognises the USA as being its prime ally in its quest to extend its moral campaign into Europe, seeing it as a country that holds values that are similar to Poland's. It is no surprise that the Polish conservative-nationalists find a natural partner in the US neo-conservatives.

5

A contradictory feature of the post-Cold War world has been that while democracy has spread to a greater number of countries than ever before, the social rootedness of the democratic State has weakened. The ability of the nation State to introduce measures to protect both its own bourgeoisie against international competition and its population against the extremities of capitalism has waned. The growing divisions between social classes and nations have undermined the social cohesion needed to secure a functioning political democracy. Despite the fact that liberal democracy and the free market were considered to be one and the same as the curtain fell on the Cold War; they have proved to be incompatible elements in a new antagonistic world order. Democracy and the free-market were the twin banners carried into EE after the fall of socialism and then raised during a succession of wars from Belgrade to Baghdad. Throughout a number of EE countries the devastation wrought by the practices of primitive accumulation (under the ideological guise of free-market economics) at once made it impossible to build secure functioning democracies.

The prospect of European integration ensured that the CEE countries continued with the policies laid down by the IMF and World Bank at the beginning of transition, whilst building the institutions of the WE democratic systems. Becoming part of the EU became the prime, and sometimes only, motive for continuing with the transition in CEE. (Andor, 2000) EU integration could be supported by liberals seeking the democratic pluralism of advanced western democracies and by the left who wanted to supplement these with the social guarantees of WE welfare capitalism. However, EU integration was continuing the destruction of those redistribution channels of the nation-state, which had survived the transition to capitalism, forcing governments to further cut welfare spending. At the same time, it was giving the neo-liberal project, of making the EU more competitive with the USA and Japan through driving down wages and cutting welfare spending, a renewed impetus. Following the entry of the CEE countries into the EU, the impulsion for continuing the course of transition was removed and replaced by an institutional framework designed to protect the liberal market economy and political democratic system.

Whilst the vast majority of the left and liberal parties in CEE supported entry into the EU, the parties of the right adopted the most eurosceptic positions. The destruction of these countries' domestic productive bases and monopolisation of large sectors of their economies by international capital, created the conditions for the growth of parties promising to prioritise the development of the domestic economy. They enunciate the frustrations and concerns of an embattled native bourgeoisie, combined with promises to improve the lives of those who have suffered the most from the transition, particularly the rural poor. Speaking out forcefully against such things as the sale of land and property to foreigners, these conservative parties identify the project of European integration as being the biggest threat to their national economy and culture. Building on the historical experience of imperialist expansion from the West, the conservative-nationalists in CEE can claim that EU expansion is its modern historical form. Once inside the EU, these parties attempt to limit the depth of the EU's integration and oppose many of its cultural liberal standards as being alien to their own national cultures. Simultaneously, these conservative-nationalist parties tend to assume pro-US positions, seeing it as a counterweight to the imperial ambitions of the major European powers and as a natural ally in their quest to build strong independent nation states in the centre of the European continent.

In Poland, a party of the conservative-right formed a government with nationalist and peasant parties little over a year after it had joined the EU. This government is comprised of three parties that had been sceptical of or opposed to EU accession.[16] Despite the scepticism of the government, the Polish population has consistently given its support to the project of European integration; and Poland's incorporation into the EU imbues WE styles of living and ways of thinking deeper into the Polish society and consciousness. However, the social effects of the neo-liberal reforms have created a high level of political instability and opened up a post-liberal phase in Polish politics. The PiS-led government believes that its conservative-nationalist agenda is the antithesis of the liberal individualism of the EU; and is inherently suspicious of attempts by the EU to impose its moral and political agenda in Poland.

6

As previously discussed, the advanced capitalist societies of WE developed sturdy, well-formed civil societies, which helped to maintain political consensual rule without the regular deployment of the repressive instruments of the state. These civil societies were able to form due to the growth of a protectionist, Interventionist State; that provided the social space and cohesion for the evolution of diverse and open societies. The growth of the Interventionist State and civil societies could occur due to the existence of a hegemonic bourgeoisie, sustained by the profits from colonial exploitation, which was able to project its own interests as being those of society at large. In contrast, the societies in EE were defined by the dominance of the coercive element of the state; weak civil societies; prevailing feudal social structures and weak bourgeoisies. These contrasting forms of civil societies and states emerged out of the uneven development of the European continent, with the advanced nature of WE capitalism partly due to the under-development of EE. The socialist period was a time when the EE countries attempted to create systems, at a structural and superstructural level, that were distinct from those in WE. After the collapse of socialism, the EE societies returned to replicating the advanced western capitalist systems. Following the division of EE in the mid-1990s, the CEE countries deepened this course, which was institutionalised through their entry into a number of financial, political and military global organisations.

The failure of a strong domestic bourgeoisie to instigate or grow out of the reintroduction of capitalism has created distortions within post-socialist Poland. Within the capitalist system, the bourgeoisie not only directs a country's socio-economic development, but also helps shape its dominant ideologies and social consciousness. In post-socialist Poland, this role has been played by international capital. Therefore, at the beginning of transition, the concepts such as freedom, openness and individualism concurred with the need to open up the Polish economy to foreign capital and allow the process of primitive accumulation to proceed. Such thinking found a level of mass support, with the majority of society backing the break-up of the party/state monopoly over socio-economic life. However, the rapid impoverishment of millions of Poles and the creation of mass unemployment and huge social inequalities destroyed this ideology's hegemonic position. The liberal ideology propagated further, demolishing the economic sectors remaining from socialism and increasingly sought to cut the social guarantees inherited from this system. Huge swathes of the country's population, who were materially and ideologically tied to the previous system, were identified as holding back the growth of a developed market economy. This liberal ideology could continue to win the support of the country's middle-class, which concentrates in foreign companies. This urban middle-class is also the section of society that instinctively holds opinions and ideas that are the most cosmopolitan, liberal and secular; due to the fact that it has benefited the most from the opening of Poland to the international economy. However, the strict connection of these ideas with liberal free-market economics drove it further into a subjective cul-de-sac, bringing it into conflict with the majority of society.

It was in these conditions that the conservative-nationalists assumed political power. It was not the case that conservative-nationalist ideology had won the majority of society over to its way of thinking; but that the political instability, caused by 15 years of neo-liberal economic reform, had left a society atomised and disillusioned. The collapse in support of the left, who had been submerged into a shrinking liberal consensus, opened the way for a new political ideology in Poland. With only 40% of the electorate voting, these parties could appeal to a section of society who felt alienated and betrayed by the system. This anger was channelled through identifying an enemy that could be blamed for their predicament: communists and liberals. The 'unholy alliance' of these two groups was held responsible for the failures of the capitalist system. The conservative-nationalists blamed this group for the sale of the country's assets to foreign buyers (even although the majority of the large-scale privatisations had been carried out by post-*Solidarność* governments); and they proposed bringing these individuals and organisations to account for their actions. The project of the conservative-nationalists devours the leaders of the post-socialist transition and aims to create a new elite formed around a conservative ideology.

The conservative-nationalist project not only divides society, but also the country's capitalist class, media, Church and intelligentsia, all of whom are split in their opinions regarding the creation of a new Fourth Republic. The previous liberal ideology is not strong enough to counter the conservative-nationalist venture, no longer commanding the overall support of the country's elite, let alone society. Following its dramatic decline at the 2005 elections, the left has been unable to articulate and formulate a coherent alternative to the conservative-nationalists.

Increasingly, opponents of the Fourth Republic are looking to the EU as an ally against the government. Just as expansion opens up the question as to whether the EU can act as a counterweight to neo-liberalism in Poland, so it also raises the issue as to whether it can operate as a palisade to the growth of conservative-nationalism in the country.

7

The EU declares itself to be a confederation of democratic European countries; and Member States are required to have created stable institutions guaranteeing democracy and the rule of law. Within the EU there are a range of societies, states, political systems and forms of capitalism. The Scandinavian Welfare-State stands alongside the Anglo-Saxon liberal model and constitutional monarchies coexist with parliamentary and presidential democracies. In post-war WE, there was an unwritten accord that parties of the far right did not enter government. However, the break up of the post-war consensus and the end of the Cold War created the political space for a growth in support for European far right parties; with a number of them either entering coalition governments or supporting them in parliament. The only time the EU has imposed sanctions upon another Member State was in 2000, when the fourteen other EU countries froze bilateral relations with Austria, after Joerg Haider's extreme right-wing Austrian Freedom Party entered a coalition government. Austria's 'diplomatic isolation' was lifted just months later, with the sanctions judged to have been ineffective and to have actually helped boost Haider's domestic popularity.

The 'Haider issue' was addressed in the Nice Treaty, finalised in December 2000, which set out how the EU should react when "a clear danger exists of a Member State committing a serious breach of fundamental rights". Article 7 of the Treaty allows for the European Council to declare the existence of "a serious and persistent breach of fundamental rights" and then it may, by a qualified majority, suspend certain rights of the country concerned.[17] In reality, it is extremely unlikely that Article 7 of the Nice Treaty would ever be activated. The Austrian experience was followed a year later by the former far right politician Gianfranco Fini being appointed as Deputy Prime Minister in Italy. The EU responded by attempting to accommodate him into the mainstream of European politics. The EU now essentially accepts the participation of far right parties in European governments, with the entry of LPR into the Polish government its latest example. Article 7 attempts to acts as a kind of informal brake on extremism within the EU, compelling governments to remain within the accepted political framework. The threshold of political acceptability inside the EU has been lowered; and parties of the far right are allowed to participate in governments, as long as they are not seen to directly and openly threaten fundamental human rights.

The conservative-nationalist government in Poland is not an aberration in Europe, but part of a political trend. The PiS government is not a far right, fascist party and, although it certainly represents a more authoritarian style of government, it is not immediately creating a dictatorship. This is a conservative government, incorporating the far right into its administration, as has been done in a number of other EU countries, but within Poland's specific post-socialist reality. Fundamentally, this breaks from all previous post-socialist governments in Poland through creating a new alliance with social layers in the countryside against other urban social classes.[18] The political system, created in Poland in 1989, gave the parliament a level of independence and power greater than that in most WE countries, with emphasis placed on the neutrality of the state and the building of a strong civil society. The conservative-nationalists question the policy of imitating the systems to the West and its concept of a neutral, secular state. They promote the politicisation of the public sphere, promulgating patriotism, religion and traditional family values. This is co-joined with a campaign of 'de-communisation' and 'anti-corruption'; which includes building new instruments of the state. The aim of the government is to create a more centralised form of government, allying with the Catholic Church against the institutions and ideals of both the left and the liberal-democratic state.

8

PiS claim that its government is continuing the unfinished *Solidarność* 'revolution', which was aborted after the leaders of *Solidarność* allied with the post-communists around a 'primitive' version of liberalism.[19] According to this version of history, the Polish post-socialist state and its institutions became inflicted with corruption and pathology. The government identifies the post-communists as being the main source of corruption within the state and as the subject of their anti-corruption campaign. The government has proposed the creation of a myriad of commissions to investigate corruption within the state; looking into issues such as privatisations, the banking sector, the legal and education system and the activity of the media. These tend to pass over the role played by the right in the building of capitalism in Poland and create identifiable enemies that can be blamed for the failings of the system.

After assuming power, PiS began to reform some of the institutions of the state and create new ones in order to carry through their political programme. They set up the Central Anti-Corruption Office (CBA) to fight corruption, with the PM selecting the organisation's head every four years. It will employ around 500 people and is able to collect information on individuals (without their knowledge) on such things as their ethnic and racial origin, political and religious opinions and beliefs, membership of political parties and Trade Unions, health, addictions and sexual life. This is accompanied by the government's campaign of 'de-communisation' or lustration; which begins by determining whether someone worked or informed for the secret police and then moves towards making a more decisive break from the socialist period and excluding individuals, institutions and ideologies connected to this system from public life. This process of 'de-communisation' has reached the upper-echelons of the military, with the government dismantling the Military Information Service (WSI) and creating new intelligence and counter-intelligence services. The government accuses the WSI of being corrupt and run by members of the ex-secret service.[20]

The government also introduced a new lustration law, allowing for the removal of people who had collaborated with the secret services from public life. This would have led to hundreds of thousands of people working in business, the media, education and government being dismissed. Previously, a special court took such decisions, however it has now been handed over to a state body: the National Remembrance Institute (IPN). The IPN is under the control of the government, with its president elected through parliament, with the project of lustration becoming a means for carrying through the government's wider political project.[21] However, the majority of the government's lustration proposals have been deemed to be illegal by the Constitutional Court, with an open political struggle ensuing between the government and the legal institutions of the Third Republic.[22] As we can see, this process of lustration and de-communisation is fraught with difficulties and uncertainties, as it is an attempt to change the country's elite and transform its institutions. This affects almost every institution of the state. Even the Church has become embroiled in scandals regarding its links with the socialist system, with the conservative wing of the clergy using the opportunity to attack the more liberal wing of the Church and those who favoured a compromise with the governments of the PZPR.[23] The process of lustration has extended beyond the post-communist camp and implicated some historical leaders of the Solidarność movement (e.g. Bronisław Geremek, Jacek Kuroń, and Lech Wałęsa) as the conservative-nationalists attempt to break from the round-table compromise and the liberal consensus of the Third Republic. The historical experience of revolutions eating their children, during the period of conservative reaction, is being repeated in post-socialist Poland.

The campaign also becomes a means for creating a new historical interpretation of history, particularly concerning the PRL. The PRL is now presented as being a criminal system that was purely imposed from the USSR. A process of charging a number of high-ranking communist officials, including General Jaruzelsk, over the imposition of Martial Law in 1981, has begun. A campaign of removing symbols, place-names and monuments commemorating the Red Army's victory over socialism is being pursued, replacing them with icons that more suitably reflect the ideology of the Fourth Republic.[24] De-communisation proceeds into a more general attack on the left. For example, the government has looked to take away property from those organisations that were deemed to have supported the socialist system. This includes the SLD, OPZZ and even the country's main teachers union (ZNP), which has been active in opposing the education policies of the conservative-nationalist government.[25] A real danger therefore exists that the campaign of lustration and de-communisation could evolve into a more general McCarthyite style attack on the left.

9

The programme of historical politics reaches back beyond communism and promotes a new conservative moral agenda in Poland. The conservative-nationalist government is using some of the institutions of the state to push forward its policy of historical politics and further its conservative moral agenda. The Minister of Culture has declared that the priority of his department is to promote patriotism in society and the government has announced the creation of a National Institute of Upbringing, designed to promote and strengthen patriotism amongst children. In addition, the Ministry of Education has begun to implement a series of reforms aimed at increasing religious and patriotic education in schools. Important episodes in Polish history, such as the struggles of the working class against Stalinism and the uprising of the Warsaw population against Nazi occupation, are interpreted and commemorated in terms that suit the government's conservative-nationalist agenda, thus stripping them of much of their political meaning and substance. The government has brought the Catholic Church further into the political arena and closed the gap between the Church and the state, forming a close alliance with the ultra-nationalist Catholic radio station *Radio Maryja*. Previous administrations had kept their distance from the radio station but members of the present government have appeared on it regularly.[26]

The government has openly stated that it is an administration for 'believers' and that one of its aims is to ensure that Catholic institutions are not discriminated against. They argue that the Church is the one institution that projects a universal system of values and have raised the possibility of a form of moral censorship being created, meaning that certain views should be excluded from the public discourse.[27] Jarosław Kaczyński has identified the social revolution in Europe during the 1960s as creating a new form of oppression, whereby people are not able to express opinions that fall outside of the accepted liberal framework.[28] Also, the government has sought to reform the media. Jarosław Kaczyński has claimed that there is no such thing as a free media in Poland, with the secret service and big business commanding large influence over journalists. He thus calls for a 're-Polonisation' of the media, bringing it into the conservative-nationalist moral framework.[29]

This promotion of a conservative ideology has been combined with a campaign against groups and individuals that are believed to contradict the government's moral values, particularly the lesbian and gay community. For the conservative-nationalists this social group symbolises the 'moral decay' of the past decade and a half. In the local governments controlled by the right, including Warsaw when Lech Kaczyński was Mayor of the city, demonstrations organised by lesbian and gay groups were banned. Shortly after PiS formed a government, a March for Tolerance in the city of Poznań, that included the demand for lesbian and gay equality, was declared to be illegal by the local council and then some of the demonstrators were beaten by the police. This was met with a number of protests both domestically and from within the EU. The technical grounds upon which these marches were forbidden was declared to be unacceptable by Poland's constitutional tribunal and then the European court of human rights declared that the banning of the marches was an act of discrimination. Following these decisions, marches organised by the lesbian and gay movement have been legally held.

Such incidents show how a combination of domestic and EU pressure compelled the government to soften its stance on this issue. Nevertheless, at the same time, some conservative-nationalist politicians increased their attacks on the lesbian and gay community. For example, the LPR MP Wojciech Wierzejski, in a letter to government Ministers, claimed that the lesbian and gay groups are connected with organised crime, similar to those organised by paedophiles, and that 'if deviants begin to demonstrate, they should be hit with batons.'[30] The Education Ministry banned a Council of Europe handbook on lesbian and gay issues from schools and there has been discussion about preventing lesbian and gays working in professions such as teaching.[31]

The government's social policies point the arrow of time decisively backwards, reaching beyond anti-communism to an anti-liberal policy that seeks to roll back the social advances of liberal capitalism. Proposals to have emerged from the conservative-nationalist ruling coalition include further restricting the abortion law and removing the teaching of evolution from the school curriculum. The most catholic-nationalist wing of the governing coalition has most resolutely pushed these policy changes, which has revealed some internal political divisions within the government.[32]

10

To what extent may we expect the policies of the government to come into conflict with the EU? It is probable that the EU will exert the most pressure on the Polish government in order to ensure that it maintains the policies and institutions that favour international capital. The EU is most likely to show concern around such things as investigations into privatisations and the banking sector. In early 2006, the government publicly opposed the merger of two Polish banks (PEKAO and Bank BPH), which was part of a European merger between Unicredito and HVB. The EU claimed that the government's opposition broke EU regulations and the government then backed down allowing the merger to go ahead. The EU may place pressure on the government if it significantly slows privatisations and/or if it favours domestic buyers ahead of international purchasers. Although the PiS-led government has slowed privatisation, it has since indicated that it will speed it up, under pressure from the objective realities of the late-transition period.[33]

The government has admitted that, as a member of the EU, it would be difficult for it to proceed with its plans for a 'property revolution', which would entail a 'fair' distribution of property that it claims was expropriated by the ex-nomenclature after 1989. Accordingly, Jarosław

Kaczyński has argued that the post-communists support the country's assimilation into the EU, because it strengthens their privileged socio-economic position and makes it unlikely that any radical changes to the country's ownership structure could be made.[34] The EU would also be likely to intervene, along with other international organisations, such as the IMF and World Bank, if the government attempts to fundamentally change the rules that govern the NBP.[35] The EU has made it clear that Poland must retain a tight budgetary policy and pressure will be placed upon it to speed up the country's entry into the *eurozone*.[36]

The EU has also expressed some concern about the anti-liberal civil and political policies of the government. In June 2006, the European parliament issued a statement identifying Poland as the leading country in the EU, where there is a 'growth in intolerance, xenophobia, anti-Semitism and homophobia'. It can already be observed how membership of the EU restrains the government and forces it to maintain certain standards. The LPR has had to tone down some of its rhetoric and radical activities, in order to become a sustainable partner in government.[37] Also, Jarosław Kaczyński visited Brussels to assure the EU that Poland is not an anti-Semitic or homophobic country and indicating that the death penalty would not be restored in Poland.[38] However, the government has calculated that, once inside the EU, the ability of the Union to sanction the activities of the government is limited. This means that, within certain limits, the government is able to proceed with its policy of creating a new Fourth Republic and seek to extend its moral revolution into the rest of the EU. Furthermore, there are sections of the government who are fundamentally opposed to EU entry and may seek to draw the country into a conflict with the Union.

The EU exerts a contradictory influence upon the conservative-nationalist government. On the one hand, it restrains it from carrying out some of the radical policies in its manifesto and many inside the coalition government instinctively react against the EU. It also exerts a pressure upon the government to continue with the neo-liberal course of reform, which could undermine the social support of the governing parties. Conversely, the government is reliant upon receiving EU funds in order to improve the country's infrastructure and invest in the nation's poorest regions, which is the biggest factor compelling the government to maintain good relations with Brussels. Importantly, a large section of these funds are designated for farmers and rural areas, which is the main bedrock of support for the conservative-nationalist administration.

The ruling coalition's economic policy is essentially one of continuation, despite its rhetoric and the fact that it has won the support of large sections of the peasantry and rural poor. Committed neo-liberals have been appointed as the key economic ministers in the government and it has maintained the tight budgetary policies of previous administrations. The government has failed to instigate any real increase in social spending and has faced growing protests by public sector employees, such as health workers and teachers, while struggling to maintain the country's public services.[39] It has not implemented many of the social policies included in its manifesto, such as housebuilding and raising pensions. However, it proposes an alternative path of capitalist development to that pursued since 1989; and is seeking to break from the liberal consensus that has dominated Polish politics throughout the transition. This meets resistance both from the representatives of international capital and by sections of the elite connected to the Third Republic. This struggle within the state is becoming ever more apparent as political instability corrodes the façade of civil society, revealing an ever opening conflict within the major institutions of the state.

CONCLUSIONS

The transition from socialism to capitalism in EE is the outcome of the global conflict existent during the Cold War. The presence of two modes of production in Europe could only be a temporary situation, with one of these systems eventually having to prevail over the other. Global capitalism proved itself to be more superior to the regional brand of socialism. However, the existence of an alternative mode of production had activated profound changes within the capitalist system itself, which, conversely, contributed to the 'golden age' of capitalism. However, the growth of welfare capitalism after WW2 did not eradicate the fundamental contradictions of this system. The global economic downturn in the 1970s, opened the way for the election of governments that sought to roll back the social gains of the post-war period and which adopted more aggressive policies towards the Socialist Bloc. The fall of the Berlin Wall, the domino collapse of the socialist states in CEE and the eventual disintegration of the USSR marked the end of the Cold War and opened up EE to the imposition of capitalist relations of production. These events gave a huge boost to the worldwide ascendancy of neo-liberalism, which not only provided the ideological background for the transition in EE but also shaped the reform of the capitalist system in the West.

Neo-liberalism, which rose as socialism in EE declined, was not a regional or temporal mode of thought but an attempt to create a universal, all encompassing ideology. By linking liberal democracy with the free-market a new unity had been created between two concepts that had previously been deemed incompatible. The memories of the 1930s, two world wars and the holocaust were fresh and personal for the post-war generation. These experiences contributed to the belief that the state should provide a social safety net and seek to reduce social inequalities, in order to maintain social and political cohesion and stability. The decline of the post-war consensus and ending of the socialist project in EE changed this point of reference. The failings of the capitalist system were now blamed on the overbearing interference of the state. The wastefulness and inefficiencies of state-owned industries were seen to be holding back the capitalist economy; and the universal Welfare States as breeding an idle and uncompetitive workforce. In turn, the deficiencies of the democratic systems were understood to be the result of the suppression of the free-market, which, if allowed to develop unhindered, would empower the individual, through widening personal choice. The unification of the free-market and liberal democracy was seen to be the true realisation of liberalism and the basis for a universal economic and political model. The initial reach of neo-liberalism was extraordinary. It set the framework for political and economic policy, both nationally and globally, that strove to remove barriers to the accumulation of capital. It was claimed that there is no alternative (TINA) to the policies of neo-liberalism, with large sections of the left even attempting to refine and claim it as their own.

Despite its proclamations of unity and universality the contradictions within neo-liberalism were intense from the outset. The idea of the free-market disguised the process of accumulation and monopolisation that was occurring internationally. Social inequalities increased, global divisions widened and poverty grew. In turn, the relative social cohesion, built during the post-war period, was shaken. Despite asserting support for individual freedom and liberal democracy, the policies of neo-liberalism lead to more conservative, authoritarian styles of government, which was evident from the *New Right* administrations of Reagan and Thatcher in the 1980s. In the post Cold War world, phenomena such as the growth of the far right and racism are reflections of global schisms and the dismantling of a bi-polar world that had restrained imperialist expansionism. The democratic system has become increasingly subordinated to the needs of private capital, which attempts to permeate all areas of social life breeding an unconstrained culture of consumerism, social frustration and disorder. This inevitably meant that the international supremacy of neo-liberalism was soon challenged and the opening up of countries to international capital blocked in many countries. Examples of this have been the alternative path of development taken in China, the rise of the left in Latin America, the resistance to dismantling the Welfare State in WE and the partial closing of some EE countries to international capital.

The area of the world where neo-liberalism gained its strongest foothold was in the post-socialist states. The process of primitive accumulation has been most intense in these countries, where an entire mode of production and its corresponding social and political systems have been transformed. The opening of the socialist economies allowed both for the expansion of capitalism into these countries and the spread of neo-liberalism globally. Whilst some of the countries of the ex-USSR partly closed themselves to international capital and centralised their political systems; the countries of CEE, driven by the prospect of EU entry, continued with the policies of neo-liberalism. These countries have a higher level of economic development than the countries to their east; they have historically had more experience of political democracy and are geographically, culturally and politically closer to WE. Their submergence into the global economy was presented as a 'return to the West' and the removal of the constraints imposed during the socialist period. Throughout the transition all socio-economic problems and political shortcomings were diagnosed as being due to the fact that the reforms had not been carried through sufficiently, with the neo-liberals prescribing yet further liberalisation and privatisation as the way to rationalise the economic and political systems. With the prospect of EU entry standing on the horizon, the transition was continued and neo-liberalism could maintain a precarious yet consistent hegemony.

The transition in CEE is in its final stages and the form of capitalism in these countries essentially determined. Low wages, high unemployment, large social inequalities, small Welfare States, and weak labour laws predominate in CEE. The entry of these countries into the EU creates further pressure for dismantling the Welfare States in WE. The CEE states are now incorporated into a multi-national structure, which limits the ability of these countries' governments to direct economic and political policy. The problem arises as to how the new EU members from CEE are able to develop and sustain the liberal democratic practices of WE, whilst economically being low cost economies on the periphery of the EU. Part of this problem may be addressed through a transfer of resources (via subsidies and funds) but this is unlikely to sufficiently counteract the opening of these economies; especially if the richer countries manage to reduce their contributions to the EU budget and further neo-liberal reform of the EU is implemented.

It is this contradiction that has spawned the conservative-nationalist government in Poland. The coming to power of political forces that have opposed the course of reform since 1989 and won political power through a campaign against the liberal course of transition reveals the level of dissatisfaction felt within sections of society. While large swathes of the population, especially the young, emigrate to WE, another section are either abstaining from the democratic process or voting against the liberal course of reform. However, the ability of the conservative-nationalists to take an alternative national capitalist course is curbed both by the dependent nature of Polish capitalism and its membership of the EU. Its professed desire to remove the 'communist and liberal elite', from its privileged positions of economic and political power, is hampered by the fact that this weak and emerging bourgeoisie was partly created and maintained by international capitalism and its institutions. Despite some symbolic actions, the conservative-nationalist administration is compelled to remain within the liberal economic framework. The electoral promises of the conservative-nationalists are unlikely to be fulfilled and the distance between the political elite and the population will widen further.[1] The government will therefore attempt to maintain its social support through driving ahead with its social conservative agenda.

The major pillar of the conservative-nationalist agenda is the programme of 'de-communisation'. The conservative-nationalists have created an identifiable enemy, which can be blamed for the system's failings. By promising to 'cleanse' the state of a 'corrupt elite' they are able to channel society's frustrations and cement social and political divisions around an historical dichotomy. However, this project is wrought with uncertainties and difficulties. Opening the Pandora's Box of 'communist collaboration' unearths a plethora of contradictory and unclear information. Attempts to fit Poland's socialist past into a simplistic schemata of friend/enemy and good/bad is an impossible and dishonest endeavour. This project is being used as a guise by the right to construct a vehicle to transform the state's institutions and their personnel; with the ultimate aim of creating a new republic. If successful this new state administration will be employed to forge a conservative ideological and political hegemony. This reaches back beyond both socialism and liberalism, bringing conservative and authoritarian structures and notions to the surface. The liberal phase of capitalist development in Poland is drawing to a close, politics will decide how its next chapter shall look.

APPENDIX ONE

PARLIAMENTARY AND PRESIDENTIAL ELECTION RESULTS (1990- 2005)[1]

A) Parliamentary Elections

TABLE A.1
1991

Party/Coalition	Percentage of Votes
Democratic Union	12.32
Democratic Left Alliance	11.99
Catholic Election Alliance	8.79
Citizens' Centre Alliance	8.71
Polish Peasants' Party	8.67
Confederation for Polish Independence	7.50
Liberal Democratic Congress	7.49
Association of Farmers	5.47
NSZZ Solidarity	5.05

Turnout: 43.2%

TABLE A.2
1993

Party/Coalition	Percentage of Votes
Democratic Left Alliance	20.41
Polish Peasants Party	15.40
Democratic Union	10.59
Labour Union	7.28
Confederation for Polish Independence	5.77
Non Party Bloc Supporting Reform	5.41

Turnout: 52.13%

TABLE A.3
1997

Party/Coalition	Percentage of Votes
Solidarity Election Alliance	33.83
Democratic Left Alliance	27.13
Freedom Union	13.37
Polish Peasants Party	7.31
Movement for Rebuilding Poland	5.56

Turnout: 47.93%

Table A.4
2001

Party/Coalition	Percentage of Votes
Democratic Left Alliance – Labour Union	41.04
Citizens Platform	12.68
Self Defence	10.20
Law and Justice Party	9.50
Polish Peasants Party	8.98
League of Polish Families	7.87

Turnout: 46.28%

Appendix 1

Table A.5
2005

Party/Coalition	Percentage of Votes
Law and Justice Party	27.0
Citizens Platform	24.1
Self Defence	11.4
Democratic Left Alliance – Labour Union	11.3
League of Polish Families	8.0
Polish Peasants Party	7.0

Turnout: 40.6%

B) Presidential Elections

Table A.6
1990

Candidate	Party	Percentage of Votes
Lech Walesa	NSZZ Solidarity	39.96
Stanislaw Tymiński	-	23.10
Tadeusz Mazowiecki	-	18.08
Wlodzimierz Cimoszewicz	SdRP	9.21
Roman Bartoszcze	PSL	7.15

1st Round – turnout: 60.6%

Candidate	Party	Percentage of Votes
Lech Walesa	NSZZ Solidarity	74.25
Stanislaw Tymiński	-	25.75

2nd Round – turnout: 53.4%

TABLE A.7
1995

Candidate	Party	Votes (%)
Aleksander Kwasniewski	SLD	35.11
Lech Walesa	-	33.11
Jacek Kuroń	UW	9.22
Jan Olszewski	RdR	6.86

1st Round – turnout: 64.7%

Candidate	Party	Votes (%)
Aleksander Kwaśniewski	SLD	51.72
Lech Wałęsa	-	48.28

2nd Round – turnout: 68.2%

TABLE A.8
2000

Candidate	Party	Votes (%)
Aleksander Kwaśniewski	*	53.90
Andrzej Olechowski	-	17.30
Marian Krzaklewski	AWS	15.57
Jaroslaw Kalinowski	PSL	5.95

Independent (supported by SLD and UP).
1st Round – turnout: 61.12%

TABLE A.9
2005

Candidate	Party	Votes (%)
Donald Tusk	PO	36.3
Lech Kaczyński	PiS	33.1
Andrzej Lepper	Self-Defence	15.1
Marek Borowski	SdPL	10.3

1st Round – turnout: 49.7%

Candidate	Party	Votes (%)
Lech Kaczyński	PiS	54.04
Donald Tusk	PO	45.96

2nd Round – turnout: 50.99%

APPENDIX TWO

GLOSSARY OF MAIN POLITICAL PARTIES

Citizen's Platform (PO): PO was created in 2001 following the relative success of Andrzej Olechowski's 2000 presidential campaign. It brought together a number of prominent politicians and different factions of the AWS and UW. The party has a liberal-conservative political platform and is the country's leading political advocate of neo-liberalism, supporting the implementation of flat tax rates at the last election. The party has been runner up in the last two parliamentary elections and its candidate Donald Tusk lost to Lech Kaczyński in the second round of the presidential elections in 2005. It is the main opposition party to PiS in parliament.

Democratic Left Alliance (SLD): The SLD was initially created as an electoral coalition in 1991, with its leading component being the **Social Democracy of the Republic of Poland (SdRP)**, which had succeeded the **Polish United Workers Party (PZPR)**. In 1999 the SLD was transformed into a single political party and became the dominant party on the Polish left, forming a government in 2001 after winning over 40% of the vote. Despite only winning 11% in 2005, the party has remained the largest party on the left and is a member of the Socialist International and Party of European Socialists. It has recently helped form the **Left and Democrats (LiD)** electoral bloc with the Democratic Party.

Freedom Union (UW): UW was founded in 1994, bringing together the two main liberal parties: **Democratic Union (UD)** and the

Liberal-Democratic Congress (KLD). The party developed in a neo-liberal direction, which was underlined when Leszek Balcerowicz became its leader in 1995. The party formed a government with AWS in 1997, but failed to enter parliament in 2001, after standing on a platform of 'building a middle class.' The party became increasingly marginalized and struggled to find a role for itself in the 'centre' of Polish politics, especially as it ruled out collaboration with the SLD. Before the 2005 elections the party renamed itself the **Democratic Party (PD)**, although it only managed to win a negligible vote in the elections. It has since entered into an alliance with the left through the structures of LiD.

Labour Union (UP): UP was formed in the early 1990s, under the leadership of Ryszard Bugaj, as an attempt to create a classical social democratic party separate from the post-communists. After failing to enter parliament in 1997 the party changed both its leadership and political strategy. Under the leadership of Marek Pol it adopted a strategy of collaboration with the SLD and entered a coalition government with them. They won no seats at the 2005 elections.

Law and Justice Party (PiS): PiS was established in 2001, bringing together different currents from the AWS, and the nationalist **Movement for Rebuilding Poland (ROP)**. The twins Jaroslaw and Lech Kaczyński lead the party, becoming PM and President respectively after winning the 2005 parliamentary and presidential elections. The first attempt at forming a political party by the Kaczyńskis was the **Centre Alliance (PC)** in 1990, after the 'war at the top' in the *Solidarność* movement. PiS combines anti-communism with strong law and order policies and seeks to break the alliance of liberals and communists, which it says has dominated Poland since the fall of socialism. The other major wing of the party includes Catholic Nationalists from the **Christian-National Union (ZCHN)**. In April 2006 four MPs and former members of ZCHN left PiS after failing to win a constitutional amendment on abortion.

League of Polish Families (LPR): LPR was set up in 2001 uniting a range of Catholic-Nationalist Groups. The party associates itself with the pre-war nationalist Dmowski and his national democratic ideology (*endecja*). The party came to prominence through campaigning against Poland joining the EU and it entered parliament for the first time in 2001. It joined the coalition government with PiS and Self Defence in

2006 and its leader Roman Giertych became Education Minister. The party has had links with the far right **All-Polish Youth (MW)**, which Giertych helped reform in the early 1990s. This organisation is a continuation of the pre-war organisation with the same name, which was involved in supporting boycotts of Jewish products and excluding Jews from universities. Recently, MW has been active on demonstrations against gays and lesbians and has strong far right skinhead element. After becoming Education Minister Roman Giertych formally separated LPR from MW, although many prominent LPR representatives in government come from MW. With the party suffering in the opinion polls and PiS competing for its electorate, LPR merged with Self-Defence to create the **League and Self-Defence Party (LiS)** in July 2007.

Polish Peasants Party (PSL): The PSL claims the political heritage of PSL the inter-war PSL. However, it is based upon the organisation and resources of the **United Peasant Party (ZSL)**, which was the loyal ally to the PZPR during the socialist period. The PSL was in coalition with the SLD between 1993-1997and 2001-2003. Both of these coalitions broke down and it has recently been surpassed as the main party of the countryside by Self Defence and was excluded from entering the PiS-led coalition government.

Self Defence: Self Defence was initially formed as a peasant's trade union in 1992. Under the leadership of Andrzej Lepper it organised road blockades, demonstrations and adopted an anti neo-liberal political stance. The party entered parliament in 2001 and became a vocal opponent in parliament to the liberal policies of the SLD, whilst continuing many of its protests outside of parliament. It fought the 2005 elections by positioning itself to the left of the SLD. However, after the elections Lepper underlined his support for capitalism and formed a coalition government with PiS. With the party suffering in the opinion polls and embroiled in corruption scandals it formed a new party **League and Self Defence (LiS)** with LPR in July 2007.

Social Democracy of Poland (SdPL): The SdPL was constructed in 2004 after a number of MPs and members split from the SLD. The most prominent of these was Marek Borowski, who became leader of the party and stood as its presidential candidate in 2005. The party has no significant programmatic differences with the SLD, but has attempted to present itself as an honest and authentic European social democratic party. The party failed to enter parliament at the 2005 elections and has since been a the forefront of advocating the left forming an alliance with the liberal centre through LiD.

Solidarity Electoral Alliance (AWS): AWS brought together a range of post-*Solidarność* parties and organisations to fight the 1997 election. It emerged as the largest electoral bloc and formed a governing coalition. However, its sole unifying factor, its anti-communism, did not prove strong enough to keep the AWS together when in power. The government was ridden with corruption and did not enter parliament at the 2001 parliamentary elections and has since disappeared from the political scene.

NOTES

1
The Politics of Transition.

1 For an analysis of Gramsci's ideas concerning the relationship between the state and civil society see Perry Anderson's (1976) seminal article: 'The Antinomies of Antonio Gramsci'.
2 This expansion of civil and social rights was not of course simply given by the bourgeoisie but was a result of the struggles of the working class and organised labour movement. The point is that the bourgeoisies in the advanced capitalist states, using the super-profits gained from colonialism, were able to improve the living standards of large sections of the working class and thereby incorporate its political parties and bureaucracies into the political process.
3 Another prominent Marxist who used the theory of Primitive Accumulation was Ernest Mandel, who understood it as being part of the uneven and combined development of capitalism on a world scale.
4 The world's most 'advanced' states owned 81% of the globe's income in 2004, compared to the 68% they controlled in 1980. At the same time the share of people living in these 'advanced' countries declined from 20% to 16%. (Freeman, 2004)
5 http://tinyurl.com/27ke7o
6 At the beginning of transition it was hoped that the government of Gaidar would allow for the sale of Russia's assets to foreign buyers, especially those connected to its oil and gas resources. However, once this government collapsed the USA and Europe backed the Yeltsin/Chernomydrin government against the communist challenge. The existence of vast energy and raw material resources has meant that Russia can maintain a healthy trade surplus without having to rely on international capital.

2
Poland and the Under Development of Eastern Europe

1 Anderson observes how Prussia and Bohemia were the only zones in the East to have witnessed real peasant uprisings, as they were the areas where towns had been traditionally stronger. This can help explain the later economic strength of Germany and Czechoslovakia.
2 On this subject Marx commented in *Grundisse*: 'If the first form of industry, large-scale manufacture, already presupposes dissolution of landed property, then the later is in turn conditioned by the subordinate development of capital in its primitive (medieval) forms which has taken place in the cities, and at the same time by the effect of the flowering of manufacture and trade in other countries (thus the influence of Holland on England in the sixteenth century). These countries themselves had already undergone the process, agriculture had been sacrificed to cattle-raising and grain was obtained from countries which were left behind, such as Poland etc, by import (Holland again).' (1993: 277-8).
3 Cereal yields were around 4:1 in the East as late as the nineteenth century, a level that had been matched in WE in the 13th century and surpassed by the 16th century. (Anderson, 1996: 261).
4 In 1800 the CEE economies stood 20% below the European average and were half the level of Great Britain. In 1860 however they were 50% below the European average and had reached only one-third Great Britain's level. (Berend, 1986: 4)
5 Germany was the most successful as it had started to modernise earliest after Prussia's defeat in the Napoleonic wars, which meant it was able to take advantage of export potentialities (helped by its western proximity) and thus supply the impetus needed for its own industrialisation. (Ibid.)
6 Although both the SPD and the Second International officially opposed colonialism and supported individual nations' right to self-determination, some currents began expressing their support for colonialism. At the Second International congress (1904) the Dutch socialist Van Kol argued that colonies were necessary for the working class to be in a position to emancipate themselves and that the enormous wealth of these countries could not be left uncultivated. In 1911 sections of the SPD Executive were against opposing German operations in Morocco as it may have hampered the SPD's electoral chances. By 1912 support for colonialism was growing within the SPD, with Bernstein claiming that Germany's imperial policy helped to create a thriving economy, which produced the necessary conditions for socialism.
7 Towards the end of WW1 a wave of radicalism spread throughout Hungary, spurred by a series of demonstrations and strikes in support of the Russian revolution. Although, an independent Hungarian republic was declared in 1918, this soon led to the demand for a socialist republic. This was chiefly due to the fact that there was virtually no independent bourgeois power, capable of leading an independent republic. The Hungarian Communist

Party (MKP) was formed in November 1918, which united (under the MKP's programme) with the Hungarian social democratic party. The new party formed the Soviet Republic of Hungary in March 1919, introducing such social policies as an eight-hour day, higher wages and free health care. This lasted until August and was eventually defeated after being surrounded militarily by entente armies including France and Romania.

8 The contradictory situation existed whereby Piłsudski, who had been connected to the left, saw Soviet Russia as Poland's main threat; while Dmowski, who was a right-wing nationalist, identified capitalist (and later Nazi) Germany as the country's major danger.

9 In the 1930s one tractor per hectare of land was 135 (England and Sweden), 400 (Italy), 840 (Poland), 820 (Hungary). (Berend and Ranki, 1977) As an idea of how the recession affected agriculture we can see that agricultural exports in the 1930s were worth 20-25% less than in the 1920s. (Berend and Ranki, 1977)

10 During this period the output of industrial workers was worth two times that of agricultural workers. (Radice, 1985)

11 65% of the population were peasants and 27% manual workers. Over 70% of the agricultural population were independent peasants, the vast majority living in extreme poverty, essentially making up a huge body of concealed unemployment.

12 In accordance with the country's level of development and geographical standing the PPS found itself outside of both the Second and Third Internationals and instead joined the *Two-and-a-Half International*.

13 The KPP was reformed as a united party in 1925. They supported the USSR in conflicts with Poland, hoping that it would help bring a socialist revolution to Poland. The KPP offered Piłsudski direct assistance in his coup attempt in 1926, which he turned down. This decision by the KPP later became know as the 'Polish mistake'.

14 Hungary was denied its traditional sources of capital, which stretched back to the period of the Austro-Hungarian Empire. After the 1929 crash a number of German banks collapsed and Austrian credit was withdrawn.

15 This latter policy was of particular importance as cartels were very strong in Poland and they had prevented the government reducing prices earlier.

16 This compares to 0.2% in the USA, 0.9% in Great Britain, 2.5% in Japan, 7.4% in Germany, 11.1% in Yugoslavia and 11.2% in the USSR (Davies, 2001) In absolute terms the USSR suffered the largest amounts of casualties during WW2.

17 In the late 1940s and 1950s not only was there intense industrialisation in CEE but also huge militarisation as Cold War divisions took shape. Both processes led to a greater demand for food, which in turn meant further collectivisation accompanied with a policy of obligatory food deliveries.

18 This latter aim was made possible by détente in the 1970s and an agreement signed between West Germany and Poland in 1970.

19 For example Czechoslovakia had a trade balance of +168 million *Kcs* with the West between 1970-72, which changed to a deficit of −16,937 million *Kcs* during the period 1973-79. (Myrant, 1988)
20 This actually meant that by 1979 Poland had become a net importer of fuels for the first time since WW2. (Poznański, 1988: 20)
21 Much of the social protest was directed against the results of these policies. For example as well as a decline in food consumption, workers employed in 'export' industries were forced to work increasingly long hours. In 1978-79 miners worked forty-two Sundays. (Tittenbrun, 1993)
22 Prominent oppositionists, such as Jacek Kuroń, Jan Lipski and Adam Michnik, created KOR. They provided support for workers and their families who were suffering repression for taking part in the protests of 1976 and linked up with the strike committees that had been created in 1980.
23 This latter point was extremely important, as there were increased shortages in the shops after Gierek's credit led growth collapse. The export of goods in such a situation was met with mass opposition.
24 By 1984 coal production had nearly reached the pre-crisis (1978) level. Between 1983-85 industrial and agricultural production grew and Polish GNP bottomed out in 1982 and then grew for the next few years. (Poznański, 1988).
25 Debt was still increasing due to compound interest, although after Martial Law the West would not grant the Polish government any more credits. The contradiction in this situation is that the economic policies pursued by the government after Martial Law were far closer to those of western banks than those put forward by *Solidarność*. It has been revealed in recent years how the American government knew of the plans to introduce Martial Law as it was being informed by a high ranking Polish general Ryszard Kukliński, who subsequently defected to America. Although they had this information they did not inform the *Solidarność* leaders who they professed to support.
26 These proposals were put to the population in a referendum in 1987. Although two thirds voted for the proposals the turnout was less than 50%.

3
The Socio Economic Effects of the Transition to Capitalism

1 The main criticism of Luxemburg has focused on her claim that capitalism would reach its natural point of exhaustion when its expansion through the periphery economies had been depleted. As capitalism stabilised in the post-war period many criticised her for not realising how capitalism was also managing to extend its own domestic consumption base and the manner in which technological progress induces investment.
2 In fact, virtually the only recession to have occurred in the socialist economies of CEE was in Poland (1979-82), when the economy was caught in a debt trap and foreign banks were exerting increasing influence over the country's economic direction.

3 In both Hungary (1956) and Czechoslovakia (1968) these theories did temporarily correlate both with the demands of the opposition and with the views of sections of the ruling elite (i.e.Nagy in Hungary and Dubcek in Czechoslovakia.) Also, the reforms of Gierek in Poland during the 1970s were partly influenced by such thinking. At the end of socialism writers such as Brus, Laski and Kowalik were advocating the implementation of a social market economy in Poland, based on the practices of the Swedish model. It was argued that there would be an inevitable long-term co-existence between the state and private sectors and they supported the gradual retreat of the state sector, operating equally with the private sector, with policies aimed at maintaining full employment. (Kowalik, 2002)
4 This naturally conflicted with the original *Solidarność* policy of self-management in the workplace, as the shock-therapists saw this as leading to workers protecting their unprofitable enterprises.
5 This has been offset somewhat by Russia's growth as an exporter of gas and oil, which has had wider political repercussions in Poland and the EU (see chapter 6.)
6 http://tinyurl.com/2npy6h
7 The eight new EU states from CEE had an average trade deficit of 7.4% in 2006, up from 5.9% in 2005. (Eurostat, 2006)
8 http://tinyurl.com/32u7q6
9 Unless otherwise stated all statistics in this chapter are taken from the Polish Statistic Agency (GUS).
10 In 2000 Poland received $45,150bn, which amounted to $1,181 per capita. In comparison the Czech Republic received $38,450bn = $3,769; Hungary $24,416bn = $3,769 and Slovakia $10,225bn = $1,893. (Szymański, 2005)
11 *Lista Największych Inwestorów Zagranicznych w Polsce,* PAIZ, December 2004.
12 It is also notable that the most successful CEE economy has been Slovenia, where there is the least amount of foreign ownership.
13 All of this is in complete contrast, for example, to the situation in China. When China had a large trade deficit, in the first half of the 1980s, 50% of all imports were connected with investment in the country's infrastructure, which then helped China to turn its deficit into a growing surplus by the second half of the decade. (Szymański, 2005)
14 This is again in total contrast to the situation in China whose heavy industry has served the new emerging light industries and services. This is particularly evident in the steel sector, which has been modernised, and now produces high-grade steel used to produce electrical goods, etc.
15 Due to the large size of the agricultural private sector in Poland the shock therapy reforms did not cause as large a fall in output as in other CEE countries where the state sector dominated. For example, between 1989 and 1993 agricultural output fell by 24% in the Czech Republic and 33% in Hungary. (Poznańska, 1996)
16 In the first year of transition Poland's GDP fell by 17%. In comparison the decline in the other CEE states were: Hungary 17%; Slovenia 29%; the

Czech Republic 24%; Bulgaria 28%; Romania 32%; and the former Yugoslavian republics 40-70% (Slay, 1994)
17 For example in 1995 shares in 514 state enterprises were allocated to 15 national investment funds. (Slay, 2000)
18 This rise in social security spending occurred despite the fact that around 86% of the unemployed in Poland do not receive any unemployment benefit. The flip side of this phenomenon is that the country has one of the highest number of people claiming sickness benefit.
19 http://tinyurl.com/2spwjx
20 http://tinyurl.com/2kcq77 Road accidents kill 16.3 out of every 100,000 inhabitants each year in Poland. This compares, for example, to Britain where it is 5.6. (http://tinyurl.com/359lhj)
21 Trybuna, 05.05.2006
22 This decline in public spending was combined with a programme of decentralising and partly privatising areas of the health service, education and pension schemes.
23 Wprost, 16.02.2003.
24 http://www.4lomza.pl/index.php?wiad=7419
25 It has commonly been asserted, by advocates of neo-liberalism in Poland, that the reason for these extended working hours is low labour productivity. While it is true that labour productivity in 2003 was less than 60% the EU15 average, this is largely due to the massive, under-developed agricultural sector, whose productivity is 20% below that in the EU15 states. In services (such as trade and hotels) labour productivity is higher than Germany and France by 20 to 74%. (Łepik, 2006; Trybuna, 30.40.2006) Another major factor that contributes to the low labour productivity in Poland is the low level of technology and machinery in many of Poland's factories.
26 Wprost, 16.02.2003; Trybuna, 25/26.03.2006; 19.06.2006
27 The number of students increased 4-5 times, from 404,000 in 1990 to 1800,000 in 2002. This has been the major success story of the transition and shows how Polish youth have energetically attempted to adjust themselves to the new reality.
28 http://tinyurl.com/3chz3l A major cause of the rise in unemployment during transition has been the decline in the number of people working in the state sector and the insufficient corresponding growth of private sector jobs. Between 1989 and 2003 state sector jobs fell from 9.3m to 3.8m (i.e. by nearly 6 million). The rise in private sector jobs during these years was marginal, growing from 8,1m to 8.4m. Less than 10% of all private sector jobs in Poland are in companies controlled by foreign capital.
29 Rzeczpospolita, 09.07.2002. This drastic situation has been partly caused by a demographic boom in Poland.
30 http://tinyurl.com/2qh76g
31 Minimum existence describes the level at which people have the means to ensure their physical survival and to maintain a level of health that allows them to work. The Social Minimum of existence describes a standard of living, of an individual or family, which corresponds to essential social needs.

32 This group makes up 34.1% of all those below the minimum existence level followed by farmers 16.7%, those retired due to sickness 16.4% and physical workers 13.3%. (Kabaj, 2005)
33 http://tinyurl.com/3bzkvn
34 Around 950 people die from tuberculosis in Poland each year (GUS).
35 Rzeczpospolita, 8-9/06/2002
36 UNDP, Poverty in Transition, New York, 1998.
37 Gazeta Wyborcza, 28/29.01.2006; Trybuna, 25/26.02.2006; 14.03.2006
38 Rzczeczpospolita, 14.10.2005
39 Gus, 2004; Le Monde Diplomatitique (Polish Edition), March 2007
40 These six regions and their levels of GDP per capita, as a percentage of the EU average, are: Lubelskie (33%), Podkarpackie (33%), Podlaskie (36%), Swiętokrzyskie (37 %), Warmińsko-Mazurskie (37%) and Opolskie (47%). All of Poland's regions have a GDP per capita that is less than 75% of the EU average. The highest is Mazowieckie, which includes Warsaw, whose GDP per capita is 72% the EU average.
41 European Commission, 2002; "Progress towards the unification of Europe", World Bank Report (2000)
42 The recent economic upturn has been accompanied by an increase in internal demand. This has been driven by lower interest rates with three quarters of the growth in domestic demand resulting from credits taken by individual consumers. However, the increase in spending by consumers is threatening a rise in inflation, which would inevitably lead to a raise in interest rates. The Polish Monetary Council is obliged to raise interest rates if inflation crosses 2.5%. (Gazeta Wyborcza, 27.12.2006)
43 This equalled more than 39% of the total amount of money available to Poland between 2004-2006, which has to be used by the end of 2008.
44 Negotiations over this budget were wrought with controversy, with the richest EU states attempting to reduce the amount that they pay into the budget. The European Commission had originally proposed that the budget should equal €994,3bn; but this was finally reduced to €862,3bn (i.e. 1.27% of EU GDP.) Two years previously Poland had been due to receive €80bn; six months earlier €75bn; shortly before the negotiations €61.5bn and finally they agreed to €59bn. (Rzeczpospolita, 19.12.2005)
45 EU funds are now being directed towards investment in the infrastructural projects needed to prepare Poland for the *Euro 2012* football championships it is hosting with Ukraine. According to estimates, the organisation of Euro 2012 in Poland will speed up the construction of 636 km of motorways, the modernisation of 1,556 km of railways, the enlargement of eight airports and the construction or enlargement of six stadiums in Gdańsk, Warsaw, Poznań, Wrocław, Chorzów and Krakow. A major problem exists concerning the rising prices of raw materials and labour costs, the latter connected to the shortage of labour due to mass emigration. No new money from the EU has been assigned for Euro 2012.
46 The countries in which labour markets are open or are in the process of removing restrictions are: Finland, Italy, Greece, Ireland, Portugal, Spain,

Sweden and Great Britain. Those that plan to open them gradually until 2009 are: Belgium, Denmark, France, Luxembourg and the Netherlands. Those that intend to keep the restrictions in place until 2009 are: Austria and Germany.
47 CBOS, 2007
48 Gazeta Wyborcza, 14.07.2006 The problem of a labour exodus is most serious in some regions in the west of the county. For example, in Lower Silesia a quarter of all anaesthetists have applied for the special certificate that allows them to work abroad; nationally the figure is 14%. In 2005 Poles living outside of the country sent back around ZŁ22bn to Poland (Guardian, 21.07.2006)

4
Poland's Fragmenting Consensus

1 The system went through a number of changes, ranging from pluralism to totalitarianism. It was formally given an initial democratic legitimacy via a national referendum (1946) and parliamentary elections (1947). These were followed by a period of pluralism, with the existence of a legal opposition and an economy based upon three sectors: state, cooperatives and private. Once the system stabilised then a period of Stalinist totalitarianism was instigated (1949-56), which abolished pluralism in the economic, political and social spheres. After the death of Stalin a degree of pluralism returned, which lasted until the *Solidarność* strikes in 1981.
2 In this chapter we will focus mainly on the first of these factors, looking in detail at the second in chapter six.
3 All figures in this chapter are taken from CBOS reports, unless otherwise stated.
4 OBOP poll, cited in Przegląd 05.09.2002.
5 By December 2005 those positively assessing the parliament had grown to 26% and the senate 28%. This followed the election of a new parliament, which usually brings an initial rise in support. However, in comparative terms these increases are small and reflect the disillusionment of the Polish population towards these institutions.
6 The increase in religiosity peaked at the beginning of transition, reaching 66% in 1991.
7 BBC poll carried out by Globalscan interviewing respondents from 22 countries (http://www.pipa.org)
8 http://tinyurl.com/3d4k2w
9 In 1989, changes had been made to the existing constitution, including abolishing the Marxist pre-amble and the leading role of the PZPR and working class.
10 This was added to in April 2006, when Axel Springer introduced a new daily newspaper on the Polish market, *Dziennik*, as a rival to Gazeta Wyborcza.
11 http://tinyurl.com/2uscao

12 http://tinyurl.com/2r495r This is a survey studying 146 states in the world with the least corrupt country in 1st place and the most corrupt 146th.
13 http://www.batory.org.pl/english/civil/index.htm
14 The two main trade union federations in Poland are *Solidarność* and the All-Polish Association of Trade Unions (OPZZ). The OPZZ was created during socialism as a rival 'independent' trade union confederation to *Solidarność*. A third trade union federation, *Forum*, was created in 2002, which presents itself as being politically independent. The fourth main trade union organisation is *August 80*. This is a more radical offshoot from *Solidarność* and is connected to the Polish Labour Party (PPP).
15 http://tinyurl.com/2oerep
16 http://news.bbc.co.uk/1/hi/world/europe/4852924.stm
17 Two main liberal parties existed in Poland at the beginning of transition: the Liberal-Democratic Congress (*Kongres Liberalno-Demokratyczny* – KLD) and the Democratic Union (*Unia Demokratyczna* – UD). The KLD believed in creating a democratic capitalist state, based upon the promotion of enterprise, privatisation and the consolidation of private ownership. (Kopczyński, 2000) UD was a consolidation of different *Solidarność* currents, which were brought together after a conflict in the *Solidarność* leadership. A strong social-liberal wing existed within the party, which included prominent individuals such as Jacek Kuroń. Kuroń represented part of the *Solidarność* left, which had given their de-facto support to the neo-liberal reforms at the beginning of transition. The social liberals hoped that the new democratic era would open up a liberal order, in which divergent social interests and aspirations could be reconciled. Despite their differences both parties won support from the same electoral constituencies: entrepreneurs, the well educated and people from the cities. However, after defeat in the 1993 elections, when the KLD failed to even enter parliament, a new party was created: Freedom Union (Unia Wolności– UW). Leszek Balcerowicz was elected leader in 1995, the social-liberal faction was marginalised and UW crystallised as a neo-liberal/conservative party, becoming a marginal party on the political scene.
18 Polish opposition leader, Adam Michnik, declared that for the vast majority of Poles 'right' and 'left' are abstract divisions from another epoch.' Similarly, Czech leader, Vaclav Havel, said that the notions of left/right gave him 'a sense of emerging from the depth of the last century.' (Jorgensoen, 1991: 43)
19 The AWS won the votes of 26.9% of managers, 34.2% of businessmen, 32.7% of office workers, 33.8% of the unemployed, 40.3% of workers and 34.2% of pensioners. In comparison, 33.8% of managers, 22% of businessmen, 31% of office workers, 25.4% of the unemployed, 26% of manual workers and 32.2% of pensioners voted SLD. (OBOP, 1997)
20 OBOP, 2001
21 This factor was mentioned most often by Poles (52%) as being the one that influenced them to vote in the EU referendum (OBOP research, quoted in Gazeta Wyborcza, 04.05.2003)

22 Despite the fact that the idea of the Fourth Republic has become associated mainly with PiS, politicians from PO originally propagated the idea.
23 PO campaigned for a 15% flat rate for income tax, corporation tax and VAT.
24 By forming a coalition government with Self Defence, PiS was paradoxically crossing the historical divide, as Self Defence, including its leader Andrzej Lepper, includes many members who were previously in the PZPR. PSL, who had twice been members of coalition governments with the SLD, were also engaged in negotiations about joining a coalition government with PiS. However, once it became clear that Self Defence would join the government this was abandoned.
25 Poland faced the unique situation of its President and leader of the governing party being identical twins. Initially after winning the election, Jarosław Kaczyński did not take up the post of PM, not least because it was felt that this would harm his brother's chances of winning the presidential elections. The relatively unknown Kazimierz Marcinkiewicz was appointed PM and formed a minority government with the support of LPR. After six months PiS formed a majority government with Self Defence and LPR. Shortly afterwards Marcinkiewicz resigned as PM and was replaced by Jarosław Kaczyński. The government has been struck by a number of political scandals, concerning both Self Defence and LPR, both of who have suffered a slump in support. In an attempt to survive politically both Self-Defence and LPR merged to form a new League and Self-Defence party (LiS) in July 2007.
26 Dziennik, 21.04.2006
27 PiS is a party that includes a number of Catholic-nationalists, whose thinking is close to the *Endecja*. In an interview, Lech Kaczyński claimed that he would have supported the May Coup in 1926 and that he sees Piłsudski as a source of inspiration. He also admitted that his brother, Jarosław, is less critical of the *Endecja*. (Gazeta Wyborcza, 13.05.2006)

5
From Stalinism to Social Democracy

1 The *Proletariat* was destroyed after the first mass strike in Poland (in the industrial town of Żyradow - 1882) when the majority of its leadership was arrested and either killed or sentenced to long prison stretches.
2 On the question of Polish independence, the Polish Marxists were in disagreement with Marx and Engels, who supported an independent Polish state. Rosa Luxemburg, who helped form the SDKPiL, was against Polish independence believing that Poland had become organically incorporated into Russia and that it was dependent on this relationship through exports, etc. According to Luxemburg, Russia was no longer a force of reaction, as it had been during Marx's time, and was now the chief revolutionary hope of the time. However, even Russian Marxists continually urged the Polish revolutionaries to fight for independence with Lenin disagreeing with

Luxemburg's opinion. It is therefore a quirk of history that the issue, which more than any other distanced Polish Marxists from other Polish socialists, was also the one that divided them from other Marxists internationally.
3 In the 1920s the KPP had given its support to Trotsky in his struggle with Stalin, who then, wrongly, regarded the KPP as one of the last surviving outposts of Trotskyism within the European communist movement.
4 For example the Peasants Party and Democratic Party remained formally independent, although subordinate, parties throughout the PRL's existence.
5 Interview with Jerzy Wiatr, Warsaw, 23.10.2002.
6 Rakowski, for example, claims that he had a basically social democratic outlook from the 1970s, looking to figures from the German SPD such as Willy Brandt (interview with Mieczysław Rakowski, Warsaw, 10.12.2002). Jerzy Wiatr argues that a social democratic current emerged within the PZPR because of the long tradition of a reformist current operating within the party (My interview with Jerzy Wiatr, Warsaw, 23.10.2002).
7 Interview with Mieczysław Rakowski, Warsaw, 10.12.2002.
8 Shortly after the formation of the SdRP a group of reformers, led by Tadeusz Fiszbach, left the SdRP to form the Polish Social Democratic Union (PUS) believing that the reforms carried out when creating the SdRP had been of a cosmetic nature. Although PUS managed to attract the majority of PZPR MPs, the party was dissolved in 1991 after pursuing a strategy of non-co-operation with the SdRP. In 1990, the Union of Polish Communists 'Proletariat' was formed, but failed to gain any electoral support. Therefore, in contrast to most other post-socialist countries, a mass party, claiming the political tradition of communism, has failed to stabilise.
9 Interview with Jerzy Wiatr, Warsaw, 23.10.2002.
10 Ten Years for Poland and Democracy. Resolution to the IV Congress of the SdRP *(10 Lat Dla Polski I Demockracji. Uchwała IV Kongresu Socjal Demockracji Rzeczpospolitej Polskiej): 54.*
11 Five other successor parties have been accepted as members of the Socialist International. These are the Hungarian Socialist Party, Bulgarian Socialist Party, Croatian Social Democratic Party, Slovakian Social Democratic Party and Lithuanian Democratic Labour Party. (Antoszewski, 2001)
12 Interview with Tadeusz Kowalik, Warsaw, 30.07.2002.
13 The political trajectory of Jacek Kuroń, who became a member of UD, shows the changes within the post-*Solidarność* left. Kuroń was the leading intellectual figure behind KOR and after publishing the open letter to the party with Modzelewski became a renowned figure within the international left. However, he gave his support to the shock-therapy reforms at the beginning of transition, claiming that in order to have socialism there must first be capitalism. In the early nineties he held the post of Minister of Labour and Social Policy (1989-1990 and 1991-1993) and stood in the presidential elections in 1995, winning 9.2% of the vote. In the latter years of his life Kuroń announced that his biggest regret was that he had supported the shock-therapy reforms. He began to associate closely with the alter-globalisation movement and opposed the Iraq war. He died in 2004.

14 Interview with Ryszard Bugaj, Warsaw, 18.07.2002.
15 The PPS was reformed through an alliance of those connected to the pre-war PPS, (including from the émigré party that continued to organise during socialism) and a younger current that came from the left of the *Solidarność* movement.
16 Kołodko had been a member of the PZPR, until it was wound up in 1990, graduating from the School of Planning and Statistics (SGPiS) in the mid-1970s. Since 1990, he has not belonged to any party, although he has twice served in SLD-led governments.
17 The fact that *third way* social democracy came out of the British labour movement is consistent with the history of the European left. Just as *third way* theorists have calculated that the market is the best mechanism for achieving socio-economic progress and have presented Anglo-Saxon capitalism as being its most efficient form, so English Fabians espoused social reform built on industrialisation and political democracy. The revisionist socialism of Bernstein took its influence from English *Fabianism*. However, its popularity within German and continental European social democracy was restricted, with Marxism having a greater influence. The utilitarian theory of the *third way*, born out of the empiricist school of British sociology, has once again been limited in its appeal in European social democratic circles. Also, it has had the most enduring influence in British social democracy due to the fact that the Blair government came into power after the Thatcher/Major governments. This has meant that it has not had to introduce the radical market reforms, that *third way* style governments would be required to do in continental Europe.
18 Interview with Jerzy Jaskernia, Warsaw, 17.06.2002.
19 Interview with Jerzy Jaskiernia, 17.06.2002
20 182 out of the 192 MPs and senators of the SLD parliamentary club initially joined the new party, with those of the PPS, the Movement of Working People (RLP) and Józef Wiaderny (leader of the OPZZ) not joining. Once the PPS had stood independently in the presidential and parliamentary elections the SLD could then claim that it was the PPS who were splitting the left. Some members of the PPS parliamentary club left to join the SLD and the party was unable to maintain itself as an independent left party capable of challenging the dominance of the SLD. After the 2001 elections, Ikonowicz resigned from the party and formed a new group called New Left (Nowa Lewica).
21 *Trybuna* is derived from the official paper of the Central Committee of the PZPR, *Trybuna Luda* and was re-launched as an 'independent newspaper of the left', under the title *Trybuna*.
22 Trybuna, 04.08.1999; Gazeta Wyborcza, 25.04.2001.
23 The conflict with Yugoslavia started almost immediately after Poland, along with the Czech Republic and Hungary, joined NATO. Ikonowicz visited Yugoslavia with a group of MPs from the SLD in protest against the war. Most significantly ex-PM Włodzimierz Cimoszewicz opposed the NATO campaign, writing a letter of protest to the US government.

24 Trybuna, 3.04.1999. Celiński was critical of UW's adoption of orthodox neoliberal policies. Speaking about the division of politics around the historical divide he argued: 'Someone must say stop to this crazy divide, this will be a programme for Poland, carried out by the SLD'. (Trybuna, 03.08.1999)
25 Interview with Jerzy Strzeliga, Warsaw, 03.07.2002.
26 'SLD – Presentation of Programme – Resolutions and Propositions of the Team' (*SLD – Prezentacje Programowe – Wnioski i Propozycje Zespołów*),Warsaw, 2001.
27 OBOP, Wybory 2001
28 Trybuna, 27-28.08.2004; Gazeta Wyborcza, 17.07.2004
29 Interview with Marek Dyduch, Warsaw, 19.06.2002.
30 The PSL were initially opposed to the appointment of Belka and, along with UP, could lend some weight to those within the SLD who wanted to pursue a more 'traditional' social democratic programme. However, these forces were not strong enough to prevent Belka's appointment, which underlined the relative strength of the President's office and liberal economic thinking within the government.
31 These spending cuts included cutting the length of time which women can claim maternity payments; reducing unemployment and sickness benefit; increasing electricity prices; increasing VAT on building; taking away students' rights to cheap travel and cutting early retirement benefits. While announcing the package in parliament Belka claimed: 'The present government is not responsible for the poor state of the economy and finances. However the government is responsible for the state. Financial improvement is not a goal in itself, but it is necessary in order to avoid a catastrophe'. (Trybuna, 30.11.2001)
32 *Predsiebiorczość-Rozwój-Praca,* Myśl Socjaldemokratyczna, 1/2002
33 Kwaśniewski made it clear that he would veto any bill, which he believed threatened the NBP/RPPs independence.
34 Representatives of international financial institutions directly intervened into this debate. During a visit to Poland an envoy of the IMF made it clear that she supported the RPP's decision not to cut interest rates and argued that its independence should not be threatened. This was repeated at a conference of the OECD and some representatives from the EU argued that if the Polish parliament passed a bill restricting the RPP/NBP's independence it would be contrary to EU membership conditions.
35 "Predsiebiorczość-Rozwój-Praca*",* Myśl Socjaldemokratyczna, 1/2002
36 The commissioner for EU expansion, Guenter Verheugen, said 'the Polish government must be conscious that this has a political meaning, concerning Poland's responsibility and credibility as a partner in negotiations.' (Rzeczpospolita, 03.12.2002)
37 Rzeczpospolita, 25-26.05.2002. Minister of Industry, Jacek Piechota, said: 'The Collapse of *Stocznia Szczecińska* would lead to the collapse of the steel works in Częstochowa, shipyards in Gdynia and Gdańsk and a whole mass of corporations related to the shipyard industry'. (Polityka, 25.05.2002)
38 *Przedsiębiorczość-Rozwój-Praca*, Myśl Socjaldemockratyczna, 1/2002.

39 A campaign in the media focused mainly on public debt, which equalled around 50% of GDP. The average public debt in the EU is over 60%, with Italy, Belgium and Greece having public debt levels of over 100% of GDP. The dependent nature of Polish capitalism meant that pressure was placed on the government to reduce its public debt. This was backed up by the Polish constitution that inscribes that if public debt crosses 60% of GDP then the next year's budget must be balanced. At the beginning of the 1990s Hausner co-operated with Tadeusz Kowalik, in advocating the creation of a Swedish model of capitalism in Poland.

40 Miller also began to express his commitment to liberal economic policy in terms that surpassed even the most ardent *third way* supporters: 'Generating national wealth and its redistribution are to a large extent separate spheres. The first is decided by the hard and objective laws of economics and the market and the second by social justice. Policies must have a liberal character because the market can only fulfill its potential in conditions of a free economy. The problems of society must not be placed on the market nor should ideology be an impediment for the free market. Economic growth will be quicker through low taxes, a low budget deficit and better management of budget resources.' (Trybuna, 09.10.2003)

41 Direct agricultural subsidies equal 55%, 60% and 65%, of the level given to EU15 countries, in the first three years of membership. These actually only reach 36%, 39% and 42%, with the government allowed to make up the difference from its own state budget.

42 Przegląd, 29.07.2002

43 The Polish Minister of Defence, Jerzy Szmajdzińsi, commented, "We are prepared to work jointly towards an agreement regarding the installation of military technology on our territory". (Trybuna, 3-4.08.2002)

44 Interview with Jerzy Wiatr, Warsaw, 23.10.2002.

45 Agora owns 3 printing companies, 15 magazines, 27 radio stations, a marketing syndicate and three Internet companies.

46 According to Jerzy Wiatr these new SLD members were made up of two groups. Firstly, those who had never been a member of any party and were not interested in ideology or programme. Secondly, by ex-PZPR members who were not part of the reformist/revisionist current and had no interest in building a social democratic party in the early 1990s. Both of these groups only joined the party, as it became a party of power and they saw it as a vehicle for furthering their own personal business interests. (Gazeta Wyborcza, 23.06.2003)

47 This information is taken from the questionnaire research on SLD members carried out for my PhD thesis. For a full description and analysis of this research see 'The Social Democratic Convictions of the SLD Active Membership', Polish Sociological Review, 1/2004

48 Between 1997 and 2001 Belka had been an adviser and consultant in the World Bank and in 2002 he served as a member of the Board of Directors in the Polish-American Freedom Foundation. In 2003, Belka was appointed as president of the Council for International Coordination in Iraq, after which

he held the post of director of economic policy for the Coalition Provisional Authority in Iraq. During his time in this post over 200 state assets, including electric, telecommunication and pharmaceutical companies, were sold. Also, the highest income tax band was cut from 45% to a linear tax level of 15%. (Trybuna, 22-23/09.2005)

49 For example, in one of the SLD's traditional strongholds, Sląsk, the membership fell from 269 to 145, with the local party secretary stating that the majority had left due to dissatisfaction with the social cuts being proposed by Hausner. (Gazeta Wyborcza, 28.11.2003)

50 The other left platform in the parliamentary elections was that organised around the Polish Labour Party (PPP). The PPP is connected to the trade union federation 'August '80' (*Sierpień '80*), which lays claim to the original ideals of the *Solidarność* movement and has some influence in the industrial region of Sląsk. PPP brought together a range of small left groups in the 2005 elections: The PPS, The Polish Communist Party, the anti-clerical party *Racja* and the Polish Ecology Party – Greens. It only gained 0.77% in the parliamentary elections and its leader and presidential candidate, Daniel Podrzycki, died in a car accident during the presidential election campaign. In 2005 a section of UP, around Izabela Jaruga-Nowacka, attempted to bring a range of groups together in the Union of the Left (UL) as a left alternative to the SLD. UL ended up standing on the SLD's list in the parliamentary elections, with Jaruga-Nowacka winning a parliamentary seat. She then resigned as leader of UL.

51 Well-known figures from the former group include Leszek Miller, Józef Oleksy, Marek Dyduch and Krzystof Janik. From the group around Kwaśniewski remain people such as Jerzy Szmajdziński and Ryszard Kalisz.

52 The influence of sections of business interests upon the left can be seen in recent developments in the Trybuna newspaper. Following the collapse of the Miller leadership, the newspaper's editor, Marek Barański, was replaced by Wiesław Debski in March 2005. The content of the newspaper became more left wing and critical of the party leadership. However, in June 2006, Barański again returned as editor and appointed Miller as head of the newspaper's programmatic council. Part of the reason for this change was the financial difficulties of the newspaper, which were made worse by the reluctance of companies to advertise in the newspaper, due to its critical position towards the SLD leadership.

53 Trybuna, 12-13.06.2004; Gazeta Wyborcza 17.06.2006

54 http://www.centrolew.pl/ The name *centrolew* originates from the alliance of left and centre parties, including the peasant parties, formed in 1929 to oppose the authoritarian regime of Józef Piłsudski.

6
Beyond European Accession

1 For example in France the companies such as Nexans and Bosch decided to raise working hours without any extra pay. Similar discussions have taken

place in Dutch and German firms (e.g. Volkswagen.) (Rzeczpospolita, 22.07.2004) A number of cases have come to light of emigrant workers from CEE working in extreme exploitative conditions. In July 2006, police raided a farm in Italy where Polish workers were fed on little more than bread and water, expected to labour in the fields for up to 15 hours a day, and beaten by guards who called themselves kapos, (Guardian, 20.07.2006)

2 An example of this tension was when German Chancellor Gerhard Schroeder complained, shortly after expansion, that the A8 countries cannot expect to have low business tax rates and receive significant subsidies from the EU.
3 Of course the opposite was also true, with those in the West rarely differentiating between the countries of the Socialist Bloc or understanding the different forms of political and economic systems that existed within EE.
4 According to research carried out by the sociology department at the Ukrainian Academy of Science 50.4% of Ukrainians are against NATO entry, with only 15% in favour. In contrast 47% support joining the EU with 20% against. (Gazeta Wyborcza, 18.11.2005)
5 Lech Kaczyński's third official visit as President was to the Czech Republic (after previously visiting the Vatican and Washington) to meet his counterpart Vaclav Klaus. They underlined their common opposition to a European state and to their commonly held values. Klaus had just vetoed a law from parliament to legalise gay relationships and Kaczyński confirmed that he would do the same in a similar situation. PiS has had discussions with the ODS, British Conservatives and Lativan TB/LNNK party about forming a new centre-right eurosceptic political group in the European parliament.
6 The leading intellectual influence behind this policy is the philosopher and political scientist Marek Cichocki, who works as an adviser to President Kaczyński and heavily influences Poland's foreign policy.
7 Rzeczpospolita, 19-21.03.2005
8 http://www.warsawvoice.pl/view/8277/ Particularly controversial was the participation of General Jaruzelski in the commemorations, after receiving an invitation from Moscow. Jaruzeslski had joined the Polish Army Units built up in the USSR during WW2 and participated in the Soviet's advance into Warsaw and Berlin.
9 This was most dramatically shown when the Estonian government removed a Soviet war memorial from the centre of Tallinn, leading to large demonstrations by the country's Russian minority.
10 Rzeczpospolita, 30.11.2005 This was done on a technicality that these products did not meet required standards.
11 In June 2006 a German satirical magazine published an article referring to the Kaczyński twins as 'potatoes'. The Polish president's office, the PM and the Foreign Minister all condemned this article as being offensive. Shortly afterwards the President cancelled a meeting arranged with the Presidents of France and Germany, with health reasons given as the official reason for his

absence. A letter signed by all the former Polish Foreign Ministers over the past 15 years condemned this decision.

12 For example, the ex-German CDU leader Edmund Stoiber has claimed that both the Czech Republic and Poland should annul the legal acts, passed at the end of WW2, to expel Germans and expropriate their property. He added that the wound would remain open as long as these laws were in place and that they contradict European law. He also called for Poland to allow residents of the former Eastern Prussian lands to return, in what he claimed would be a 'noble gesture'.

13 In January 2007, the USA made a formal request to the Polish and Czech governments, which would result in the NMD radar equipment being situated in the Czech Republic and missile launchers in Poland. The Polish/Czech facility would constitute the single largest part of the NMD program outside of the USA. It was this decision that prompted Vladmir Putin to accuse the USA of establishing, or trying to establish, a "uni-polar" world and then announing, that Russia would freeze its compliance with the 1990 Conventional Forces in Europe treaty.

14 When Pinochet was under house arrest in London at the end of the 1990s the MPs Marek Jurek and Michał Kamiński joined a delegation from Poland to visit the former dictator. During a debate in the European parliament commemorating the beginning of the Spanish Civil War, LPR MEP (and father of its leader Roman Giertych) Maciej Giertych, praised Franco for defeating communism in Spain. He was backed by the PiS MEP Marcin Libicki who said "I agreed with Giertych's statement entirely". (New Warsaw Express, 07.07.2006),

15 http://tinyurl.com/39qjrz

16 LPR was strongly against Poland joining the EU and campaigned for a 'no' vote. Self Defence argued that the entry conditions were not favourable for Poland and that individuals should make their own decision as to how they voted. At one point PiS announced that it would not support Poland's accession, as the conditions were not favourable. Although they changed this policy, they refused to take part in any pro EU campaign with the SLD-led government.

17 This procedure is supplemented with a 'preventive instrument' that is very hard to activate. The text reads: "On a reasoned proposal by one third of the Member States, by the European Parliament or by the Commission, the Council, acting by a majority of four fifths of its members after obtaining the assent of the European Parliament, may determine that there is a clear risk of a serious breach by a Member State of principles mentioned in Article 6(1), and address appropriate recommendations to that state. "The values and principles are spelled out as follows: "The Union is founded on the principles of liberty, democracy, respect for human rights and fundamental freedoms, and the rule of law, principles which are common to the Member States." (http://tinyurl.com/2mg3yu).

18 This can therefore be defined as a form of Bonapartism, described by Gramsci as being 'an equilibrium of the conflicting urban classes, which

obstructs the mechanizm of normal democracy – i.e. parliamentarism.' (Gramsci, 1991: 216)

19 Taken from a speech by Jarosław Kaczyński to a PiS congress (Gazeta Wyborcza, 06.06.2006)
20 The WSI was established in 1990 after the intelligence and counter intelligence services were closed down. Jarosław Kaczyński appointed Antoni Macierewicz as Deputy Defence Minister, giving him responsibility for liquidating the WSI. Macierewicz was Minister for Internal Affairs in the Olszewski government in the early 1990s. He rose to prominence when he published a list of names of individuals (including the then President Lech Wałęsa) whom he claimed had cooperated with the communist secret services. The publication of the 'Macierewicz list' was one of the contributing factors that led to the collapse of Olszewski's government. In February 2007 Macerewicz published his report on the disbanded WSI claiming that a clandestine Soviet trained group of the military elite had exerted its control over business and public life. Lech Wałęsa was criticised for failing to monitor the WSI when he was President, who in turn called Jarosław Kaczyński 'a fool' and threatened to sue the Defence Minister for slander. The report also alleged that the Russian secret services had infiltrated the Polish secret services both before and after the collapse of socialism. (New Warsaw Express, 23.02.2007)
21 Pressure to increase the lustration process was given impetus in February 2005, when the journalist Bronisław Wildstein stole a working list of 240,000 names from the IPN and published it on the Internet. The list did not distinguish between those who were working for or being investigated by the secret service. Wildstein was sacked from his job at the newspaper Rzeczpospolita and in May 2006 he was appointed by the new government as head of the Polish public television network: *Telewizja Polska*.
21 The constitutional court declared that the aim of lustration should not be one of revenge and that there should be a guarantee of legal defence. It also decided that the lustration of a number of professions (such as education and the media) is illegal, which essentially undermined the government's whole lustration project. The day before two of the tribunal's members had been removed after the government obtained files from the IPN that allegedly showed they had collaborated with the secret services.
23 This was most dramatically shown in January 2007 when the new Archbishop of Warsaw, Stanisław Wielgus, stood down moments before his inauguration. Wielgus, who had been appointed by the Pope, was accused of working with the former communist secret services.
24 The government has proposed a law that would remove 'communist symbols' from Polish cities and towns, although this will not concern monuments situated in cementaries. (Dziennik, 16.05.2007)
25 A proposal by LPR, supported by PiS, aims to take away property from those organisations that 'propagated Marxism and Communism in Poland'. This project is laden with legal difficulties regarding the issue of reprivatisation. (Gazeta Wyborcza, 24.02.2007)

26 When PiS announced the formation of a stability pact with Self Defence and LPR in February 2006, it did so exclusively to *Radio Maryja* and its television counterpart *TV Trwam*. In protest, journalists from other stations boycotted the following press conference. The level of involvement of the radio station and its founder Father Rydzyk in politics even led to the Vatican sending a letter to the Polish Catholic Church asking for them to limit the station's political activity.
27 Gazeta Wyborcza, 07.08.01.2006, 20.07.2006
28 Dziennik, 29-30.07.2006
29 Gazeta Wyborcza, 17.02.2006
30 http://tinyurl.com/3c7h3w
31 On the week that the 2007 Warsaw March for Tolerance was held, the Education Ministry announced that it was introducing a directive forcing the directors of schools to protect its pupils from 'homosexual propaganda'. (*Trybuna*, 17.05.2007)
32 In April 2007 six PiS MPs, led by Speaker of the House Marek Jurek, resigned and created a new party: Right Wing of the Republic (PR). The direct reason for these resignations was the failure of efforts to introduce anti-abortion amendments into the constitution.
33 Government data shows that gross privatisation revenue at the end of December 2006 totalled zl.622 million, accounting for merely 11.3 percent of the original annual target. The government states that this low level of privatisation was due to the lack of pressure for privatisation, relative to previous years, due to high tax revenues. However, in 2007 the government plans to significantly increase the pace of privatisations, aiming to sell a total of 139 companies. (Warsaw Voice, 10.01.2007)
34 Dziennik, 22-23.07.2006
35 The government criticizes the banking system, claiming that it was created to support Balcerowicz and the liberals and controlled by the post-communist nomenclature, thus creating corruption within the system. PiS believe that the NBP should be based on the American Federal bank, which is responsible not only for price stability, but also for economic growth and employment. They also consider the high level of foreign ownership of banks as being unhealthy for the economy. (Kowalik, 2006) Balcerowicz's term as head of the NBP came to an end in January 2007 and Sławomir Skrzypek, who is relatively unknown and inexperienced but politically close to Lech Kaczyński, replaced him.
36 The government has ruled out a quick entry into the *eurozone*, although it states that it wants Poland to join by the end of the decade.
37 For example, Roman Giertych visited Jedwabne, a town where hundreds of Jews were killed by Poles during WW2 and stated that there was no room for anti-Semitism in Poland. Also, he urged the youth wing of the LPR to restrain from attacking demonstrators during the 2006 March for Tolerance in Warsaw. On the other hand, as PiS increasingly wins the support of the LPR's constituency, the party becomes more radical on some issues (e.g. abortion) in order to distance itself from PiS.

38 Previously, Lech Kaczyński had said that he has always been a supporter of the death penalty, and that the future development of European civilisation and culture could lead to the re-introduction of the death penalty inside the EU for violent or sexual crimes. Any EU Candidate State must abolish the death penalty and Poland signed the ratification of protocol number 6 to the European convention on human rights, which prohibits the use of the death penalty in peace-time.
39 Moves have been made to erode the free nature of the health service. For example in April 2006 the Ministry of Heath proposed charging people ZŁ20/50 for a visit to the doctor. (Trybuna, 15-16.04.2006) Also, during the health workers protests over pay in 2007 some voices were raised within the government about privatising the health service.

Conclusions

1 This situation is not unique to Poland, but is a phenomenon that exists throughout CEE. An example of this was the riots in Hungary in September 2006 after the Socialist Party PM, Ferenc Gyurcsany, admitted that his party had lied prior to the elections. The Hungarian Socialist Party had promised to increase public spending but then introduced a set of austerity measures to cut spending under pressure from the IMF and EU.

Appendix One

1 From the 1993 elections onwards only those parties that crossed the 5% threshold and electoral blocs that crossed 7% entered parliament. Only those parties that managed this are included in these tables.

BIBLIOGRAPHY

Adorno, T & Horkheimer, M (1997) *Dialectic of Enlightenment*, London: Verso.
Agh, A (2000) 'Party Formation Process and the 1998 Elections in Hungary: Defeat as Promoter of Change for the HSP' *East European Politics and Societies*. **14**, 2: 288-312.
Alexander, J (1978) *The Dialectic of Individuation and Domination: Weber's Rationalisation Theory and Beyond*. London: Blackwell.
Ali, T. *Revolution from Above: Where is the Soviet Union Going?* London: Hutchinson.
Ambrose, S (1993) *Rise to Globalism. American Foreign Policy Since 1938*, New York: Penguin Books.
An Outline of the History of the CPCz, (1980) Prague: Orbit Press Agency.
Anderson, P (1965) *Towards Socialism* in Anderson P (ed) *Origins of the Present Crisis* London: New Left Review.
Anderson, P (1976) 'The Antinomies of Antonio Gramsci' *New Left Review* **100**, 17-43.
Anderson, P (1976a) *Considerations on Western Marxism* London: Verso.
Anderson, P (1992) *English Questions* London: Verso.
Anderson, P (1992a) *A Zone of Engagement* London: Verso.
Anderson, P (1994) *Introduction to Mapping the West European Left* in P. Anderson & P. Camiller (eds) *Mapping the West European Left*, London: Verso.
Anderson, P (1996) *Passages from Antiquity to Feudalism* London: Verso.
Anderson, P (1997) *The Europe to Come* in P. Anderson & P. Gowan (eds) *The Question of Europe* London: Verso.
Anderson, P (1998) *The Origins of Post-modernity* London: Verso.
Anderson, P (2000) 'Renewals' *New Left Review* **1**: 7-17.
Anderson, P (2001) 'Testing Formula Two' *New Left Review* **8**: 5-23.

Anderson, P (2002) 'Force and Consent' *New Left Review* **17**: 5-16.
Anderson, P (2006) 'Inside Man' *The Nation* April 2006.
Andor, L (1996) 'Decline and Rise of the Left Communists, Socialists and Social Democrats in Hungary' *Newsletter Global Alternative Media Associatio'*: 25.
Andor, L (2000)*Hungary on the Road to the European Union: Transition in Blue* London: Praeger.
Antoszewski, A (2002) *Sousz Lewicy Demockratycznej w Polsim systemie Partyjnym in Europejska Lewica Wobec Szans i Wyzwan XXI Wieku* Kraków: Trans Krak.
Arato, A (1991) *Revolution, Civil Society and Democracy* in Z Rau (ed) *The Re-emergence of Civil Society in Eastern Europe and the Soviet Union* Boulder: Westview.
Ascherson, N (1982) *The Polish August. What Has Happened in Poland?* London: Penguin Books.
Ash, T G (1991) *The Polish Revolution* London: Penguin Books.

Balcerowicz, L (1994) *Socialism, Capitalism and Transformation* Budapest:Central European University Press.
Balcerowicz, L (1996) *Polish Economic Reform in a Comparative Perspective* in Baczko, T (ed) *The Second Stage of Polish Transformation* Warsaw: Polish Scientific Publishers.
Balcerowicz, L & Gelb, A (1995) *Macropolicies in Transition to a Market Economy: A Three Year Perspective,* in, *Proceedings of the World Bank Annual Conference on Development Economics 1994*, Washington DC: The World Bank: 45-48.
Bartlett, D (1998) 'Has the East Really Become the South? Ownership Structure and Economic Policy' *Politics and Society* 25, 2: 203-229.
Barysch, K (2003) 'Will EU Money be the Tune for New EU Members Catch-Up Song?' *World Bank Transition Newsletter* 14/4-6.
Bauman, Z (1994), *After the Patronage State — A Model in Search of Class Interests* in Mokrzycki, E & Bryant, G (eds), *The New Great Transformation? Change and Continuity in East-Central Europe* London: Routledge.
Bernstein, E (1967) *Evolutionary Socialism* New York: Schocken Books.
Berend, I (1986) *The Crisis Zone of Europe — An Interpretation of East Central European History in the First Half of the Twentieth Century* Cambridge: CUP.
Berend I & Ranki, G (1977) *East Central Europe in the Nineteenth and Twentieth Centuries Budapest:* Akademiai Kiado.

Berend I & Gyorgy R *(1977)* Under-Development and Economic Growth, Studies in Hungarian Economic and Social History *Budapest: Akademiai Kiado.*

Berglund, S & Dellenbrandt, J (1994) *The New Democracies in Eastern Europe* USA: Edward Elgar publishing Ltd.

Bernhard, M (1996) *Civil Society after the First Transition* Communist and Post-Communist Studies 29/3: 309-330.

Bielasiak, J (1995) 'Substance and process in the Development of Party Systems in East Central Europe'. Paper presented at the *V Congress of the International Council of Central and East European Studies.*

Bieler, A and Morton, A 2004, 'A Critical Theory Route to Hegemony, World Order and Historical Change: Neo-Gramscian Perspectives in International Relations' *Capital and Class,* 82, pp 85-113.

Blackledge, P (2001) 'Realism and Renewals: Perry Anderson and the Prospects for the Left' *Contemporary Politics* 7/4: 263-281.

Blit, L (1971) The Origins of Polish Socialism 1878-86, London: CUP.

Boggs, C (1995) *The Socialist Tradition – From Crisis to Decline* London: Routledge.

Borowski, J (2000) *Poland and the EMU: An Optimum Currency Area?* Warsaw: Friedrich Ebert Stiftung.

Borysanyi, G (1968) *Some Problems of the Policy of the MSzDP in* The *Period Between the Two Wars (1919-39) Studies on the History of the Hungarian Working Class Movement* Budapest: Akademiai Kiado.

Bozóki, A (1997) 'Between Modernisation and Nationalism: Socialist Parties Under Post-Socialism', Working Paper #7 Budapest: Central European University.

Bozóki, A (2001)*Globalists vs Localists:* 'A Historic Debate and the Position of the Left in Hungary' *Central European Political Science Review* 2/4 175-199.

Bożyk, P (1997) *Gradualism versus Shock-therapy* in Pickel, A and Wiesenthal, A *The Grand Experiment Debating Shock-therapy, Transition Theory and the East German Experience,* Boulder Westview Press (2000)

'Problemy Trzeciej Drogi' *Myśl Socjaldemocrkratyczna* **2**: 24-27.

Brada, J (1997) *A Critique of the Evolutionary Approach to the Economic Transition from Communism to Capitalism* in Pickel, A & Wiesenthal, A *The Grand Experiment Debating Shock-therapy, Transition Theory and the East German Experience* Boulder: Westview Press.

Brus W & Łaski K (1991) *From Marx to Market,* Oxford: Claredon Paperbacks.

Bryant, C (1995) *Transformation and Continuity in Contemporary Britain* in Bryant G & Mokrzycki, E (eds) *Democracy, Civil Society and Pluralism* Warsaw: IfiS.
Bryant, C (1993), *Economic Utopianism and Sociological Realism* London: Penguin.
Bryant G & Mokrzycki, E (1995) *Introduction: Democracies in Context* in Bryant G & Mokrzycki M *Democracy, Civil Society and Pluralism* Warsaw: IFiS Publishers.
Bugaj, R (2002), *Dylematy Finansów Publicznych Przekształkcenia w Gospadarce Polskiej* Warsaw: Instytut Nauk Ekonomicznych.
Bugaj, R (2002a) *Ustrojowa Zmiana pod Kontrola Liberalnych Elit* in *Polskie Przemiany Uwarunkowania i Spory*, Stowarzyszenie Studiów i Inicjatyw Społecznych Warsaw: Stowarzyszenie Studiów i Incicjatyw Społecznych
Bugaj, R *Czy Tak Dalej Być Musi?*, Rzeczpospolita, Warsaw: 6/7, 07, 2002b.
Bugaj, R (2005)*Polski Sektor Finansów Publicznych w Okresie Transfomacji* in *Polska Transformacja Ustojowa* in, *Polska Transformacja Ustrojowa*, Warsaw: Fundacja Inowacja.
Bukharin, N (1929) *Imperialism and World Economy* London: Martin Lawrence.
Butler, DE & Rose, R (1960) *The British General Election of 1959 London*: Frank Cass.
Butler, D & Stokes, D (1974) *Political Change in Britain* London: Macmillan.

Castle, M & Taras, R (2002) *Democracy in Poland* Cambridge: Westview.
Celiński, A (2000) 'Problemy Trzeciej Drogi' *Myśl Socjaldemocrkratyczna* 2: 27-32.
Chomsky, N (1994) *World Orders, Old and New* New York: Pluto Press.
Chang, H & Nolan, P (1997) *Europe versus Asia: Contrasting Paths to the Reform of Centrally Planned Systems of Political Economy* in Pickel, A & Wiesenthal, A *The Grand Experiment Debating Shock Therapy, Transition Theory and the East German experience* Boulder: Westview Press.
Cook, L & Orenstein, M (1999) *The Return of the left and its Impact on the Welfare State in Russia, Poland and Hungary* in Cook, L, Orensten, M & Rueschemeyer, M *Left Parties and Social Policy in Post-Communist Europe* Oxford: Westview Press.
Connor, W & Płoszajski, P (1992) *Escape From Socialism. The Polish Route* Warsaw: IfiS.

Cox, R (1987) *Production, Power and World Order: Social Forces in the Making of History.* New York: Columbia University Press.

Crewe, I (1986) *On the Death and Resurrection of Class Voting: Some Comments on How Britain Votes* London: Political Studies.

Crewe I & Sarvlik B (1983) *Decade of Realignment* Cambridge: CUP.

Crossland, A (1964) *The Future of Socialism* London: Jonathan Cape Paperback.

Cumpers, R & Kandel, J (1999) *European Social Democracy: Transformation in Progress* Bonn/Amsterdam: Fredrich Ebbert Stiftung.

Czykier-Wierzba (1995) *Polish Agriculture Policy and its Integration with the EU* Gdańsk: Gdańsk University.

Daianu, D (2002) *Is Catching-UP Possible in Europe,* Warsaw: TiGER Institute.

Dahrendorf, R (1959), *Class and Class Conflict in an Industrial Society* London: RKP.

Dauderstadt, M, Andre, G & Markus, G (1999) *Troubled Transition Social Democracy in East Central Europe* Bonn/Amsterdam: Friedrich Ebert Stiftung.

Davies, N (1981) *Gods Playground – A histrory of Poland* Colombia: Colombia University Press.

Davies, N (2001) *Heart of Europe. The Past in Poland's Present* Oxford: Oxford University Press.

Day, S (2000) *From Social Democracy of the Polish Republic (SdRP) to Democratic Left Alliance (SLD)* in Kubiak, H & Wiatr, J (eds) *Between Animosity and Utility Political Parties and Their Matrix* Warsaw: Scholar.

De Angelis, M 1999 'Marx's Theory of Primitive Accumulation: A Suggested Reinterpretation' London: University of East London.

Despincy-Zochowska, B 2003, *Restructuring Polish Agriculture: The Case Study of State Owned Agricultural Enterprises*, Extraordinario, 6: pp1-20.

Domański, H (1998) 'Two Transformations and Social Mobility' Polish Sociological Review 4/124: 313-333.

Domański, H. (2000) 'Death of Classes in Poland? Electoral Voting and Class Membership in 1991-1997' *Polish Sociological Review* 2/130: 151-179.

Domański, H. (2001*) Wzrost Merytokracji i Newrónosci Szans in Jak Żyją Polacy* Warsaw: IfiS.

Domański, H. (2002) *Ubóstwo w społeczeństwach postkomunistycznych* Warszawa: ISP.

Dziewanowski, MK (1976) *The Communist Party of Poland* Cambridge: Harvard University Press.

Ekiert, G (1991) 'Democratisation Processes in East Central Europe, A Theoretical Reconsideration' *British Journal of Political Science* 21: 285-313.

Ferrera, M, Hemerijck, A & Rhodes, M (2001) *The Future of Social Europe: Recasting Work and Welfare in the New Economy* in Giddens, A (ed) *The Global Third Way Debate* Cambridge: Polity Press.

Fodor, E, Hanley, E & Szelenyi, I (1997) 'Left Turn In Postcommunist Politics: Bringing Class Back In?' *East European Politics and Societies*, 11, 1: 190-224.

Foldes,G (1997) *The Positions and Problems of the Hungarian Social Democracy* Budapest: transcript.

Franciszek, T (2005) *Rolnictwo a Procesy Tranformacji I Europejskiej integracji Gospodarki Polskiej 1989- 2004* in *Polska Transformacja Ustrojowa*, Warsaw: Fundacja Inowacja.

Freeman, A and Kagarlitsky, B (2004) *The Politics of Empire: Globalisation in Crisis* London: Pluto Press.

Frenkel I (1998) *Employment and Under Employment In the Private Sector of Agriculture* Warsaw: Wies i Rolnictwo.

Fukuyama, F (1992) *The End of History and the Last Man* London: Penguin Books.

Fukuyama, F (2006) *America at the Crossroads* New Haven: Yale University Press.

Gamble, A (1988) *The Free Economy and the Strong State: The Politics of Thatcherism* Durham: Duke University Press.

Giddens, A (1998) *The Third Way. The Renewal of Social Democracy* Cambridge: Polity Press.

Giddens, A (2001) *The Global Third Way Debate* Cambridge: Polity Press.

Giddens, A, Hutton, W (2001) *On the Edge, Living with Global Capitalism* London: Vintage.

Głowczyk, J (2001) *Społeczne Konsekwencje Transformacji Ustrojowej W Polsce* Oświata i Wychowanie 1/731: 24-27.

Glyn, A (1997) *Wasted Sacrifices: Real Wages and Reconstruction in Eastern Europe* in Pickel, A & Wiesenthal, A *The Grand Experiment Debating*

Shock-therapy, Transition Theory and the East German Experience Boulder: Westview Press.

Gortat, R (1994) *The Development of Social Democracy in Poland* in Waller, M, Coppieters, B & Deschouwer, K (eds) *Social Democracy in a Post-Communist Europe* Oregon: Cass.

Gowan, P 1997. 'The Dynamics of EU Expansion' *Labour Focus in Eastern Europe*, No. 57.

Grabowska, M (2004) *Podział Postkomunistyczny* Warsaw: Scholar.

Gramsci, A (1991) *The State and Civil Society* in *Selections From Prison Notebooks* London: Lawrence & Wishart Ltd.

Gramsci, A (1991a) *The Modern Prince* in *Selections From Prison Notebooks* London: Lawrence & Wishart Ltd.

Gramsci, A (1991b) *Americanism and Fordism* in *Selections From Prison Notebooks* London: Lawrence & Wishart Ltd.

Grzymała-Brusse, A (1998) 'Reform Efforts in the Czech and Slovak Communist parties and the Successors, 1988-1993' *East European Politics and Societies* 12/3: 442-471.

Grzymała-Brusse, A (2002) *Redeeming the Communist Past. The Regeneration of Communist Parties in East-Central Europe:* Cambridge CUP.

Habermas, J (1985) *The Theory of Communicative Action*, Great Malvern: Beacon Press.

Habermas, J (1991) *What Does Socialism Mean Today?* in Robin Blackburn ed. *After the Fall: The Failure Communism and the Future of Socialism* London: Verso.

Haralambos, M & Holborn, M (1992) *Sociology Themes and perspectives* London: University Tutorial Press Ltd.

Higley, J, Pakulski, J & Wesołowski, W (1998) *Post Communist Elites and Democracy in Eastern Europe* London: Macmillan Press.

Hudson, K (2000) *European Communism since 1989* London, Macmillan (1996) *Continuity and Change: The Post-Communist Left in Contemporary Hungary* http://www.psa.ac.uk/cps/huds/pdf.

Inglehart, R (1977) *The Silent Revolution* Princeton: Princeton University Press.

The Changing Structure of Political Cleavage in Western Society in Dalton, R, Flanagan, S & (1984) Beck, P (eds) *Electoral Change in Advanced Industrial Democracies* Princeton: Princeton University Press.

Iwiński, T (2002) 'O Problemach i Dylematach Integracji Europejskiej' *Myśl Socjaldemokratyczna'* 2: 17-29.

Janik, K (2001) *Sousz Lewicy Demokratycznej – Nowa Partia czy Nowa Oferta Programowa* in *Lewica Wobec Szans i Wyzwan XXI Wieku* Kraków: Trans Krak.

Jaskiernia, J (1998) *Dylematy i szanse lewicy* in *Problem Główny współczesnej Polskiej lewicy* Warsaw: Kazimerza Kelles Krauza.

Jasiewicz, K (2003) *Portfel Czy Różaniec? Wzory Zachowań Wyborczych Polaków W Latach 1995-2001* in Markowski, R (ed) *System Partynjny i Zachowania Wyborcze* Warsaw: PAN ISP.

Jorgensen, K (1992) *The End of Anti-Politics in Central Europe* in Lewis, P (ed) *Democracies and Civil Society in Eastern Europe*, London, Macmillan.

Kabaj, M 2005, *Syndrom Polskiej Transformacji*, in, *Polska Transformacja Ustrojowa*, Warsaw: Fundacja Inowacja.

Kabaj, M & Kowalik, T (1995) *Who is Responsible for Postcommunis Recession* World Bank Transition Newsletter July August 1995.

Kaser M.C & Radice E.A (1985) *The Economic History of Eastern Europe 1919-1975* New York: Oxford University Press.

Kellner, D (1989) *Critical Theory, Marxism and Modernity* Cambridge: Polity Press.

Kerr, C et al (1962) *Industrialisation and Industrial Man* London: Heinemann.

Kochanowicz, K (1989) *The Polish Economy and the Evolutin of Dependency* in Chirot, D (ed) *The Origins of Backwardness in Eastern Europe* London: University of California.

Kocór, M & Masłyk, T. (2000) *The Political Beliefs of Poles and their Party Affilitations. An Expresssion of an Emerging Democracy* in Wiatr, J & Kubiak, H (eds) *Between Animosity and Utility Political Parties and their Matrix* Warsaw: Scholar.

Kolarska-Bobińska, L (1994) *Aspirations Values and Interests* Warsaw: IfiS

Kolarska-Bobińska, L (2002) *Polska Scena polityczna Po Wyborach Parlamentarnych 2001Roku* in *Przyszłość Polskiej Sceny Politycznej Po Wyborach 2001 Warsw: ISP*.

Kołodko, G (1994) *Strategia Dla Polski* Warsaw: Poltext (2001) 'Globalisation and catching-up: from Recession to Growth in Transition Economies' *Communist and Post-Communist Studies* **34**: 279-322.

Konrad, G and Szelenyi, I (1979) *The Intellectuals on the Road to Class Power: A Sociological Study of the Role of the Intelligentsia in Socialism* New York: Owl Pen Books.

Kopczyński, M (2000) *The Formation of Post-Solidarity Political Parties. The Case of the Union of Freedom* in Kubiak, H & Wiatr, J *Between Animosity and Utility Political Parties and Their Matrix* Warsaw: Scholar.

Kornai, J (1992) *The Socialist System: The Political Economy of Communism* Princeton: Princeton University Press.

Kornai, J (1993) *Transformational Recession: A General Phenomenon Examined Through the Example of Hungary's Development* Budapest: Institute for Advanced Study.

Kornai, J (1997) *The Principles of Privatisation in Eastern* Europe in Pickel, A & Wiesenthal, A *The Grand Experiment Debating Shocktherapy, Transition Theory and the East German Experience* Boulder: Westview Press.

Kowalik, T (2002) *True to Oneself: An Appreciation of Włodzimierz Brus Labour Focus on Eastern Europe* **72**: 81-101 .

Kowalik, T. (2003) *Rosa Luxemburg, Accumualtion of Capital, With a new introduction by Tadeusz Kowalik* London-New York: Routledge Classics.

Kowalik, T. (2003a) *Mój 'Przyjaciel Jurek Hausner' Przegląd, 23.03.2003.*

Kowalik, T. (2006) *'Poland's Sudden Shift to the Right'* Paper presented at the 12th Workshop Euromemorandum Group, Burssels September 2006.

Kowalewski, M (2006) *'50 Years Since the Poznań Uprising'* International Viewpoint IV379.

Krejci J & Machonin P (1986) *A Laboratory for Social Change* Oxford: Macmillan.

Kubik, J (1994) *The Power of Symbols against the Symbols of Power* USA: University Park.

Kurczewska, J (1995) *Democracy in Poland: Historical Context and Tradition. Democracy, Civil Society, and Pluralism* in Bryant C and Mokrzycki E (eds) Warsaw IfiS PAN.

Lawson, K, Rommele, A & Karasimeonow, G (1999) *Cleavages, Parties and Voters* London: Praeger.

Lemke, C & Marks, G (1992) *The Crisis of Socialism in Europe* USA: Duke University Press.

Lenin, V (1967) *The Development of Capitalism in Russia* Moscow: Progress Publishers.

Lenin, V (1970) *Imperialism, the Highest Stage of Capitalism* Beijing: Foreign Languages Press.

Leon, A (1946) *The Jewish Question — A Marxist Interpretation* www.marxists.org/subjct/jewish/leon/index.htm.

Łepik, R (2005) 'Czy w Polsce Możliwe jest Podnoszenie Płac? *Rynku Pracy"* nr 6 (150).

Lewis, P (1993) *Poland's SLD: The Communists who came in from the Cold* Labour Focus on Eastern Europe **3**: 29-34.

Livingstone, K (1998) *How Deep Will the Downturn Be?* London: Socialist Economic Bulletin.

Luxemburg, R (1963) *The Accumulation of Capital* London: Routledge & Kegan Paul Ltd.

Luxemburg, R (1986) *Reform of Revolution* London: London: Militant Publications.

Ługowska, U (2002) 'Samoobrona Versus the Establishment: Poland's 'Self Defence' Party in the Year Since the Election' *Labour Focus on Eastern Europe* 72: 63-81.

McGowan, F (2001) *Social Democracy and the European Union: Who's Changing Whom?* in Martell et al.*Social Democracy Global and National Perspectives* New York: Palgrave.

Mach, B & Wesołowski, W (1997) *Politicians in Times of Transformation: Transformational Correctness or Genuine Differences in Perception?* Berlin: Fur Sozialforschung.

Markowski, R (2002) *Polski System Partyny Po Wyborach 2001 Roku* in *Przyszłość Polskiej Sceny Politycznej Po Wyborach 2001* Warsaw: ISP.

Machejek, A & Machejek, J (2001), *Dogońmy Europę* Łódź: Hamal Books

Mandel, E (1978) *Late Capitalism* London: Verso.

Mandel, E (1991) *Beyond Perestroika* London: Verso.

Mandel, E (1995) *The Long Waves of Capitalist Development* London: Verso.

Marcusse, H (1964) *One Dimensional Man* London: Routledge.

Markowski, R & Cześnik, M (2003) *Polski System Partyjny: Dekada Zmian Instytucjonalnych* in Markowski, R (ed) System Partynjny i Zachowania Wyborcze Warsaw: PAN ISP.

Marshall, T H (1992) *Citizenship and Social Class* London: Pluto Perspectives.

Marx, K (1993)*Grundisse* London: Penguin Books.

Mencinger, J (2002) 'Slovenia: Alternative Economic Policies in Action' *Der Offentliche Sektor- Forschungs-B* Erichte **3-4**: 58-63.

Merkel, W (2001) *The Third Ways of Social democracy* in Giddens, A (ed) *The Global Third Way Debate* Cambridge: Polity.

Milei, G (1968) *The Historical Path of the Emergence of the Hungarian Party of Communists* in *Studies on the History of the Hungarian Working Class Movement* Budapest: Akademiai Kiado.

Modzelewski, K (2006) 'Jaruzelski UtorowałDroge Balcerowiczowi' *Le Monde Dpplomatique Edycja Polska'* Nr 10: 4-5.

Mokrzycki, E (1997) *Od Protokapitalizmu do Posocjalizmu: Makrostruktualny Wymiar Dwukrotney Zmiany Ustrou* in *Elementy Nowego Ładu* Warsaw: IfiS PAN.

Mokrzycki, E (2001) *Jak Mamy Demokrację?* in *Jak Żyją Polacy?* Warsaw: IfiS PAN.

Morawski, W (1992) *Economic Change and Civil Society in Poland* in Lewis P *Democracies and Civil Society in Eastern Europe*, London, Macmillan.

Naimark, N (1979) *History of the Proletariat,* USA, Colombia University Press.

Nairn, T (1965) *The Nature of the Labour Party* in Anderson, P (ed) *Origins of the Present Crisis* London: New Left Review.

Nałęcz, T (2000) 'Problemy Trzeciej Drogi' *Myśl Socjaldemocrkratyczna* 2: 35-38.

Nieckarz, S. 'Milliardy do Spłacenia' *Przegląd* 6th May 2002.

Nolan, P (1995) *China's Rise, Russia's Fall* Basingstoke: Macmillan.

Newman, O & De Zoysa, R (2002) 'The Third Way Alternative: America's New Political Agenda?' *Contemporary Politics* 6, 3: 231-247.

Olivova, V (1972) *The Doomed Democracy – Czechoslovakia in a Disrupted Europe 1914-38,* London: Sidgwick & Jackson.

Orenstein, M (1998) 'A Genealogy of Communist Successor Parties in East-Central Europe and the Determinants of their Success' *East European Politics and Societies* 12, 3: 472-487.

Ost, D (1990) *Solidarity and the Politics of Anti-Politics* Philadelphia: Temple University Press.

Ost, D (1993) 'Labour, Class and Democracy', *ILWCH*, 45: 453-466.

Ost, D (1995) 'An Introduction: Shock-therapy and its discontents' *Telos* 92: 107-112.

Ost, D (2000) 'The Salience of Class, not of Class Voting' *Polish Sociological Review,* 2, 130: 183-186.

Padgett, S & Patterson, W (1991) *A History of Social Democracy in Post-War Europe* London: Longman.

Palma, G (1978) 'Dependency: A Formal Theory of Underdevelopment of a Methodology for the Analysis of Concrete Situations of Underdevelopment?' *World Development* 6: 881-924.
Pamlenyi, E (1975) *A History of Hungary* London: Collets.
Perelman, M 1997 *Classical Political Economy; Primitive Accumulation and the Social Division of Labour,* Durham, NC: Duke University Press.
Pickel, A (1997) *Authoritarianism or Democracy? Marketisation as a Political Problem* in Pickel, A & Wiesenthal, A *The Grand Experiment Debating Shock-therapy, Transition Theory and the East German Experience* Boulder: Westview Press.
Piławski, K (2005) 'Dokąd zmierza Polska Lewica' *Przegląd* Socjalistyczn 4-5: pp11-28.
Polonsky, A (1972) *Politics in an Independent Poland 1921-39* New York: Oxford University press.
Popper, K (1943) *The Open Society and its Enemies* Princeton: Princeton University Press.
Poznański, K (1996) *Poland's Protracted Transition Cambridge*: CUP.
Poznański, K (1997) *Instituional Perspectives on Post-Communist recession in Eastern Europe* in Pickel, A & Wiesenthal, A *The Grand Experiment Debating Shock-therapy, Transition Theory and the East German Experience* Boulder: Westview Press.
Poznański, K (1999) *Wielki Przekręt Klęska Polskich Reform,* Warsaw: Towarzystwo Wydawnicze i Literackie.
Przeworski, A (1993) *Economic Reform, Public Opinion and Political Instituions: Poland in the Eastern European Perspective* in *Economic Reforms in New Democracies A Social Democratic Approach* Cambridge: Cambridge University Press.
Przeworski, A (1985) *Capitalism and Social Democracy*, Cambridge: Cambridge University Press.

Rakowski, M (2001) *Nurt liberalny w PZPR i Jego Rola na Drodze do Socjaldemokracji* in *Europejska Lewica Wobec Szans i Wyzwań XX1 Wieku* Kraków: Trans Krak.
Riddle, J (ed) (1984) *Lenin's Struggle for a Revolutionary International* New York: Pathfinder Press.
Ringold, D (1999) *Social Policy in Postcommunist Europe: Legacies and Transition* in Cook, L, Orensten, M & Rueschemeyer, M (eds) *Left Parties and Social Policy in Post-Communist Europe* Oxford: Westview Press.

Rueschemeyer, D (1999) *Left Parties and Policies in Eastern Europe after Communism: An introduction* in Cook, L, Orensten, M & Rueschemeyer, M (eds) *Left Parties and Social Policy in Post-Communist Europe* Oxford: Westview Press.

Rueschemeyer D & Wolchik, L (1999) *The Return of Left-Orientated Parties in Eastern Germany and the Czech Republic and their Social Policies.* in Cook, L, Orensten, M & Rueschemeyer, M (eds) *Left Parties and Social Policy in Post-Communist Europe* Oxford: Westview Press.

Ringold, D (1999) *Social Policy in post-Communist Europe: Legacies and Transition* in Cook, L, Orensten, M & Rueschemeyer, M (eds) *Left Parties and Social Policy in Post-Communist Europe* Oxford: Westview Press.

Rose, A (1999) 'Extraordinary Politics in the Polish Transition' *Communist and Post-Communist Studies* 32, 2: 195-210.

Rose, R (1997) 'Where are Post-Communist Countries Going?' *Studies in Public Policy 28* University of Strathclyde: 92-108.

Rychard, A (1998) *Institutions and Actors in a New Democracy, The Vanishing Legacy of Communist and Solidarity Type Participation in Poland*, in, Rueschemeyer, D et al *Participation and Democracy East and West* New York: ME Sharpe.

Sachs, J (1994) *Shock-therapy in Poland and Perspectives of Five Years*: Tanner Lecture Manuscript.

Schumpter, J (1942) *Capitalism, Socialism and Democracy*, New York: Harper & Row.

Shaw, M (2001) *Social Democracy in the Global Revolution: An Historical Perspective* in Martell, L et al (ed) *Social Democracy Global and National Perspectives* New York: Palgrave.

Shields, S 2003, *The Charge of the Right Brigade: Transnational Social Forces and the Neoliberal Configuration of Poland's Transition*, New Political Economy, 8/2, 225-243.

Sik, O (1967) *Plan and Market under Socialism* Prague: Czech Academy of Sciences.

Slay, B (2000) 'The Polish Economic Transition: Outcome and Lessons' *Communist and Post-Communist Studies* 33: 49-70.

Slay, B (1994) *The Polish Economy Crisis Reform and Transformation* Princeton: Princeton University Press.

Slocock, B & Smith, S (2000) 'Interest Politics and Identity Formation in Post-Communist Societies: the Czech and Slovak trade Union Movements' *Contemporary Politics*: 6, 3: 215-231.

Soros, G (1998) 'Towards a Global Open Society' *Atlantic Monthly* January 1998.

Soros, G (1999) *The Crisis of Global Capitalism: Open Society Endangered* New York: Public Affairs.

Stabrowski, F (2002) 'Poland's Union of labour: the Dilemma of the Non-Communist Left in Post-Communist Poland' *Labour Focus on Eastern Europe* 72: 4-63.

Stammers, N (2001) *Social Democracy and Global Governance* in Martel, L (ed) *Social Democracy Global and National Perspectives* New York: Palgrave.

Stefanowski R (1992) *PPS 1892-1992* Warsaw: Institute Wydawniczy Książka i Prasa.

Stabrowski, F (2002) 'Poland's Union of Labour: the Dilemma of the Non-Communist Left in Post-Communist Poland' *Labour Focus on Eastern Europe* 72: 4-63.

Szczerbiak,A (1998) 'Electoral Politics in Poland: The Parliamentary Elections of 1997' *The Journal of Communist Studies and Transition Politics* 14, 3: 58-84.

Szczerbiak,A (2001) 'Explaining Kwaśniewski's Landslide: The October 2000 Presidential Election' *The Journal of Communist Studies and Transition Politics* **17**: 78-108.

Szczerbiak,A (2001) 'The New Polish Political Parties as Membership Organisations' *Contemporary Politics* **7**, 1: 57-71.

Szelągowska, A (2004) *Kapitał Zagraniczny w Polskich Bankach,* Warsaw: Poltext.

Szacki, J (1994) *Liberalism After Communism* Hungary: Central European Press.

Sztompka, P (1996) 'Trust and Emerging Democracy, Lessons From Poland' *International Sociology* **11**, 1: 37-62.

Szumlewicz. P (2006) 'Antysocjalna transformacja' http://www.lewica.pl/index.php?id=9706.

Szymański, W 2005, 'Przyczyny I Skutki Nadmiernego Uzależnienia Gospodarki Od Kapitału Zewnętrznego', in *Polska Transformacja Ustrojowa*, Warsaw: Fundacja Inowacja.

Tarkowski, J (1994) *Władza I Społeczeństwo w Systemie Autorytarnym* Warsaw: ISP.

Taylor, J (1952) *The Economic Development of Poland 1919-50* New York: Cornell University Press.

Teichova, A (1985) *The Czechoslovak Economy*: London and New York: Routlege.

Thompson, E (1963) *The Makings of the English Working Class* New York: Vintage.
Tismaneanu, V (1992) *Reinventing Politics* New York: The Free Press.
Tittenbrun J (1993) *The Collapse of 'Real-Socialism' in Poland* London: Janus Publishing.
Trotsky, L (2004) *The Revolution Betrayed* New York: Dover Publications.

Vincze, S (1968) *The Struggle for the First Independent Proletarian Party*, in, *Studies on the History of the Hungarian Working Class Movement*, Budapest: Akademiai Kiado.

Waller, M, Bruno, C & Deschouwer, K (1994) *Social Democracy in a Post-Communist Europe* London: Frank Cass, UK.
Wetherly, P (2001) 'The Reform of Welfare and the Way We Live Now: A Critique of Giddens and the Third Way' *Contemporary Politics* 7, 2: 149-171.
Wesołowski, W (1994) 'The Destruction and Construction of Interests Under Systemic Change: a Theoretical Approach' *Polish Sociological Review* 4, 108: 273-294.
Wesołowski, W (1996) *The Formation of Political Parties in Post-Communist Poland* in Pridham, G & Lewis, P *Stabilising Fragile Democracies* London & New York: Routledge.
Wesołowski, W (1998) 'Political Actors and Democracy: Poland 1990-1997' *Polish Sociological Review* 3, 119: 226-247.
Wesołowski, W (2000) 'Democratic and National-Liberal Leadership in Times of *Transformation' Polish Sociological Review* 4,132: 366-386.
Wheaton, B (1986) *Radical Socialism in Czechoslovakia*, New York: Columbia University Press.
Whyman, P (2001) 'Can Opposites Attract? Monetary Union and the Social Market' *Contemporary Politics*, 7, 2: 113-129.
Wiatr, J (1991) *Zmierzch Systemu* Warsaw: Fundacja im. Kazimierza Kelles-Krauza.
Wiatr, J (1998) *Strategiczny Wybór Dla Polski* in *Problem Główny Współczesnej Polskiej Lewicy* Warsaw: Fundacji. im Kazimierza Kelles-Krauza.
Wiatr, J (1999) *Political Parties and Cleavage Crystallization in Poland, 1989-93* in Lawson, K, Rommele, A & Karasimeonov, G *Cleavages, Parties and Voters* London: Praeger.
Wiatr, J (2000) *Socjaldemokracja Wobec Wyzwań XXI Wieku* Warsaw: Kazimierza Kelles-Krauza.

Wiatr, J (2000a) *Lasting Cleavages and the Changing Party System in Poland: 1989-1999*, in, Kubiak, H & Wiatr, J. *Between Animosity and Utility Political Parties and Their Matrix* Warsaw: Schola.
Wiatr, J (2000b) 'Dokąd Prowadzi Trzeciej Drogi' *Myśl Socjaldemokratyczna* 2: 39-46.
Wiatr, J (2003) *Polska Droga do Demokracji* in *Demokracja Polska 1989-2003* Warsaw: Scholar.
Winiecki, J (1997) *Institutional Barriers to Poland's Economic Development* London: Routledge.
Winiecki, J (1997a) *Introduction: Seven Years Experience* in Winiecki, J (ed) *Institutional Barriers to Poland's Economic Development* London: Routledge.
Wnuk-Lipiński, E (1995) *After Communism, a Multi-Disciplinary Approach to Radical Change*: Warsaw: Institute of Political Studies.
Wnuk-Lipiński, E (1993) *A Left Turn in Poland – A Sociological and Political Analysis*, Warsaw: Instytut Studiów Politycznych Polskiej Akademii.

Ziblatt, D (1998) 'Adaptation of Ex-communist parties to Post-Comunist East Central Europe' *Communist and Postcommunist Studies* 31, 2: 119-137.
Zubek, V (1995) 'The Phoenix out of the Ashes: The Rise to Power of Poland's Post-Communist SdRP' *Communist and Post-Communist Studies* 28, 3: 275-306.
Zweig f (1994) *Poland Between the Two World Wars – A Critical Study of Social and Economic Changes* London: Secker & Warburg.

NEWSPAPERS AND MAGAZINES
Dziennik
Financial Times.
Gazeta Wyborcza
Le Monde Diplomatique (Polish Editio).
New Warsaw Express
NewsWeek (Polish Edition)
Polityka.
Przegląd.
Rzeczpospolita.
The Guardian.
The Economist Trybuna.
The Warsaw Voice
Wprost.

RESEARCH AGENCIES

Public Opinion Research Centre (CBOS).
Centre for Opinion Poll Research (OBOP).
Central Statistics Agency (GUS).
Eurostat
Polish Information and Foreign Investment Agency (PAIiIZ).

INTERVIEWEES

Ryszard Bugaj: A leading left politician and economist from the *Solidarność* movement. He helped to form and then led UP until 1998 when he resigned over its increasing close links with the SLD.

MP Marek Dyduch: Former SLD General Secretary and MP during the second SLD-led government.

MP Jerzy Jaskiernia: Leader of the SLD parliamentary caucus during the second SLD-led government.

Tadeusz Kowalik: Leading left economist in Poland, who was an advisor to the unions during the famous Gdansk Strikes during the 1980s. He was a member of UP, leaving shortly after Bugaj resigned as leader.

Mieczyslaw Rakowski: Last General Secretary of the PZPR. Although he is not officially a member of the SLD he strongly connected with the party and edits the journal *Dzis*.

MP Jerzy Szteliga: Former SLD MP who has openly admitted to having worked with the secret police during socialism.

Jerzy Wiatr: A leading intellectual of the SLD and former MP, who was a prominent figure of the PZPR during socialism

INDEX

1929 Crash, 37-40, 179
9/11("nine-eleven"), 21, 134
abortion, 90, 96, 97, 101, 118, 121, 123, 135, 137, 150, 160, 173
absolute state, 12, 29
absolutism, 28
accession eight states (A8), 8, 74-6, 100, 144, 150, 192
Afghanistan, 137, 150
Agora, 135, 190
American, 14, 16, 18, 20, 37, 56, 99, 124, 134, 145, 147, 149-150
Anderson, Perry, 11-12, 20, 28-29, 102, 124, 177, 178
anti-communist, 83, 106, 109, 150
anti-corruption, 156
anti-politics, 82, 84
anti-semitic, 34, 161
anti-semitism, 30, 44, 161
August '80 Trade Union, 185, 191
Auschwitz, 41
Austria, 3, 28-9, 56, 155
Baghdad, 151

Balcerowicz, Leszek, 54, 63, 116, 121, 126, 173, 185
Baltic states, 3, 8
Bauc, Jarosław, 127
Bauman, Zygmunt, 44
Belarus, 3, 22, 34, 37, 147
Belgrade, 151
Belka, Marek, 128, 130, 137, 189, 191
Berlin Wall, 2, 8, 21, 55, 112, 145, 163
Bernstein, Eduard, 31, 177, 188
Bielecki, Jan, 62
Bierut, Bolesław, 42
Blair, Anthony, 124, 135, 138, 188
Bolshevik, 1, 115
Bonapartism, 193
Borowski, Marek, 137-8, 171, 174
bourgeoisie, 12-13, 21, 26, 29-30, 33, 35, 37, 50-2, 57, 80, 82, 98, 102, 104, 114, 151-3, 166, 177
Britain, 38, 124, 135, 144, 178, 179, 182, 184
British Conservative Party, 148, 192

Brus, Włodzimierz, 52, 181
Brussels, 77, 161
Brzeziński, Zbigniew, 144-5
Budapest, 29, 112
budget deficit, 65, 77, 97, 127, 130-1
Bugaj, Ryszard, 53, 65, 116, 121, 173
Bukharin, Nikolai, 32
Bulgaria, 29, 40, 42-3, 75
capitalism, 1-7, 10-27, 30-5, 40, 48, 50-3, 55-8, 64-7, 72, 78-84, 90, 98, 101, 111-4, 117-8, 122, 124, 142-3, 151, 153, 155, 157, 160, 163, 165-6, 174
catholic (Church), 4, 35, 41-2, 98, 101, 104, 109-110, 116, 120, 126, 135, 138, 150, 156, 159, 167, 173, 195
catholicism, 35, 90, 102
Central Anti-Corruption Agency (CBA), 157
Central Bank, 97, 99
Central-Eastern Europe (CEE), vii, 2-8, 17, 20-30, 33, 36-43, 45-6, 49, 51-3, 55-8, 61, 74-5, 78, 80, 83-6, 90, 99, 103, 110, 114, 117, 134, 142-147, 149-153, 163, 165, 179, 181
Celiński, Andrzej, 126, 189
Centre Alliance Party (PC), 104, 107, 109, 173
centrolew, 140, 192
Chernomydrin, Viktor, 177
China, 56, 164, 181
Christian Democratic, 106
CIA prisons, 145
Cichocki, Marek, 192
Cimoszewicz, Włodzimierz, 138, 169, 189

Citizens' Movement Democratic Action (ROAD), 121
Citizens Platform (PO), 106-9, 140, 171, 172, 186
citizenship, 15, 29, 86
Civil Democratic Party (ODS) (Czech), 148, 192
civil society, 6, 12, 14, 16, 19, 24, 26-7, 29, 79, 82-4, 100, 110, 156, 162, 177
Clintonomics, 124
cold war, 1-2, 18-20, 82, 118, 143-6, 150-1, 155, 163-4, 179
colonialism, 10, 177- 178
Comecon, 55, 81
Cominform, 42
Common Agricultural Policy (CAP), 101
communism, 8, 41, 80, 107, 110, 158, 160, 173, 175, 195
communist, 8, 37, 114-5, 177, 188, 195, 196
Communist International, 8
concordat, 98, 102, 123
conservatism, 19-20, 25, 107, 118, 135
conservative, 7, 19, 40, 78, 84, 103, 106-110, 120, 126, 136, 139-140, 143, 148-150, 152, 154, 156-161, 164-6, 172
Conservative-Nationalist, 140-141, 148, 152, 154, 158, 161, 166
constitution, 3, 36, 67, 90, 97-8, 123, 135, 148
corruption, 2, 90, 99, 106-107, 135-9, 156-7, 175
Council of Europe, 160
Crossland, Anthony, 15, 180

Czech Republic, 3, 29, 33, 36, 56-57, 66, 72, 75, 98, 106, 113, 133-4, 148, 150
Czech Republic, 3, 36, 57, 66, 72, 75, 98, 106, 113, 133-4, 150, 181, 193
Czechoslovakia, 33-4, 37-8, 40, 43, 47, 114, 178, 193
de-Communisation, 25, 98, 105, 118, 139, 156-8, 166
Democratic Left Alliance (SLD), 62, 64-5, 87, 105-7, 118-140, 158, 170, 172-4, 186, 187, 188, 191
Democratic Party (PD), 137, 140, 173
Democratic Union (UD), 121, 173, 185
Deutscher, Isaac, 115
Dmowski, Roman, 35, 37, 39, 108, 173
Dolnosląskie, 73
dual society, 68, 85
Dyduch, Marek, 191
Dziennik, 185
Eastern Bloc, 4, 9, 41, 55, 103, 149
Eastern Europe (EE), v, 1-5, 8, 10-13, 17-24, 26-32, 40-1, 50, 54, 57-8, 79, 84, 98, 112-114, 126, 143-149, 151, 153, 163-4
egalitarianism, 88
emigration, 69, 76
endecja, 35, 37, 39, 108, 110, 116, 186
England, 31, 178-9
enlightenment, 84
European Union (EU), viii, 3, 5, 7-9, 21, 25-6, 55-8, 64, 66, 69, 72, 74-7, 91, 97, 99, 101, 106-7, 111, 118-9, 127-1355, 137, 142-152, 155-6, 159-161, 165-6, 174, 183, 192, 193
EU Accession, 9, 145
EU15 Countries, 73, 75-76, 133, 143, 190
European Central Bank (ECB), 22
European Constitution, 144
European Council, 155
Euro 2012, 183-4
eurosceptic, 148, 152
eurozone, 77, 161
extraordinary Politics, 54, 62
F-16 Planes, 134
Fabians, 31, 188
Fascism, 25, 41 114, 149
Fascist, 35, 40, 115, 156
feudal, 6, 11-12, 28-31, 33, 50, 113, 153
feudalism, 11, 23, 28, 30, 34, 50, 56, 80
Fiszbach, Tadeusz, 187
flat-tax Rate, 107, 132, 185, 186
Fordism, 13
foreign direct investment (FDI), vii, 57-9, 72, 99
Forum Trade Union, 184
Fourth Republic, 107, 109, 111, 136, 154, 158, 161, 186
France, 21, 56-7, 145, 150
Franco, Francisco, 150, 193
Frankfurt School, 15
Freedom Party (Austria), 155
Freedom Union (UW), 62, 65, 105-6, 119, 124, 126-7, 130, 136-7, 170, 172-3, 185
Fukuyama, Francis, 18, 20, 181
Gaidar, Yegor, 177
Gazeta, Wyborcza, 126, 185

General Association of Trade
  Unions (OPZZ), 118, 125,
  158, 184, 188
Geremek, Bronisław, 158
Germany, 3, 21, 28-9, 34-5, 39,
  41, 55-7, 66, 98, 115, 133,
  145-9, 178, 179, 180, 182,
  184, 193
Gianfranco, Fini, 155
Giddens, Anthony, 16, 18-19,
  124
Gierek, Edward, 44-5, 47, 89,
  180, 181
Giertych,
  Jędrzej, 109
  Maciej, 218, 193
  Roman, 108, 139, 174, 193
glasnost, 18
globalisation, 2-3, 14, 22, 142-3
Gomułka, Władysław, 42, 44
Gorbachev, Michail, 48, 53,
  83-4
Gramsci, Antonio, 5, 11-13, 82,
  102-103, 110, 112, 177, 194
growth and stability Pact, 77
Haider, Joerg, 155
Hapsburg Empire, 28
Hausner, Jerzy, 132, 137, 190
Havel, Vaclav, 185
Hegel, Georg, 16
hegemony, 5, 11-13, 31, 41, 85,
  97, 102, 109, 113, 117, 124,
  140, 143, 165, 166
historical bloc, 5, 7, 12-17, 20,
  25, 79, 85, 109, 111, 142
historical politics, 110, 148, 158
Holland, 56, 133, 178
holocaust, 4, 41, 163
homophobia, 161
Hungary, 17, 29, 33, 36-9, 43,
  47, 53, 57, 63, 66, 72, 75,
  106, 113, 119, 133-4, 178-9,
  181-2, 189, 196
Hungarian Communist Party
  (MKP), 179
Hussein, Saddam, 20
Ikonowicz, Piotr, 122, 189
imperialism, 11, 32, 51
industrial revolution, 1, 103
Inglehart, Ronald, 16, 19
intelligentsia, 23, 35, 44, 46, 53,
  81, 83, 85, 89, 108, 124, 154
International Monetary Fund
  (IMF), 21, 41, 48, 77, 151,
  161, 189
interventionist state, 12, 14, 20,
  153
Iraq, 20, 91, 133-7, 145, 150,
  191
Janik, Krzysztof, 191
Japan, 17, 21, 55, 67, 151
Jaruga-Nowacka, Izabela, 191
Jaruzelski, Wojciech, 47, 98,
  158, 186, 193
Jewish, 34-5, 175
Jews, 30, 34-5, 41, 174
July 8th Movement, 117, 121
Jurek, Marek, 193, 195
Kaczyński,
  Jarosław, 110, 139, 159, 161,
  186, 193, 194
  Lech, 104, 107, 149, 159,
  186, 192, 193
Kadar, Janos, 53
Kalecki, Michał, 52
Kalisz, Ryszard, 191
Kamiński, Michał, 193
Keynesian, 17
Keynesianism, 14, 52
Klaus, Vaclav, 192
Kołodko, Grzegorz, 43, 122-3,
  130-2, 188

Index

Kornai, Janos, 53, 64, 184
Kowalik, Tadeusz, ix, 52, 65, 105, 121, 181, 190
Kukliński, Ryszard, 180
Kuroń, Jacek, 44, 158, 170, 180, 185, 187-8
Kwaśniewski, Aleksander, 105, 109, 116-120, 126-8, 131-4, 137-8, 140, 146-9, 170
Labour Union (UP), 118, 120-1, 123, 125, 127, 140, 170, 173, 189
Lange, Oscar, 52
Law and Justice Party (PiS), 106-8, 110-111, 138-9, 148-150, 152, 156-7, 159-160, 171-4, 186, 192, 193-4, 195
League of Polish Families (LPR), 106, 108, 111, 139, 155, 160-1, 173, 186, 195
League and Self-Defence (LiS), 174, 186
Left and Democrats (LiD), 140, 172-175
Lenin, Vladimir, 32, 34
Lepper, Andrzej, 171, 174,186
lesbian and gay, 90, 159, 160
liberal, 1, 6-7, 15, 17-20, 22, 24-5, 31, 33, 69, 73, 75-9, 84-6, 90, 99, 102-111, 116-121, 123, 125-6, 132, 135, 137-8, 140, 143, 147-166, 172-5
Liberal-Democratic Congress (KLD), 173, 185
liberalism, 5-6, 13, 15, 17-20, 24-5, 52-3, 62, 75, 80, 84-5, 88-89, 97, 99, 102, 104, 106, 110, 118, 120, 124, 135, 143-144, 155-156, 163-6, 172

Lipski, Jan, 180
Lithuania, 34, 41, 114
Łaski, Kazimierz, 52, 181
Łódź, 29
Lubelskie, 70, 73, 183
Lukashenko, Alexander, 147
lustration, 105, 119, 139, 157-8
Luxemburg Rosa, 5, 11, 32, 51-2, 115, 180, 187
Maastricht Treaty, 21-2, 77
Macieriewicz, Antoni, 194
Małopolska, 69
Mandel, Ernest, 185, 177
march for tolerance, 159, 195
Marcinkiewicz, Kazimierz, 186
Marshal Plan/Aid, 21, 41, 55, 86
Marshall T H, 15
martial law, 47-8, 81, 116, 120, 158, 180
Marx, Karl, 11, 82, 179, 187
Marxism, 15, 32, 52, 80, 115, 176, 188, 195
Marxist, 11, 15, 31-2, 51, 112, 114, 177, 185, 187
Masaryk, Tomas, 33
Mazowiecki, Tadeusz, 54, 104, 169
Mazowieckie, 72, 183
McCarthyite, 158
meritocracy, 19, 136
Michnik, Adam, 126, 135, 180, 185
Middle East, 21, 145
Military Information Service (WSI), 157, 194
Miller, Leszek, 123, 126, 128-9, 132, 136-7, 190, 191
minimum wage, 46, 72, 74, 76, 123

Ministry of Education, 158, 160, 195
Modzelewski, Karol, 44, 47, 121
Molotov-Ribbentrop Pact, 149
Monetary Policy Committee (RPP), 99, 183, 189
Moscow, 115, 149-150
Nałęcz, Tomasz, 125
Narodniks, 32, 114
National Bank of Poland (NBP), 63, 126, 129, 161, 189
National Institute of Upbringing, 158
National Missile Defense System (NMD), 91, 150, 193
National Remembrance Institute (IPN), 157, 194
Nazi, 39, 41, 82, 103, 112, 114-115, 149, 158
Neo-Conservative, 20, 151
neo-liberal, 6-7, 17, 19-21, 23, 25, 52, 54-5, 76-7, 84, 86-87, 101-2, 104-5, 107, 109-110, 113, 117, 119-122, 124, 126, 128, 142, 144, 151-4, 161, 165, 173, 174, 185
neo-liberalism, 19, 24, 85
Netherlands, 28, 99
New Democracy, 122
New Left, 189
New Right, 19, 164
New World Order, 2
Nice Treaty, 155
nobility, 12, 28-30, 35
nomenclature, 47, 57, 98, 160
North Atlantic Treaty Organisation (NATO), viii, 3, 21, 91, 97, 99, 118-9, 126, 137, 144, 146, 150, 189, 192

Olechowski, Andrzej, 105, 170, 172
Olejniczak, Wojciech, 137-8
Oleksy, Józef, 191
Olszewski, Jan, 105, 170, 194
orange revolution, 146
Organisation for Economic Cooperatin and Development (OECD), 66-7, 190
Ost, David, 24, 79, 82, 109, 186
patriotism, 30, 33, 110, 115, 156, 158
Party of European Socialists (PSE), 120
peasantry, 14, 28, 30-1, 33, 38, 42, 108-9, 113, 122, 162
perestroika, 18
Piłsudski, Józef, 34-5, 37, 40, 110, 114-5, 179, 192
Pinochet, Augusto, 150
PKN Orlen, 135
Plekhanov, Georgi, 31
Podkarpackie, 70, 73, 183
Podlaskie, 67, 73, 183
Pol, Marek, 122, 125, 173
Polish Communist Party (KPP), 37, 41, 115, 179, 187
Polish Humanitarian Organisation, 70
Polish Labour Party (PPP), 185
Polish Peasants' Party (PSL), 62, 106, 117, 119, 121-2, 127-8, 132, 169-170, 174, 186, 189
Polish Peoples' Republic (PRL), 41, 47, 80, 103, 118, 120, 122, 127, 130, 136-9, 158

Polish Social Democratic
    Union (PUS), 187
Polish Socialist Party (PPS),
    35-6, 38, 114-5, 117, 122,
    125, 179, 188-9, 191
Polish Teachers' Union (ZNP),
    158
Polish United Workers Party
    (PZPR), 42, 44, 46-9, 89,
    98-9, 103, 115-121, 125-6,
    136-9, 158, 172, 174, 186,
    187, 189, 191
Polish Workers' Party (PPR),
    115, 117, 191
political cleavage, 103, 105
Polsat Television, 135
Pope John Paul II, 83, 106, 116
popiwek tax, 61, 62
positivism, 33
post communist, 1, 8, 104-5,
    107, 110, 117-119
post-socialist, 1, 3-8, 23-7, 50,
    61, 64, 66, 77, 80, 85-6, 90,
    102-105, 108, 113, 119, 131,
    135, 138, 142, 148, 153, 154,
    156, 158, 165
post-war, 13-14, 16-19, 41-2,
    67, 80, 83, 112, 143, 149,
    155, 163, 164
post-war consensus, 15, 19,
    155, 164
poverty, 2, 5, 6, 22, 38-9, 49,
    70, 73, 77-8, 85-6, 107, 113,
    125, 147, 164, 183
Poznań, 42, 159, 183
Prague, 44, 112, 176, 188
pre-capitalist, 11, 14, 23, 27, 61,
    78-9, 83, 86, 97, 102, 104,
    111, 118
primitive accumulation, 5, 7,
    11, 13, 17, 21-2, 25, 43, 46,
    51, 80, 85, 103, 132, 142,
    151, 153, 165, 177
privatisation, 53, 56-8, 61-5, 87,
    89, 92, 100, 122-3, 129, 136,
    146-7, 160, 165, 195
proletariat, 10, 31, 32, 80, 82
Proletariat (political
    organisation), 114, 186
Prussia, 3, 178, 183
Prussian, 28
Putin, Vladimir, 147, 193
PZU Insurance Company, 129,
    135
Racja (political party), 191
radical centre, 19, 124
Radio Maryja, 159, 195
Rakowski, Mieczysław, 116,
Reagan, Ronald, 19, 124, 164
recession, 2-3, 22, 36-40, 45,
    55, 61-2, 142
Red Army, 34, 41, 114-115, 158
revolution, 1, 12, 18, 27, 34, 36,
    40, 48, 84, 103, 113-114,
    146-8, 150, 156, 159-161
Right Wing of the Republic
    (PR), 195
Rolicki, Janusz, 125-6
romanticist, 30
round table talks, 49, 53
Romania, 29, 41, 43, 75, 179,
    182
Rumsfeld, Donald, 134
Russia, 3, 8, 12, 22, 28-32, 34-5,
    41, 53, 55-7, 107, 113-116,
    143, 145-150, 177-9, 181,
    187, 193-4
Russian Revolution, 8, 34, 112,
    113, 178
Rydzyk, Tadeusz, 195
Rywin, Lew, 135
Rywingate, 136

Sachs, Jeffery, 53, 188
Sanacja, 35, 37, 39, 110
Schmitt, Carl, 25
Schroeder, Gerhard, 124, 192
Schumpeter, Joseph, 15
Second International, 178
secularism, 25, 104
Self-Defence (Samoobrona), 106, 108, 111, 168-9, 174, 186, 193
self-managed republic, 47, 49, 81, 84
self-management, 47, 49, 52, 81, 83, 104
Serbia, 29
shock therapy, 49, 53, 54, 61-2, 65, 70, 84-5, 87, 98, 103-5, 116-8, 121, 126, 188
Sik, Otta, 52, 188
Sikorski, Radosław, 149
Siwec, Marek, 134
Slovakia, 3, 33, 57, 66, 72, 75
Slovenia, 8, 181
social democracy, 18, 32, 40, 118-119, 124, 132-134, 138, 140, 191
Social Democracy of the Kingdom of Poland and Lithuania (SDKPiL), 114, 187
Social Democratic Movement (RDS), 121
Social Democratic Party - Germany (SPD), 31, 124, 134, 178, 187
Social Democratic Party of the Republic of Poland (SdRP), 117-9, 121, 125, 169, 172,
social democratic, 1, 7, 14, 18, 40, 112-3, 116-7, 120-2, 124, 127, 130, 132, 134-7

Social Democratic Party of Poland (SdPL), 137, 138, 140, 171, 174
socialism, 1-10, 13, 16-18, 20-6, 31, 40, 42-3, 49-50, 54- 6, 61, 66-8, 74, 80-2, 84-7, 90-1, 98, 101, 103-5, 109, 111, 113-4, 117, 122, 125, 136, 139, 142-3, 145, 149, 151, 153-4, 158, 163, 166, 173
Socialist Bloc, 1, 3-4, 8, 20, 26, 43, 49, 87, 142-5, 163
Socialist International (SI), 8, 120, 172
Solidarity Electoral Alliance (AWS), 62, 65, 105, 124, 127, 130, 136, 170, 172-5, 185
Solidarność, 46-9, 81, 83-4, 98, 103-4, 109-110, 116, 118, 120-1, 124, 126-7, 146, 154, 156, 158, 173, 180, 181, 184, 188, 191
Soviet, 3, 34, 41, 49, 55, 57, 80, 83, 112-115, 117, 143, 147, 149, 150
Soviet Union, 3, 34, 41, 57, 143, 149
Stalin, 42, 113, 115, 149, 184
Stalinism, v, 8, 115, 158
Stalinist, 8, 41, 112, 114, 184
Stambuliski, Aleksandur, 40
Star Wars II (see NMD), 134
state farms, 61, 70
Stocznia Szczecińska Shipyard, 130, 189
Stoiber, Edmund, 193
Strauss, Leo, 25
subsidies, 22, 46, 48, 58, 60- 61, 5, 74-5, 77, 88, 92, 101, 122, 131-3, 144, 165
successor parties, 113, 120, 138

Suchocka, Hanna, 62
superstructure, 13, 25, 102
surplus value, 51, 143
Sweden, 3, 28, 184
Szlachta, 30, 33
Szmajdziński, Jerzy, 190, 191
Telewizja Polska, 194
Thatcher, Margaret, 19, 124, 164, 188
thick line policy, 98, 117
Third Republic, 97, 110, 140, 157, 162
third way, 7, 18-19, 105, 124, 127, 136, 138-9, 140-1, 188, 190
TINA, 164
trade union, 21, 46-47, 81, 98, 100, 120-121, 174
triangulation, 124, 134
Trotsky, Leon, 32, 113, 187
Trotskyism, 212
Trybuna Newspaper, 125, 189
Turkey, 151
TV Trwam, 195
Two-and-a-Half International, 179
układ, 107
Ukraine, 3, 34, 37, 41, 56, 146, 151, 192
unemployment, 2, 6, 34, 36-8, 52, 60-2, 64-5, 69, 74, 76-8, 86, 107, 113, 122, 128-9, 131, 139, 147, 153, 165
Union of the Left, 191
United Peasants' Party (ZSL), 119, 174
Union of Poles (Belarus) UoP, 147
Union of Soviet Socialist Republics (USSR), 20, 34, 39, 41, 43, 47-8, 55-6, 80, 83-4, 114-5, 118, 136, 142, 146, 149, 158, 163, 165, 179
United States of America (USA), 2-3, 8, 13-14, 16, 18, 20-1, 37, 53, 57, 91, 122, 124, 129, 133-5, 143-7, 151, 193
Vatican, 98, 102, 123, 192
Wałęsa, Lech, 47, 55, 105, 119, 146, 158, 194
Warmińsko-Mazurskie, 67, 73, 183
Warsaw, ix, 4, 33-4, 41, 44, 72, 80, 115, 117, 148-9, 158- 9, 183
Washington Consensus, 21, 144
Western Europe (WE), 2-3, 5-6, 10-12, 14, 21, 25-7, 29-33, 40-1, 43-4, 49, 53-5, 58, 67-69, 72, 75, 77, 82-4, 103, 106, 112, 120-1, 124, 130, 143-5, 149, 151-3, 155-6, 164-6, 178
welfare state, 14-15, 18, 21, 87, 127, 136, 164
Wiaderny, Józef, 188
Wiatr, Jerzy, 80, 134, 187, 190
Wielgus, Stanisław, 195
Wielkopolska, 69
Wierzejski, Wojciech, 160
Wildstein, Bronisław, 194
Witos, Wincenty, 37, 108
Workers' Defence Committee (KOR), 46, 180, 188
working class, 12-14, 16, 19, 23, 31, 33, 44, 46, 48-9, 51, 80-1, 83, 109, 113, 116, 118, 121, 124, 158
World Bank, 21, 22, 48, 151, 161

World War One (WW1), 3, 8, 35, 40, 114-5, 178
World War Two (WW2), 4, 13-14, 21, 39, 41, 81, 101, 114, 116, 147, 149, 150, 163, 180, 193

Yalta Treaty, 149
Yeltsin, Boris, 177
Yugoslavia, 17, 21, 114, 126, 179, 182
Zachodniopomorskie, 67

www.ingramcontent.com/pod-product-compliance
Lightning Source LLC
Chambersburg PA
CBHW061442300426
44114CB00014B/1795